D1526049

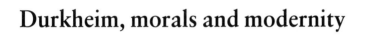

Durkheim, morals and modernity

McGill-Queen's Studies in the History of Ideas

1 Problems of Cartesianism
Edited by Thomas M. Lennon,
John M. Nicholas, and John W. Davis

2 The Development of the Idea
of History in Antiquity
Gerald A. Press

3 Claude Buffier and Thomas Reid:
Two Common-Sense Philosophers
Louise Marcil-Lacoste

4 Schiller, Hegel, and Marx:
State, Society, and the Aesthetic Ideal
of Ancient Greece
Philip J. Kains

5 John Case and Aristotelianism in
Renaissance England
Charles B. Schmitt

6 Beyond Liberty and Property:
The Process of Self-Recognition in
Eighteenth-Century Political Thought
J. A. W. Gunn

7 John Toland: His Methods,
Manners, and Mind
Stephen H. Daniel

8 Coleridge and the Inspired Word
Anthony John Harding

9 The Jena System, 1804–5:
Logic and Metaphysics
G. W. F. Hegel

10 Consent, Coercion, and Limit:
The Medieval Origins of
Parlimentary Democracy
Arthur P. Monahan

11 Scottish Common Sense in
Germany, 1768–1800:
A Contibution to the History
of Critical Philosophy
Manfred Kuehn

12 Paine and Cobbett:
The Transatlantic Connection
David A. Wilson

13 Descartes and the Enlightenment
Peter A. Schouls

14 Greek Scepticism:
Anti-Realist Trends in
Ancient Thought
Leo Groarke

15 The Irony of Theology and the
Nature of Religious Thought
Donald Wiebe

16 Form and Transformation:
A Study in the Philosophy
of Plotinus
Frederic M. Schroeder

17 From Personal Duties towards
Personal Rights:
Late Medieval and Early Modern
Political Thought, c.1300–c.1650

18 The Main Philosophical
Writings and the Novel *Allwill*
Friedrich Heinrich Jacobi
Translated and edited by
George di Giovanni

19 Kierkegaard as Humanist
Discovering My Self
Arnold B. Come

20 Durkheim, Morals and Modernity
W. Watts Miller

Durkheim, morals and modernity

W. Watts Miller

McGill-Queen's University Press
Montreal & Kingston • London • Buffalo

© W. Watts Miller, 1996

First published in 1996 by UCL Press
The name of University College London (UCL) is a registered
trade mark used by UCL Press with the consent of the owner.

Published simultaneously in Canada by
McGill-Queen's University Press
3430 McTavish Street
Montreal
Quebec
H3A 1X9

Printed in England.

Legal deposit third quarter 1996
Bibliothèque nationale du Québec

ISBN: 0-7735-1444-9

CANADIAN CATALOGUING IN PUBLICATION DATA
Watts Miller, William, 1944–
Durkheim, morals and modernity

(McGill-Queen's studies in the history of ideas)
Includes bibliographical references and index.
ISBN 0-7735-1444-9

1. Ethics. 2. Modernism. 3. Durkheim, Emile,
1858–1917. I. Title. II. Series.

HM216.W38 1996   1701.1   C95-920921-2

Contents

Acknowledgements   vii

Introduction: Durkheim's project   1

Part I "America"

1 Developing a moral science   25

2 Towards a new spirit of the laws   47

3 The division of labour   73

4 The organic self   95

5 Modern ills and modern ideals   117

Part II The kingdom and the republic

6 Virtue ethics: duty and the good   141

7 Rational ethics: autonomy   163

8 From the kingdom of ends to the republic of persons   185

9 A secular religion?   207

10 The cult of man   229

Conclusion: from "is" to "ought"   251

Notes   263
References   271
Index   283

To Elizabeth

Acknowledgements

This book has been long in the making, and is dedicated, with all my heart, to my wife, Elizabeth Anne Watts Miller. I also very much wish to acknowledge affections and debts to my parents, Bill and Margaret, and to my colleague, critic and friend, Bill Pickering.

A collective acknowledgement is to the *équipe* of the Centre for Durkheimian Studies, Oxford – especially Nick Allen, Mike Gane, Mike Hawkins, Joseph Llobera, Steven Lukes, Herminio Martins, Susan Steadman-Jones, Ken Thompson, John Torrance and, again, Bill Pickering. This book would not have been possible without the encouragement, division of labour and "collective creative ferment" of the *équipe*. Other collective acknowledgements are to the *Maison Française*, Oxford, which has regularly hosted the Centre's seminars and conferences, to my tutors at the University of Edinburgh, especially the late Jimmy Littlejohn, to French colleagues, especially Philippe Besnard, and to colleagues in the University of Bristol, especially Kieran Flanagan, David Milligan and Theo Nichols.

An especial, individual acknowledgement is to Etienne Halphen, Durkheim's grandson, for the cover photograph and for general support. Other, diverse, individual acknowledgements are to Leslie Abraham, Jeffrey Alexander, Michael Banton, Jackie Bee, the late Helen Bloom, Mark Cladis, Charles-Henry Cuin, Steve Fenton, Jean-Claude Filloux, Ian Hamnett, Doreen Harding, Andrew Harrison, David Hirschmann, François-André Isambert, Hans Joas, Claudette Kennedy, Peter Lopston, Hans-Peter Müller, Onora O'Neill, Liz Paton, Edo Pivcevic, Robert Reiner, Vernon Reynolds, the late David Rosenberg, Caroline Schimeld, Justin Vaughan, Sylvia Walby, Michael and Jackie Watts Miller, Kate Williams, Xu Yi-li and Zheng Hang-sheng.

For a' that, an a' that,
It's comin yet for a' that,
That man to man the world o'er
Shall brithers be for a' that.
(Robert Burns 1795)

Introduction: Durkheim's project

Durkheim has been compared with Columbus, who in seeking a new route to old kingdoms instead discovered America. In seeking a new route to ethics Durkheim instead discovered sociology (Gurvitch 1938: 279).

This book examines and in the end supports Durkheim's search for a passage from "is" to "ought". But his project is of interest for other reasons. It involves, not least, a communitarian defence of individualism. It suggests, in the case of sociology, the need for a new look at Durkheimian America. It leads, in the case of ethics, to an account that is impressive in its stature. It can seem in many ways a development of Hume. It is above all an engagement with Kant.[1]

Durkheim's route from science to ethics does not settle for instrumental rationality, which advises on means to ends just taken as given, or even seen as rationally undecidable. His concern is with the rational deliberation of ends themselves. He wants a sociologically informed enquiry that can identify, clarify and rework ideals, but also adjudicate on them. It is still to adjudicate them, even though he argues for acceptance of the basic ethic of our time.

He sums this up as the "human ideal". It is the universalist ethic of the "human person". It demands, as the city of modern citizenship, a "human *patrie*" – or, in a neo-Kantian term, a "republic of persons". It means everyone's flourishing as an "autonomous centre of thought and action". It requires a "broad, truly human culture". It is perverted by the "sordid commercialism" that reduces morality to interest. It finds expression in the aspirations, however utopian, of the French Revolution. These will not go away. They are rooted in the modern world. Attempts to reject them will prolong the "sad conflict" of class and deepen social and moral malaise.

1

It is odd to see Durkheim as a political conservative. Yet is he a philosophical conservative? He criticizes the idea that we can escape the ethic of our time to invent or appeal to something completely different. Indeed, it is why he can seem to subvert political through philosophical conservativism. Yes, we should accept our own local ethic – and it is the universalist ethic of the Revolution. In fact he is not a philosophical conservative, just as he is not a philosophical radical, and for the same reason. He wants to base ethics on a sociological understanding of things. Provided there is this basis, views about reform can be as limited or as far-reaching as may be. Usually he sees a need for far-reaching reform.

It is a permanent need: "there is and will always be . . . a free field open to our efforts" ([1893b] 1902b: 336; t.344).[2] A distinction running through his thought is between the imagination and the will. Anthropology, history, ethics itself and a "human culture" all require an ability to reach out to and imagine other ways of life. It is not the same as a power to will them, and Durkheim is concerned, not just with what we can imagine, but with what we can will. It is also a concern with what we can hope. The human ideal is rooted in our world – if only in the collective consciousness as a collective imagination, willing and hoping for its dream of the good society.

"America"

It is naïve to complain about Durkheim's optimism if we do not reflect on the role in ethics of hope. There is anyway a certain desperation in his search for reforms that can work to realize the modern human ideal and overcome forces that work against it. He is sometimes tempted to locate these forces outside of modernity itself, whether in tradition or in the "contingent", "accidental" causes of a passing crisis. Part I of this book discusses these temptations. But the main aim is discovery of his sociological "America". It charts – in his very early writings, in his Latin thesis on Montesquieu's *Spirit of the laws*, in his main thesis on *The division of labour*, in *The rules of sociological method*, in *Suicide* and elsewhere – the development of, we might say, a "strong internalist programme" for understanding modernity. What does it involve?

Durkheim is all for science's empirical detective work, but all against empiricism and those who, "under the guise of positivism", spread "mystery everywhere" (1897f: 288). He insists he is a *rationalist*" ([1895a] 1901c: ix; t.33). Science must concern itself with the observable. But it is to track, via this, an underlying logic in the world. His criticism of Montesquieu is not that he looks for such a logic, but that he is not patient and thorough enough in doing so.

Durkheim never refers, in writing in Latin, to "phenomena". He refers to "things", distinguishing between the obvious and others that lie hidden and out of sight. He makes the same distinction in French, but without clearly marking it as between "phenomena" and the hidden. He refers to "things", "facts" and "phenomena" so interchangeably that hidden realities can be phenomena. An explanation is that even the hidden world of, say, Newtonian gravity is still a world of Kantian phenomena, which, unlike "noumena", can still be tracked through empirical detective work and scientific, theoretical reason.

Science, in Durkheim's view, does not work with an empiricist or positivist idea of causality just in terms of observable regularities. It looks beyond these for a logic, a rationale, in things. He subscribes to an idea of causality as necessary connexion – along with Montesquieu, Kant and indeed Hume himself, according to Durkheim's own teacher and "master", Emile Boutroux (1926: 100).[3]

So social science must look for a social world's rationale, its real, underlying, constitutive dynamic. Durkheim finds this, in the case of the modern world, in the division of labour. But it also includes, and has to include, the human ideal. The division of labour and the human ideal are essential, interacting and interdependent elements of the dynamic – its Montesquieuan "structure" and "principle". They make up the core ideal logic Durkheim describes as the spontaneous division of labour.

What difficulties does it run into, and what generates them? The internalist programme, though not excluding "accidental" causes that lie outside society's dynamic, insists on looking for causes that lie within it. Indeed, it is because the dynamic must contain such possibilities that it must be made up of a complex of elements and cannot be monolithic. The problem, even so, is to explain how modern ills have their source in the same dynamic as modern ideals, to see how they are part of this yet are also "pathologies" deviating from and working against it. But it is a problem the internalist programme both sets up and sets out to solve. It is the key to the argument about the division of labour's abnormal forms, to *Suicide*'s diagnosis, alongside individualism's human ideal, of individualism's pathologies, and to various worries elsewhere, all centred round the possibility, contained in our world's dynamic, of its own self-generated collapse.

The beginnings of the internalist programme can be found in Durkheim's first academic publication, a review identifying a modern Scylla and Charybdis. Either there is a "conflict of unfettered egoisms", with its source in individualism and resulting in an oppressive, class-divided society. Or, in reaction, there is a growth of the concentrated, unlimited power of a "despotic socialism" (1885a: 96). The preface to the new edition of *The division of labour* sees the two dangers as one. It argues, in effect, that a libertarian regime of atomized individuals is the police regime of a coercive, not very minimalist, "hypertrophied state" (1902b: xxxii; t.28).

It is clear that Durkheim's list of modern ills includes tendencies inherent in our society towards authoritarianism. It is also clear, working through the list, that "egoism" means very different things. As in the early review it is connected with class conflict and is the unfettered, morally unconstrained pursuit of self-interest. This is part of a pathology later diagnosed as *anomie* – unfettered, morally unconstrained and limitless desire; its opposite is fatalism, a crushing of desire. "Egoism" is then reworked as essentially a disease of the intellect, a self-absorbed withdrawal that numbs feelings of attachment to our milieu. Its opposite is an altruistic overattachment, a crushing of self. So, going back to authoritarianism, there is also a general worry over "anarchy". This involves a chaos of opinion, a collapse of the free thought that is part and parcel of the human ideal into subjectivism, scepticism, antirationalism, nihilism, etc. Far from being postmodern, such things are built into modernity.

Durkheim insists on cohesion, without which freedom is impossible – but is just as insistent on freedom, without which modern cohesion is impossible. He looks to the spontaneous division of labour as a basic dynamic bringing both. He also forms out of the dynamic a set of further conditions, countering risks of its collapse and essential for its realization. They are:

  (a) the organic self
  (b) intermediate groups
  (c) a culture of man
  (d) a cult of man

The organic self and intermediate groups are mainly discussed in Part I of this book, a culture and cult of man in Part II.

Durkheim develops an account, not just of individualism, but of individuality. It is tied up with his view of modern "organic society". It might be baptized, therefore, as the "organic self". It lies in our incompleteness, attaches us to one another through our differences and in a commitment that can take the strain of our hurts, wounds and disputes. It is introduced in *The division of labour*, through the paradigmatic cases of friendship and the family.

The organic self is about sentiments of attachment and solidarity, but even more about Durkheim's opposition to vague, general appeal to these sentiments by themselves. He insists on their rootedness in particular definite relationships. Indeed, this is one of the places where he can seem, in his views, so Humean. Particular connexions of family and friends are of vital importance in our lives. They are the source of concern for others, of the feelings, motivations and commitments that are essential for morality and cannot be stirred up just by reason. Human ethical life needs anchorage in particular definite relationships, with the particular definite loyalties bound up with them. There is therefore the Humean problem of their compatibility with the need – above all in the modern world – for enlarged, extensive morals. How can the organic self attach us not only to the immediate but to the abstract other?

The Durkheimian answer is complex. Intermediate groups and a culture and cult of man are all part of it. Intermediate groups draw us into the life of wider society. Durkheim sees in them an escape route from atomized, unorganized individuals and the authoritarian state. But they are also an escape from imprisonment in the loyalties of the traditional, confined community. It is a search for groups that, in locking us into particular connexions, lock us into the world.

He hopes to find them in the occupational groups of the socio-economic division of labour, reconstituted as self-governing corporations. They are definite but interlinking groups, in a central sphere of life, that offer the cohesion we need in the arguments in which we work out and work for the aspirations to freedom and justice of the modern human ideal. They can take on a whole range of functions. But they are above all a moral force and the road, not least, to the active, meaningful and informed involvement of democratic citizenship.

This very much opposes Durkheim to certain varieties of liberalism. These look to a state with a fixed, constitutional framework of law, within which individuals are then free to go their separate ways, never having to come together to argue towards a collective line on an issue. There is little or no place left for citizenship, and they are essentially anti-political strains of liberalism. Durkheim belongs to the pro-political tradition, which finds expression in Constant's *Ancient and modern liberty*, Tocqueville's *Democracy in America* and Mill's *Representative government*. This is again tied up with his dynamic view of the human ideal as something involving a continuing, indeed growing, "multitude of disagreements" around it ([1893b] 1902b: 147; t.174), and a continuing development and unfolding of aspirations: there will always be a "free field open to our efforts". A conception of justice might crystallize for a time. It must remain open to the processes involving us as citizens in its interpretation, and in its change and evolution in new directions.

It is also why there is a need, if we are to stay together in these processes, for something that Durkheim sees as completely fundamental, given the nature of the modern world, its individualism, free thought and human ideal. It is the need for cohesion without consensus.

It is only if we grasp this, and give up idylls of a community of belief, that we can understand the determination – even desperation – of his search for attachment, in all our differences and disagreements. It is this search that takes him to the organic self, intermediate groups and, underlying both, the interlinkage of the division of labour. A republic, just because it is committed to the human ideal, rules out cohesion through a far-reaching, substantive consensus, and must draw on other sources of solidarity. But why does Durkheim look to the division of labour as a basic source of this, as well as of modern ideals, and what, bound up with its dynamic, might be a basic source of modern pathologies?

The division of labour is *not* just the other side of the market. As the division of labour develops, so, no doubt, does the market. But it is the division of labour, not the market, that generates solidariness. It is the division of labour, not the market, that is involved in the individuality of the organic self. It is the division of labour, not the market, that can give rise to respect for persons, autonomy, and other values of the human ideal. The internalist programme looks for the roots in the modern world both of its pathologies and of its ideals and aspirations. The trouble with the market as the driving force of things is that it might explain the pathologies, but not the aspirations.

Durkheim's main thesis introduces the division of labour through the organic self and particular connexions. It prepares the way for his critique, in going on to enlarged society, of emphasis on the relationship then involved in market exchange. To concentrate on this, and marginalize the division of labour, is to concentrate on the "superficial" and "transient". It is an *échangisme* in which we go to the market, get what we can from one another, and then, our business done, steal off. It is a recipe for instrumentalism, treating persons as if things, valued only for their utility. Persons have to be ends in themselves, integrated in one's own consciousness as one's own ends, as in the consciousness of the organic self, and through sustained, interlocking relationships in which there is this interpenetration of selves.

Criticism of instrumentalism – whether involving self-interest or a collective interest, which limits moral concern to one's own group – is not necessarily criticism of interest as such. Durkheim might be unenthusiastic about interest, yet accepts rather than denounces it. In fact he is clear about its involvement in the division of labour itself and not just in the market. The division of labour separates and opposes us in our interests, even at the same time that it is a way of uniting us, taking the strain of our conflicts, and regulating them. Part of the story might be that this is in our mutual interest. It is not, and cannot be, the whole story.

Durkheim opposes attempts to reduce morality to negative rights. Attitudes that respect rather than instrumentalize others depend on positive moral fellow feeling – "Justice is full of charity" ([1893b] 1902b: 91; t.121–2).

He is even more against attempts to reduce morality to interest. We require an identity – as individual, or as member of a particular group, or as "man" – that defines our interests in the first place. We again require a positive moral concern that transcends interest and the slide into instrumentalism. The need for a pre-existing identity and solidarity, before the play of interest, underlies the argument, one of the most famous in the whole thesis, that "all in the contract is not contractual" (*ibid.*:189; t.211).

The thesis itself is a sustained view of ethical life as dependent on attachment to one another and society as ends, rooted as such in the character of the organic self. It is then a sustained argument that this is dependent, in the modern world, on definite, interlocking relationships in a division of labour.

But a common complaint is that Durkheim has little to say, in all this, about class. It is in a way misdirected. Durkheim maps out the ideals that criticize the inequalities and injustices of the "sad conflict of class" ([1897c] 1970a: 251), and is clear where the values critical of our society must have their source – the nature and dynamic of our society itself. Do Marxists appeal to God, metaphysics, universal reason or whatever instead? But it is also essential to block the reduction of ethical life to interest, and Durkheim does just that, in looking beyond the market – as well as idylls of community – to the division of labour, the human ideal and a republic of persons.

It is part of all this that he has the resources for a theory of class. Jean-Claude Filloux has done most, nowadays, to explore them (Filloux 1971, 1977, 1993). What might be stressed here?

We must go to the internalist programme for an explanation of inequality and class, not just as survivals from the past, but in terms of forces continuing to generate them. We must also notice how, as part of the general programme to "clarify" basic ideals, Durkheim sees aspirations to equality as inherent in the modern social world but then reworks them in two rather different versions. The ideal of equal opportunity is the most obvious. The most fundamental is the ideal of a society in which everyone can develop and flourish. He makes a simple logical slip when he says that equal opportunity is a sufficient condition of everyone's developing and flourishing. What about his claim that it is a necessary condition?

This, if correct, completely rules out a republic of everyone's developing and flourishing, because, for all kinds of reasons, the liberalism of completely equal life chances is an illusion. Indeed, *The division of labour* has long inspired gloominess amongst commentators – for example, in a review by Durkheim's associate, Célestin Bouglé (1903: 107), quoted and discussed, also in gloom, by Philippe Besnard (1993a). It has also inspired wonder, from the beginning, at Durkheim's optimism – for example, in the review by Gabriel Tarde (1893: 625) and in the complaint by Steven Lukes that Durkheim assumes an identity between "the ideal and the about-to-happen" (Lukes 1973: 177). In a way this hits the nail on the head, since it is because the human ideal is the ideal, *en marche*, of modernity's dynamic that we should embrace it. In a way it does not, since it overlooks worry in the internalist programme at the dynamic's built-in problems and risks.

There is at least one worry, however, that needs reassessing. The liberalism of equal life chances is not just impossible. It is undesirable, in that it assumes an abstract society of abstract individuals, which contradicts everything Durkheim stands for – a republic of everyone's developing and flourishing, in the particular, definite connexions of particular, different and diverse milieux. For the same reason the republic need not be classless, given Durkheim's view of classes as cultural rather than simply economic groups. What matters is that it is not class divided, which means that the main obstacles to it include market instrumentalism, exploitative contracts and relationships, a system of degraded and desocialized labour, and denial, not of equal chances to move into any position but of opportunity to develop and flourish in whatever position.

This rethinking of things is consistent both with the basic social ideal Durkheim holds up to us as rooted in the modern world, and with the kind of change and reform he sees as necessary to realize it. Is such change likely? The ambivalence between optimism and gloom is built into the internalist programme: the human ideal is part of modernity's dynamic, and so are the forces working against it. But there is a need to return, in the end, to the role in moral life of imagination, the will and hope. To sustain commitment to the ideal, we must imagine, will and hope for the coming, despite everything, of the republic.

> For a' that, an a' that,
>   It's comin yet for a' that,
> That man to man the world o'er
>   Shall brithers be for a' that.

The kingdom and the republic

Boutroux, in justly celebrated lectures on Kant given in 1896–7, interprets the kingdom of ends as a republic of persons (1926: 373). The problem of seeing the kingdom as a republic has emerged, in writing this book, as an important way of trying to understand Durkheim's ethical theory, which is very much an engagement with Kant. The theory is above all set out in the lectures on moral education, probably first given, not in 1902 as has been thought, but in 1898–9 (Besnard 1993b).

The lectures begin with the worry that the modern world – and Durkheim especially has in mind the French republic – demands a secular, rational, enlightened approach to morality, but this risks destroying morality itself. It is nonetheless possible to understand, without diminishing, the "majesty" of the moral realm (1925a: 139; t.122).

Part II of this book starts with Durkheim's republican account of the moral kingdom, in the sense of the essential, universal elements of morality that have to be understood if we are not to destroy it. It then goes on to his account of autonomy, which involves the very understanding of these elements, as stressed by Georges Gurvitch (1938: 280). But autonomy is also, and more importantly, "enlightened acceptance" of the social and moral realities of our time. This sounds odd. Indeed, Durkheim so criticizes the idea's original, authoritative articulation by Kant that it might be asked if he is any longer talking about autonomy in a meaningful sense at all. So there is next an attempt to do something he himself does not do. It is to show how, step by step, we can rework Kantian as Durkheimian autonomy, to see them as more or less two expressions of the same thing.

This on its own cannot republicanize the kingdom, in the sense, now, of an ideal ethical commonwealth. An obstacle remains: God. Kant's necessary postulates of morality are, as well as autonomy, an immortal soul and God. Durkheim dismisses the immortal soul, and in a way dispenses with God, although leaving it unclear if the replacement is man or society. But he is insistent that the modern secular ethic must continue to be, in some sense, a religion, and again and again talks of it as a "cult" of man. Trying to sort out what he means by this, and why it is so important for him, is essential for understanding the nature of his ethical theory itself.

There are at least four great questions at the core of any ethical theory of interest and stature, and Durkheim wrestles with all of them. They are:

(a) what is a moral character?
(b) what is the nature of moral motivation?
(c) what is the nature of the right and the good?
(d) who is the moral judge?

For Durkheim, the moral judge cannot possibly just be the individual.

Yet, in the modern case, it cannot just be society. The answer has to be something like the individual as man. This will be brought out in discussing autonomy. Autonomy of course affects all the other questions. They must first be considered via his view of morality's universal elements.

Durkheim, it clearly emerges, works with virtue ethics. He is very much concerned with character, motivation and the will. He argues, with force, against their reduction just to dispositions needed to act as pre-existing definitions of the right or the good require (that is, the reduction of ethics to answers to question c). He is also very much concerned with "individual morality". This is his term for the branch of ethical life and reflection concerned with duties to oneself, integrity, self-respect, developing and flourishing. Like Hume and Kant, he does not see ethics as simply legislation of relations with others, let alone talk just of rights, without asking what they are for or what to do with them.

In discussing questions of character, motive and the will, the lectures on moral education involve a further development of the theory of the organic self. Self-discipline becomes an essential virtue, in addition to the solidarity, engrained in the conscience, of attachment to one another and society as ends. It is also a development of the moral analysis in *The division of labour*'s original introduction, which does not at all go into self-discipline as a virtue, but just emphasizes a set of obligatory rules. Moreover, this is despite making the point that solidariness is "the very source of morality" (1893b: 10; t.415), and despite all the concern with solidariness and attachment in the book as a whole.

Durkheim connects attachment with "the good" and the spirit of discipline with "duty", to see an irreducible dualism between these, but with an underlying source in society. Many things seem involved in it, including a dualism between ideals and rules, but also, and not least, a dualism between Humean sentiment and Kantian reason and will. We are motivated to the good and the ideal by positive sentiments of attachment to one another and to society. We are motivated to duty and the rule by respect for the moral law's imperative authority, and by the will to control and order the crowd of our desires. Like Kant, Durkheim talks of "obligation" to refer not to the content of duty but to the imperativeness moving and constraining us to act on it. It is in this sense that he insists that there cannot be a morality without obligation. Hence, too, his worry that ethics might destroy morals, in demanding a rational, self-legislated law that collapses its obligatoriness. *Autonomie* risks *anomie*.

This is to criticize Kant himself, who envisages – at least as a "holy" ideal – a morality without obligation. It is even more to criticize Jean-Marie Guyau, who introduces the notion of *anomie* in his influential book, *A sketch of a morality without obligation or sanction* (1885: 3, n.1; t.4). But Guyau sees *anomie* as an ideal, not a malaise, and as a humanly realizable, not holy, ideal of spontaneous, non-dutiful morals. He expands on this in *The non-religion of the future* – in which he also attacks talk of a "cult" of man (1887: 391; t.445). Durkheim knew both books very well. It is via Guyau, plus Kant, that his own belief in a cult of man will be examined, but in the context, too, of his commitment to autonomy.

He is concerned, as he says, with "autonomy of the will". As autonomy of the person it is about the essential virtue of self-knowledge. But it is in understanding that our autonomy has to be a collective, historically evolving achievement. It lies in discovery of a social and moral reality and its rationale. Hence it lies in collective processes of enquiry, with science's republic of enquirers as the paradigm. Thus, in this collective aspect of things, Durkheimian autonomy very much involves, like Kantian autonomy, a proceduralism. The identity of the ethical judge is also a procedural issue. But the ethical judge could be the individual, informed by collective public reasoning, rather than the collective itself, and in the Durkheimian case is the individual as man.

An issue here concerns the human culture, spanning science, history and the arts, needed by the Durkheimian citizen. It is a general way of entrenching the human ideal, yet is of especial importance for autonomy. The lay republic is threatened by authoritarianism and dogma in the name of expertise, but also, in reaction, by mistrust and scepticism about any claim to knowledgeability. Autonomy depends on a human culture that can address the difficulty through some sort of general, critical understanding, in the lay republic, of claims and arguments in the republics of this or that specialism.

A rather different problem is that Durkheim concentrates on procedural autonomy without drawing out its substantive social and moral implications. Of course he is committed to the social and moral ideal of a republic. Yet could autonomy, as "enlightened acceptance", endorse some highly illiberal, nightmarish world instead? It is important to try to show how and why it cannot. Autonomy entails a republic, although in a risk-strewn rather than a straight and sunny deductive path. Durkheim is a liberal, but not by chance.

But if it is by necessary connexion, what has it to do with autonomy as freedom of the will? Durkheim rejects the standard, soft routes to the compatibility of science and freewill. These reduce causality to contingency, or freewill to sociopolitical freedom, or both. Instead, like Kant, Durkheim takes the hard route. He wants – and, it is argued, gets – autonomy of the will *and* necessary connexion.

Indeed, this is a basic answer to the worry that ethics might destroy morals. With Durkheim, as with Kant, autonomy lies in respect for the moral law and discovery of its objective necessary rationale. But in that case why should Durkheim want to entrench respect in a "cult"? And why should Kant see belief in God and an immortal soul as necessary moral postulates? It is worth noting, given the interest they both took in Rousseau, how Durkheim's lectures on the *Social contract* report its argument for a civil religion, which reinforces morality's authority through the following principles: "the existence of God, the future life, the sanctity of the laws" ([1918b] 1953a: 194; t.134).

The notion of a cult of man has a long history in French republican thought, never took on, and even or especially as articulated by Durkheim is highly problematic, all of which is brought out by W. S. F. Pickering (1990, 1993a,b). The Durkheimian approach to religion, including a religion of man, has, of course, been much discussed. Three main recent interpretations are analyzed by François-André Isambert (1992), who sees the most authoritative as that of Pickering (1984), and there is again the question of what might be added.

But the concern, here, is with Durkheim's approach to modern secular ethics and morality, rather than religion as such, and concentrates on the aspects of his view of religion that seem the most relevant to this concern. These involve three interconnected emphases – on beliefs and sentiments at the core of the *conscience collective*, on faith, and on sacredness.

It is not an accident that Durkheim so often runs "beliefs and sentiments" together. "Belief", in line with contemporary French usage, is not simply cognitive, like "knowledge", but can include an emotive dimension, even a moral commitment, in a feeling of certainty. So, for example, there might still be a need to believe, even when we know, that there is a God, since there is a need, not just for a cognition, but for an emotive, intensely held sense of conviction and certainty. Similarly, and with the arrival of enlightenment, it might not be enough just to know that the modern social ideal is the human ideal. It might still have to be an entrenched and, however secular, "religious-like" belief.

This is clearly to emphasize the importance of the issue of motivation, rather than just of the nature of the right or the good. It is also a way in which, even with the arrival of enlightenment, there is still the dualism of reason and sentiment, with a need for both and neither reducible to the other. But it is not the only way. When Durkheim talks of "faith", he might very often just mean "belief", in the sense so far discussed. He again and again insists, however, that there is and will always be a need to go beyond knowledge. The autonomy of a complete understanding of things is a guiding but unrealizable ideal, and it is part of enlightenment to recognize the limits of knowledge in the very effort to extend them. So what happens when there is a need, even in enlightenment, to act beyond the limits of knowledge? We might reason, as best we can in this situation, in scientifically and philosophically disciplined ways. But the question remains, and Durkheim's answer is that ethical life requires that we act on the basis of belief, conviction, commitment and, in a word, faith. Guyau's answer is that the very idea of enlightenment requires, on the contrary, acceptance of moral and metaphysical uncertainty and risk.

Guyau is perhaps the first to claim that sociology must become "the science of risks" (1885: 216; t.126). His work is very much about modern enlightenment as an age of *anomie*, doubt, risk – and, above all, moral and metaphysical risk. There has been a reinvention, nowadays, of "the risk society" (Beck 1986). But it can seem tamer fare. In any case Durkheim himself develops, through his internalist programme, a powerful social theory of risks. These are risks systematically built into our world, and threatening not just the individual but liberal society and culture itself. The issue – doubt versus faith – that is articulated in the disagreement between Guyau and Durkheim is crucial for liberal culture and for ideals, which they both share, of enlightenment and of a republic of persons. An attempt will be made to identify a solution. But even if it is possible to sustain, let alone get to, a culture involving this, there is an in-built risk of collapse, via faith, into an authoritarianism that undermines and betrays the republic, or, via doubt, into a scepticism that undermines and paralyses commitment to it.

The issue is also connected with how, if at all, it is possible to secularize Kant's kingdom of ends and address his argument for God. It is at bottom an argument that ethical life requires hope. Durkheim never goes into it as this. He just talks, vaguely, of God as a metaphor for society. But if, more precisely, God represents hope, more care is needed before dispensing with Him.

Guyau remarks that, in religion, we can hope because we believe, and argues instead that we can believe because we hope (1885: 240; t.148). The idea of hope through belief captures the essence of Kant's argument for God as a necessary moral postulate. It also captures the essence of Durkheim's secular substitute: hope for a republic through belief in a dynamic working to bring it about. But it is necessary to add in belief because there is hope, since hope helps to sustain the very belief on which the dynamic depends – our own belief in and commitment to the human ideal itself.

Hope is a sentiment, just as it is a motive. All this again keeps the dualism of reason and sentiment in place, just as it is again to emphasize the importance of the issue of motivation, of the human ideal's entrenchment as a real, living, social ideal. It is undoubtedly an issue that helps to power Durkheim's constant appeal to a "cult" of man, in which the human person has become the "sacred" centre of the modern moral world. But his concern, here, is also of great, indeed original and seminal, importance for ethical understanding of the nature of the right and the good.

Durkheimian "sacredness" involves, in the first place, a constative–constitutive theory of moral belief. That is, to state and constitute something as a core moral belief, we have to state it in a special, "sacred" linguistic register, having the right emotive force, drawing on the resources of metaphor and of rhetoric and symbolism generally, and contrasting with registers appropriate for other, "profane" things (so that a way in which ethics might destroy morals is through the use of such registers).

But it is also a communicative theory. That is, it is concerned with how, through a register having the right emotive force, drawing on the resources of rhetoric, etc., something is not only stated and constituted but transmitted as a core moral belief throughout a group or society as a whole. This merges with the issue of motivation, of ideals that are real, living, social ideals, with a widespread, meaningful commitment to them. It leads on, at the same time, to Durkheim's stress

15

on symbols of all kinds. These include the ritual as symbolic action, the emblem as a symbol of identity, the icon as a symbol with sacrality transferred on to it from the thing it represents, and the *logos*, or the word itself, as a sacred text. So, as we read in *The elementary forms* : "social life, in all its aspects and in every period of its history, is made possible only by a vast symbolism" (1912a: 331; t.264). But an essential point of the argument is that symbolism does not just express or reinforce already existing beliefs. It helps to create and constitute them (*ibid.*: 329–31; t.262–4).

This is tied up with the idea of great periods of creative collective ferment. The idea first surfaces in an early review article on the French Revolution ([1890a] 1970a: 224; t.41). It reappears in a discussion of judgements of value and of reality, which cites the Revolution as one of these periods, ushering in a new era's ideals, and hope of the imminent coming of "the kingdom of God on earth" ([1911b] 1924a: 134; t.92). It again appears, with the Revolution as the example, in *The elementary forms*, and underlies the idea, in lectures of 1913–14 on pragmatism and sociology, of "mythological truths" – beliefs not just rooted in, but constitutive and creative of, a social reality (1955a: 175–8; t.86–8).

Durkheimian "mythological truths" and their symbols are constitutive in the philosophical sense that they enter into a society's very description. The case of the Revolution underlines how they are creative in a historical way. Indeed, it means that the human ideal is not simply a product of the division of labour. It has its own sources in the collective creativeness of the Revolution. But on both the historical and philosophical fronts the Revolution involves invention of the "individual" and "man" as the central modern identities. There is then every need for a powerful symbolism that constitutes, communicates and entrenches, in a "cult" of man, everyone's sacredness as a person.

It is necessary, after all, to struggle against and disempower the "vast symbolism" sustaining old regime ideology. It is necessary, too, to combat the instrumentalism continually secreted, via the market, by the modern world's own dynamic. But there are other reasons, lying in the human ideal itself. A community of commitment to it cannot be a community of belief, involving a widespread substantive consensus, even in the case of the development of a particular local society as a human *patrie*. Durkheim is generally opposed to the idea of a global *patrie*, but is nonetheless committed to global ethics and a universalism of our place and time, demanding respect for persons everywhere, aspiring to a human fraternity, and condemning man's inhumanity to man wherever, in our world, it may occur. His vision then seems to be of a global evolution of different societies, cultures and traditions, each developing their own particular versions of the human ideal around its basic, common search for everyone's status and sacredness as a person in a republic of persons. It is therefore a vision of human fraternity in which there may be continuing conflict between the traditions as well as within them, yet in which the strains of this can be contained by a basic sense of attachment, with a cult of man as an essential part of it.

From "is" to "ought"

Durkheim's first great work, *The division of labour*, begins with the statement that it is "above all an attempt to study the facts of moral life according to the method of the positive sciences" ([1893b] 1902b: xxxvii; t.32). The point made, Durkheim wants to drive home another. Like any science and its pursuit of knowledge as such, the science of morals is "theoretical". But it is also of vital importance for interests that are "practical". It helps to identify social problems, to propose reforms and to clarify, correct and decide on ideals. In sum, the science of morals is the key to ethics, or, as he says, "art". He attacks "mystics down the ages" who deny that one can inform and guide the other (*ibid.*: xli; t.36).

Durkheim's last work, the introduction to a long-projected book on morality, ends with a promise to investigate "how practical conclusions may be derived from these theoretical, scientific studies" (1920a: 97; t.93). Just as the theoretical refers to science, the practical again refers to "art", in this case, ethics. He writes, earlier in the introduction, that every science gives rise to an "art", but that morality is different, because "none of these techniques legislates on ends", whereas morality "consists, above all, in positing ends" (*ibid.*: 85; t.83). So when he talks of moral science's "practical" conclusions he remains set on it as the key to ethics, helping to clarify, rework and decide on ideals and ends.

In wanting, all along, a moral science that informs moral art, Durkheim insists, all along, that they are different things. As in his

Latin thesis, science "is of more service to art the better it is kept distinct from it" (1892a: 15; tf.34; t.7). As in his main thesis: "If we carefully separate theoretical from practical problems, it is not to neglect the latter; it is, on the contrary, to be in a better position to solve them" ([1893b] 1902b: xxxix; t.33). It is a recipe for misunderstanding to translate his *science de la morale* as a "science of ethics". For Durkheim, a "science of ethics" is a contradiction in terms and nothing to do with his project, which is for moral science as a rational basis of moral art. But this art, concerned with what ought to be, cannot itself constitute a science, concerned with what is. Hence his criticism of Montesquieu:

> What is the case is not discussed in one part of his book, what ought to be in another, but art and science are so mixed together that there is often an imperceptible passage from one to the other. (1892a: 23; tf.45; t.16).

Durkheim is less restrained in the article on the Revolution, in condemning the political sciences so-called and their "half-theoretical half-practical bastard speculations" ([1890a] 1970a: 225; t.42). He says the same years later in a review endorsing Lucien Lévy–Bruhl's *Ethics and moral science* and attacking ethical systems, with their theoretical-cum-practical mix, as a "bastard conception" ([1904a(5)] 1969c: 467; t.29–30).

So again there is no change in Durkheim's position. But it is itself a mixture, of the subtle and the naïve. The subtlety is seeing "is" and "ought" as distinct while looking for ways of connecting them. The naïvety is wanting, as in the criticism of Montesquieu, one part of an enquiry that is just about "what is the case", another just about "what ought to be". This can be brought out through his own appeal, in the thesis on Montesquieu, to an idea of the "normal". It is a dual-purpose concept, serving scientific and evaluative interests simultaneously. The result is that, even if a discusssion concentrates on the "normal" from the perspective of science and makes no attempt to explore its implications from the perspective of ethics, it inevitably contains such implications. Looking for them is the whole point of looking to the "normal" as a bridge between moral science and moral art.

Durkheim never gave up the idea of the normal. It develops into the internalist programme's key argument about an underlying dynamic and rationale. The argument becomes the route from "is" to "ought", via what becomes his basic ethical position. This is not so much: *the real is the rational is the good*. It is more: *the real and its rationale are the good*.[4]

Its beginnings can be seen in the article on the Revolution. Durkheim asks his readers to approach the ideals of 1789 as social facts, instead of arguing over them as philosophical principles. They then emerge as expressions, however inadequate, of an "underlying reality" ([1890a] 1970a: 218; t.36). There can also be understanding of their absolute, religious-like character, something "found in all creative epochs, in all periods of a new and audacious faith" (*ibid.*: 224; t.41). Moreover, they have become general, persistent beliefs, surviving over time and spreading well beyond the country of their birth. They therefore "depend, not on local and accidental circumstances, but on some change which has taken place in the structure of European societies". He continues:

> It is only when it is known with some precision what this change is that it is possible to be definite about the status of the principles of 1789 and to say if they constitute a pathological phenomenon, or indeed, on the contrary, if they simply represent a necessary transformation of our social consciousness. (*ibid.*)

They are not of course pathological, but indeed, on the contrary, a necessary transformation of our social consciousness. We know, apart from the give-away rhetoric, that Durkheim had already done enough work on his thesis on the division of labour to know this (1888c: 257–9). So starting with the ideals of 1789 as facts, he is out to establish them as the ethic of our time, which ought to be accepted as such, even when he goes on to ask, again rhetorically:

> do not all the difficulties with which modern peoples struggle come from the pain we experience in adapting the traditional structure of societies to these new and unconscious aspirations at work on them for a century? (*ibid.*: 224–5; t.42)

We might note the complex relationship between ideals and structures. Changing structures are the basis of emerging ideals – but these are also formed in a creative collective ferment, and become aspirations that help to change the traditional system. We must especially note the two routes to the "normal": observation of general, persistent phenomena, and, more fundamentally, search for a dynamic and rationale.

A worry, driving the internalist programme's development in the Latin and in the main thesis, is the possibility that the two routes might diverge, so that something becomes general that is nonetheless pathological in terms of an underlying rationale. It is again a recipe for misunderstanding Durkheim's project if we just fix on "normality" as an affair of the general. It is the real and its rationale that matter. This becomes clear in the lectures on moral education. It is again evident in a series of engagements with philosophers in the 1900s.

Durkheim insists, in a debate with Dominique Parodi: "All moral systems have their own rationality. All moral forces have their reality. All of them are natural and consequently rational, like the rest of nature" (1910b: 60; t.66). A debate of especial interest is with Gustave Belot. It is concerned with ideas on ethics and moral science Belot had first set out in articles – reviewed by Durkheim – and then in a book (Belot 1905–6, 1907). Durkheim thinks Belot works with two ideas of the rational, and accepts the first but rejects the second. The first, which he accepts, is "an objective rationality, immanent in reality, a rationality given in things themselves, which the inquirer *discovers, brings out,* but does not *create*". The second is "a rationality the mind has to construct, create and not just detect" (1908a(2): 190; t.54). How, Durkheim goes on to ask, is it possible to pass from one rationale to the other? It is not, and Belot protests against the categorical distinction foisted on him (Durkheim 1908a(2): 193–4; t.57–8). So might Durkheim himself, given his own view of ideals and aspirations that are both socially rooted and socially creative. But he repeats his question, aimed against Belot's supposed appeal to a completely new, completely different rationale: "how does the objective study of moral facts permit the determination of new ends, different from those existing morality assigns to conduct?" (*ibid.*: 194; t.58). It does not, and Durkheim is affirming not changing his position, the crux of which is the development of "new" aspirations out of an existing but dynamic social and moral reality. As in *The division of labour*, we cannot create an ethic completely different from "the ruling one" ([1893b] 1902b: xli; t.35–6). As in the review of Belot himself, the study of social and moral reality is the only rational way we have to understand the dynamic of things and "the ideals that strive to realize themselves" ([1907a(4)] 1969c: 583).

The discussion of Durkheimian moral science *and* ethics that remains the most authoritative is by Georges Gurvitch (1937, 1938). The main other discussions are by R. T. Hall (1987, 1993), François-André Isambert (1990, 1993c), and Ernest Wallwork (1972). But all retreat, if in different ways, from defence of Durkheim's project of moral science as the key to ethics. Indeed, Hall sees a basic change of approach somewhere around the 1900s. But he construes the *science de la morale*, in its early days, as a science of ethics; dates the "bastard" criticism to the Lévy-Bruhl review when it is there from the start; thinks that the question pressed on Belot expresses a sense of defeat; passes over talk of the real and its rationale; and interprets, in an anodyne way, moral science's "practical" implications for moral art. It is a "change" from something Durkheim was always against to mere advice on means to ends.

In contrast, Gurvitch sees Durkheim as committed, all along, to the project of a science of morals as the key to ethics. It is just that he is opposed to it as misbegotten. He sees Lévy-Bruhl as opposed to it too – and he might be, although clearly wanting to get from "is" to "ought" in his reply to critics in a new edition of his book (Lévy-Bruhl 1910: xii–xvii). A lot turns on the exact route, but also on Gurvitch's rejection of grandiose ethics and appeal to the phenomenological approach of Frédéric Rauh's *Moral experience*. Thus, his rejection of the Durkheimian project is above all of Durkheimian "metaethics" and the "semi-sociological, semi-metaphysical" equation at its heart. The equation is: "Society = Mind = the Supreme Good" (Gurvitch [1937] 1961: 69; 1938: 280). It is not difficult to justify this reading. In a way it corresponds with the reading suggested here: "the real and its rationale are the good." Again, a lot turns on Durkheim's insistence on science's empirical, phenomenological detective work – but as part of a rationalism that looks for a logic in things. It also turns on the role of claims we can and must subject to argument, yet that are speculative, even apparently unsettlable, and perhaps at the core of most or all social science research programmes. They are nonetheless "empirical" in that they are about the world, and even though inescapably evaluative in their import. Gurvitch seems to think it possible to get away from such claims altogether, both in social science itself and in ethics. Here it is taken it is not.

Part I

"America"

Chapter One

Developing a moral science

Durkheim's early work is of considerable interest. Apart from his two theses, it consists of reviews, articles and lectures, including his inaugural lecture of 1887 in a new appointment in social science at the university of Bordeaux. The best place to start is with his preoccupation with "real" man.

Real versus abstract man

Durkheim again and again describes the "real" man, usually in an attack on "abstract" man. In his inaugural lecture he says:

> The real man, whom we know and whom we are, is more complex; he is of a time and place, he has a family, a city, a country, a religious and political faith, and all these and many other concerns come together, combine in a thousand ways, cross and crisscross in their influence so that it is not at first sight possible to tell where one begins and another ends. ([1888a] 1970a: 85)

It is an argument about our social situatedness that connects with a number of other arguments, about solidariness, morality's roots in the real, and identity.

Solidariness is "the condition of social life" ([1886a] 1970a: 207), and "the very source of morality" (1893b: 10; t.415). Indeed, as attachment to one another and society as ends, it *is* morality, and only real man can be moral man.

"The ideal has no basis unless it keeps its roots in reality" ([1893b] 1902b: xxxix; t.34). Ethics cannot guide and perfect morals without a knowledge of reality: "The ideal constructed by it would otherwise just be a work of poetic fantasy, a purely subjective conception with no possibility of actualization in the world of facts, since with no relationship with them" (1888c: 274). The reality Durkheim has in mind clearly has to do with real man's social situation and situatedness. But it is also of interest to note his talk of "poetic fantasy" versus the "world of facts". It is the first expression of the theme of what we can imagine versus what we can will. Moreover, in an important article on German moral science, Durkheim was already beginning to define "facts" – including moral sentiments and aspirations – as things resistant to change at will (1887c: 44–5; t.72–3), a view articulated in the Latin thesis (1892a: 20; tf.41; t.12), and again in *The rules* ([1895a] 1901c: 29; t.71).

This ties up with the argument about identity, since our identity is something basic that we cannot just change at will. The identity argument is itself very much tied up with attachment to one another as ends and our social situatedness, for it is all about ends that are constitutive of the self and part and parcel of who we are. It is a long-standing argument, going back to Durkheim's first publication: "The real man, the man truly man, is integrally part of a society which he wills as himself, since he cannot withdraw from it without degeneration and collapse" (1885a: 95). It is repeated in various forms thereafter, including in the discussion paper on moral facts: "To will a morality other than that implied by the nature of society is to deny the latter and, in consequence, oneself" ([1906b] 1924a: 54; t.38).

The identity argument is an important Durkheimian route, via real man, from "is" to "ought", and we shall have to return to it. Let us pursue, at this point, another question. Who or what is abstract man?

There are three Durkheimian candidates, and one of them might come as a surprise, since it is an oversocialized conception of man. Durkheim's long-running campaign for a *sui generis* social science certainly opposes attempts at biological or psychological reduction. But he is as much as anything against these because they are one-dimensional. He criticizes Gumplowicz for a similarly one-dimensional account of the world of society, sealing it off from "the world of life" (1885c: 634). All along and from the outset, Durkheim is interested in how, in "life", the social, psychic and physical aspects of our existence interact, or even conflict. Indeed, a reason for talking, here, of the organic self is its resonance with this interest in the embodied self and the different facets of "life".

Durkheim is also against the invention of a single, world-historical man, as in stories of an unfolding World Spirit. In the German moral science article he attacks Wundt's belief in "*one* moral ideal which develops in all actual moralities; *one* humanity of which particular societies are merely the provisional and symbolic embodiments" (1887c: 141; t.121). He repeats the attack, only without mentioning Wundt, in *The division of labour* ([1893b] 1902b: xxxviii; t.33).

However, the main target of his campaign against abstract man is undoubtedly the idea of an unchanging, socially decontextualized, essential man. Sometimes he condemns particular theorists working with this conception. Sometimes he condemns them *en bloc* – "the philosophers", with their timeless ideal of "the person", or "the economists", with their belief in "the individual" as a natural, thoroughgoing egoist. What is his case against such model characters?

He accepts that abstraction has a role, but not that it licenses just anything. It must be based on observation and experiment ([1890a] 1970a: 220; t.38). It "consists in isolating part of reality, not in making it disappear"(1887c: 39; t.66). A possible response is that *homo economicus*, say, has such a basis. But this is to agree with Durkheim that an abstraction's value depends on its realistic credentials. A more radical response is that abstractions not at all claiming to be realistic can still have value if they generate successful predictions. Durkheim would have been unimpressed. His concern is with science as an understanding and explanation of the world, not as a magical, who-knows-why, predictive technique. He certainly objects to abstract man as part of an anti-sociohistorical, essentially deductive approach: the theorist does not stir from the study to investigate and discover how things *are*, but simply announces some axioms, then reasons from these how things *must be* ([1888a] 1970a: 84–5). Again, either it is conceded that models of man should pass an empirical, realistic test, or it is necessary to give a more radical and more problematic defence of not bothering with such tests at all.

Indeed, "rational reconstructions" deducing social life from the abstract individual are incoherent. The point is developed in *The division of labour*, and especially in the argument that all in the contract is not contractual. But the point had already been made in an early review. A contract does not arise in a void and create something wholly new. It assumes and is itself created and regulated by an already existing society. It is "a spontaneous adaptation of two or more individuals to each other, in conditions determined by the social and physical milieu in which they find themselves placed"(1886b: 662). It can be added, if it needs to be added, that, just as the contract is made as a convention of a real, historical, already existing society, so the contracting individuals are themselves already real, flesh and blood, highly social characters. "Rational reconstructions" are incoherent because the contracts between abstract individuals from which they attempt to derive social life already smuggle in and presuppose it.

In sum, Durkheim builds up a powerful case against abstract man. But there are also problems with real man, and let us now examine them.

One shows up in *The rules*. Durkheim criticizes the "nominalism" of historians and, somewhat confusingly, the "extreme realism" of philosophers ([1895a] 1901c: 76–7; t.108–9). What is going on? The trouble with emphasizing real people and their very different social situations is that it might rule out the very idea of a comparative social science. This must steer clear of the abstract sands of philosophers, concerned only with the general and universal. It must do so without heading straight for the concrete rocks of historians, concerned only with the detailed and particular. Durkheim sees and seeks to avoid the difficulty long before *The rules*, in his inaugural lecture.

He tackles the view, common amongst historians, that the circumstances of social life are so complex, variable and diverse that they "resist all generalization" and "do not lend themselves to comparison" ([1888a] 1970a: 81). He sees history and sociology not as rival but as distinct and complementary disciplines. Sociologists need to draw on detailed evidence, while historians need a more general view to sift through it and to ask "the questions which limit and guide their researches" (*ibid.*: 108). In suggesting what this more general view might be, Durkheim accuses Comte of working with an abstract idea of society, as if, at bottom, there is only a "single social type" (*ibid.*: 88–9). He praises Spencer for his interest in "distinguishing different social types" (*ibid.*: 93). Durkheim himself always insists on a comparative social science that seeks to understand particular societies through important characteristics that they share and that differentiate them, as a type, from others. The idea of the normal is bound up with this, and it is unDurkheimian to define the normal in terms of a particular, individual society. He makes clear in *The division of labour* that a whole society can be in some way deviant compared with others of the same type (1893b: 34; t.432), and in a famous footnote sees England as in certain respects abnormal compared with Europe ([1893b] 1902b: 266, n.4; t.282, n.30). Perhaps, in other respects, it is a pathological case today.

It is consistent with all this that he still recognizes and indeed looks for things that are very general or even universal, such as "the formation of the *conscience collective*, the principle of the division of labour", etc. ([1886a] 1970a: 214). Or as he says in the Latin thesis: "just as all societies, however different, have something in common, so there are certain laws found in every society" (1892a: 29; tf.53; t.22). But the point is made in a context emphasizing how much laws, morals and so on vary between social types. The same is true when he says in *The division of labour*: "it is a fundamental duty everywhere to ensure the existence of one's country." This comes in the middle of a long argument driving home sociohistorical variation, and is to contrast earlier societies with our own. They could not have survived if they had had "the respect for individual dignity which we profess today" (1893b: 21; t.423).

It is misleading to take the claim about duty to one's country out of context, to claim that the "early" Durkheim is a universalist rather than a relativist in his ethical theory (Wallwork 1972: 164). Durkheim – "early" or "late" – is both, always recognizing moral universals while always emphasizing every social type's own morality. The most important statement of his ethical theory, the course on moral education, analyzes duty and the good as moral universals while emphasizing autonomy as an aspiration of the modern human ideal.

Indeed, the contrast Durkheim himself wants to make, between traditional demands of duty towards one's society and the modern demand of "respect for individual dignity", takes us to another problem for real versus abstract man. It concerns the content of the modern *conscience collective*, which, as Durkheim announces in *The division of labour*, is this ethic of respect for individual dignity. It is an ethic, as he repeatedly says, of the individual in general, in the abstract and as man. Yet he repeatedly criticizes abstract man. So how can he defend and attack the selfsame thing?

It is again unpromising to divide Durkheim up into "early" and "late", or in this case the "very early" and "not so late". The main ideas of *The division of labour* were in place many years before its publication, as we know both from Durkheim's own lectures and from the testimony of his student and nephew, Marcel Mauss (introduction to [1928a] 1971d: 27; t.32). Part of the answer is to distinguish support for the human ideal's version of abstract man from attacks on the moral cripple, *homo economicus*. The fundamental answer is that Durkheim defends moral individualism on methodologically holist, sociohistorical grounds, and attacks its deduction from man as a methodological axiom-cum-atom. As he says in *The division of labour*, the ethic of the individual draws all its force from society ([1893b] 1902b: 147; t.172), and in a later article: "individualism is itself a social product, like all moralities and all religions" ([1898c] 1970a: 275, n.1; t.70, n.4).

There is a snag, to do with the arguments about situatedness and identity and how they are connected. In an article of 1887, a statement of one argument leads on, in the same page, to a statement of the other:

> The real and concrete man changes along with the physical and social milieu which envelops him, and morality, completely naturally, changes with men . . .
> The individual is integrally part of the society into which he is born; this penetrates him from all sides; to withdraw and isolate himself from it is to diminish himself. (1887a: 337)

The two arguments more or less merge in a review of Alfred Fouillée:

> the milieu in which [the individual] acts, the atmosphere which he breathes, the society which surrounds him, all this reaches into him, stamps, shapes and fashions him, without his seeing it, without his feeling it and above all without his complaining about it; for it is also that which constitutes the best part of himself. ([1885b] 1970a: 172–3)

This is Durkheim in full collectivist throttle. It can happen throughout his work, and the snag is that we cannot just assume that his identity argument can as readily accommodate "liberal" as other socially situated selves, or as readily attach us to a "liberal" as to any other social world. He does not at all come across, from the argument, as someone out to champion individual freedom. Yet this is what he is out to champion. The ethic of our place and time – stamping, shaping, fashioning, penetrating us from all sides, and to deny which is to deny the nature of our society and in consequence to deny ourselves – is an ethic of freedom. Just as the Revolution combined ideals of liberty *and* fraternity, the thesis of *The division of labour* is that the dynamic of the modern world makes for autonomy *and* solidarity ([1893b] 1902b: xliii–xliv; t.37–8). How does the thesis develop in Durkheim's early work, and how can a sociology of real man ground an ethic of abstract man?

Particular connexions, enlarged society and modern man

The inaugural lecture criticizes Spencer for just emphasizing modern freedom:

> Individual freedom is always and everywhere limited by social constraint, in the form of customs, *mores*, laws, regulations. And, since in proportion to the growth in volume of societies the sphere of action of society increases at the same time as that of the individual, a legitimate complaint against M. Spencer is for having seen only one side of reality, and perhaps the less important. ([1888a] 1970a: 96)

The German moral science article criticizes Ihering for just emphasizing modern regulation:

> With progress, the human person more and more emerges from the surrounding physical or social milieu and assumes a sense of a distinct identity; the freedom which is enjoyed increases at the same time as social obligations. Here is an obscure phenomenon, contradictory in appearance, and which, to our knowledge, has not yet been explained. Social progress has two sides which seem to exclude each other; therefore most of the time there is seen only one. (1887c: 54; t.84)

Take the passages together, and we have the thesis of *The division of labour*. Moreover, its underlying ideas must have been taught in

31

Durkheim's first lecture course at Bordeaux, given his summary of that course in the opening lecture of the following year. Two very different types of society had been analyzed, involving two very different types of solidarity. "Mechanical" solidarity, as he had called it, is "due to the similarity of consciences, to the community of ideas and sentiments". "Organic" solidarity, as he had called it, is "a product of the differentiation of functions and of the division of labour". Strictly speaking, it can be said that the two types of solidarity have never existed without each other. But mechanical solidarity dominates life in primitive societies, where tradition and custom govern people's activities down to the last detail. In contrast, organic solidarity very much characterizes modern society. This *allows its members their independence while strengthening the unity of the whole*" (1888c: 258; italics added).

Durkheim unfortunately does not remind his students how. The answer, to speculate, might be filled in from *The division of labour* itself. If society continues to shape us, it is not into the same mould, but into individuals, constituting increasingly diverse, distinct and independent centres of thought and action. As such, we are particular personalities, linked through particular relationships, norms and functions. So this is a highly concrete picture of individuality and integration, yet brings in abstract man in a number of interconnected ways. One is the enlargement of society through the division of labour. Another is a continuing need for a shared identity, however general, and for shared beliefs, however general. Another is the dependence of respect for the empirical individual on respect both for everyone's status as a person and for "the person" itself as a collective idea and representation. So we can get both freedom and cohesion, and ground an abstract ethic on a concrete sociology.

Or can we? Durkheim's first review is an enthusiastic piece on Schaeffle, in which he often seems to speak in his own voice. He is certainly interested in a "cult of the ideal". It concerns the internal mental world of the individual, yet does not isolate us in that world: "On the contrary, there is no more powerful link binding men to one another. For the ideal is impersonal; it is the common good of humanity" (1885a: 87). This points ahead to Durkheim's own insistence on morality as an affair of "impersonal ideals", and to his own commitment to the modern "human ideal". But the review is important for a number of other reasons. One, as we have seen, is concern with the risk inherent in modernity of collapse either into individualism's conflict of "unfettered egoisms" or into a "despotic socialism": Schaeffle's solution, which Durkheim obviously endorses, is corporatist reform (*ibid.*: 96). Another is concern at a narrow "blind patriotism" and hope for a "cosmopolitanism" that, instead of destroying, can harmonize with "national life" (*ibid.*: 90) – pointing ahead to hope for a human *patrie*. Another, however, is worry over how such routes to modernity's human ideal rather than internal collapse might come about. Durkheim criticizes appeal just to a sentiment of solidarity, abstracted from relationships that are "simple, obvious, tangible, escaping no one". The problem, to which he does not suggest a solution, is how solidarity with a wider society and its human ideal can arise from relationships entailing only a "limited horizon" (*ibid.*:100).

He soon sees the answer in the division of labour. The difficulty that persists, and indeed develops as part of the internalist programme's development, is to do with virtuous versus vicious circles in the modern dynamic's self-realization versus self-collapse. The virtuous circle is once the intermediate groups of corporatist reform and the human cult and culture of a human *patrie* all get going. The vicious circle is that they cannot get going, thanks to the forces that make them necessary.

Is there an even more basic difficulty? From the outset, Durkheim is against up in the air talk just about sentiments and ideals. It escalates their centrality into all-importance, ignores their roots, and is no way to understand society, or, which also matters, to try to reform it. From the outset, he emphasizes the need for definite, "tangible" relationships, and for understanding of underlying social structures, movements and processes. From the outset, he tries to negotiate a way through all this that steers clear of the dogmatic wastelands of extreme "materialism" on the one hand and extreme "idealism" on the other. The basic difficulty is not so much doing so, as escaping the pigeonholing of him, from the outset, in just such terms.

Boutroux makes a thinly veiled attack on Durkheim in arguing that the division of labour, far from being a "mechanical" necessity, involves "an end, the cessation of the struggle for life", and is a "more or less intelligently conceived means of realizing this ideal" (Boutroux 1895b: 131–2; t.199–200). A reviewer of *The rules* accuses Durkheim of constructing "a sort of blind algebra" (Anon. 1895: Jan. supplement, 1). Views, at a 1911 conference, of Durkheim's conversion to idealism are reported by Augustin Guyau (1913: 221), who nonetheless complains that Durkheim's "system oscillates between the sociological materialism of Marx and the voluntarist idealism of Fouillée" (*ibid.*: 136). Indeed, with Fouillée replaced by Parsons, this is a theme that preoccupies Jeffrey Alexander (1982, vol. 2).

On the one hand, the 1887 inaugural lecture insists that the *conscience collective* merely records realities without creating them; it expresses underlying social processes more or less faithfully, and "does nothing more" ([1888a] 1970a: 194). On the other, an earlier review insists that "it is *mores* which shape the law and which determine the organic structure of societies" (1885c: 632), while a review of the same year as the lecture praises J-M. Guyau's account of birthrates, which shows that "the causes are above all moral", and that "until now only religion has combatted Malthusian doctrines and practices" (1887b: 304; t.29–30). But the 1890 article on the Revolution, as we have seen, involves the development of a complex overall view of the relationship and interaction between ideas and structures.

One of the complexities is crucial for understanding the argument of *The division of labour*. This is the difference between wanting a world-historical evolutionary story and an account of change and development in particular societies. In summarizing his inaugural lecture course, Durkheim summarizes the world-historical argument of his later thesis. The increasing division of labour and volume and density of societies constitute "probably one of the principal factors dominating all history" and "the cause which explains the transformations through which social solidarity has passed" (1888c: 259). It is to make this point that *The division of labour* makes the famous claim: "Everything happens mechanically" ([1893b] 1902b: 253; t.270). It is to make a different point that the German moral science article makes the less famous claim: "everything happens mechanically, and *mores* produce moral consequences without these having been intended or foreseen" (1887c: 120; t.97).

But if we return to *The division of labour*, take an interest in world-historical evolution, and look for a world-historical factor running through it, Durkheim offers morphology and so some sort of "materialism". He discounts, as logic requires, ideas that are local and culturally specific. He also discounts appeals to a World Spirit. Then unless his critics come out and announce there is such a Spirit – timeless or unfolding, let us not quibble – this exhausts the "idealist" possibilities.

Or it does so if, to repeat, we want to identify a factor running through all of human social evolution. It is different once we turn our attention, like Durkheim himself, to local social worlds. Accounts of them, like his own, can let in an active role for ideas while keeping out "idealism" as much as "materialism".

Let us leave things there for the moment, to take up other issues.

Morality and the *conscience collective*

Durkheim sees such close links between morality and religion that he has difficulty in distinguishing them:

> What difference is there between religious prescriptions and the injunctions of morality? They are equally directed at members of one and the same community, and supported by sometimes identical, always analogous sanctions; finally, their violation arouses in consciences the same feelings of anger and disgust. ([1886a] 1970a: 193; t.19)

The passage is of interest as Durkheim's earliest statement of morality as a matter of obligatoriness and of sanctions expressing the reaction of a *conscience collective*. The review as a whole is of interest, containing in germ the irreducible dualism of duty and the good. Morality has authority over us and imposes itself as "a social discipline" (*ibid.*: 206). It also involves positive fellow-feeling and attachments, and "solidarity comes, not from outside, but from within" (*ibid.*: 212).

The inaugural lecture concentrates on the element of obligatoriness, but across the board, to cover "judgements", "maxims" and "beliefs" that are shared throughout a society and that "exercise a sort of ascendancy over the will, which feels constrained to conform to them" ([1888a] 1970a: 102).

The moral analysis in *The division of labour*'s original introduction concentrates on obligatoriness too, but of "rules of conduct". It was suppressed in the new edition, perhaps because its view of morality was too one-sided and "dour" (Isambert 1993a: 126–7), or perhaps because it distracted too much attention away from the rest of the book (Besnard 1987: 25, n.4). It certainly contrasts with the rest of the book's concern with positive attachments, the aspirations of the human ideal and the development of autonomy – as well as with the account of duty itself in the lectures on moral education – and, although it tells us something about the *conscience collective*, we anyway have to turn to the rest of the book to find out more.

The adventures of the *conscience collective*, from *The division of labour* on, still get their fullest discussion from Gurvitch (1963, vol. 2: 1–58). But let us stress a number of things here. The *conscience collective* always very much involves strong convictions and beliefs, including strong sentiments of morals. These are always felt with an obligatory force. In *The division of labour* they are conceived as shared beliefs, "common to the whole society" and existing in the collective bit of everyone's consciousness, as against diverse, personal beliefs existing in the individual bit, so that there are "two consciousnesses in us" ([1893b] 1902b: 74; 105). This sees off the spectre of an independently existing "group mind". It can still be seen off with increasing insistence, from *The rules* on, that what we think and feel arises, as in times of collective ferment, through collective ways of thinking and feeling. It might come closer with increasing insistence, from *Suicide* on, that individual ideas of a collective idea never capture it, that individual thought and experience, even in contributing to and drawing on collective thought and experience, never comprehend it: "collective thought is only feebly and incompletely represented in each individual consciousness" (1955a: 204; t.104). Indeed, in *The division of labour* itself, the human ideal at the core of the modern *conscience collective* is precisely something around which there is "a multitude" of different and conflicting interpretations ([1893b] 1902b: 147; t.172). Then even if none of this entails a group mind, it has far-reaching implications, as we shall see, for autonomy, enlightenment and modern cohesion around a "cult" of man.

The division of labour's original introduction is very clear that "if we define the moral rule by the sanction attached to it, it is not because we consider the sentiment of obligation as a product of the sanction". On the contrary, it is because the sanction is the outward sign and symbol, "accessible to observation", of the obligatoriness constitutive of a moral rule (1893b: 25; t.426). In fact, the symbolism of the sanction is part of a whole theory in which "ideas" must have an active social role: strong sentiments of morals react, when offended, with condemnation or other sanctions that not only express the sentiments but reinforce and reproduce them. But the theory as developed by Durkheim remains incomplete. It also requires a theory of responsibility concerned with who or what it is seen as appropriate to subject to a sanction, something developed in a brilliant, undeservedly neglected book by Durkheim's student and successor at the Sorbonne, Paul Fauconnet (1920).

The division of labour's original introduction also contains one of Durkheim's most important attacks on the attempts of "moralists" to deduce everything from a few axioms. Moral life, far from running on a few principles, involves "a great number of special precepts" (1893b: 16; t.419). So when the introduction goes on to define morality in terms of rules, the context implies detailed, specific rules. His earlier discussions of obligatoriness do not necessarily imply this, and indeed do not usually talk of rules at all. They refer to *mores*, customs, precepts, maxims, beliefs, norms, even judgements.

Mores and customs again have to do with the specific, whereas precepts, maxims and beliefs could be very general. But *mores* and customs also have to do with unreflective tradition, whereas precepts and maxims may belong to a more "rational" world – as may rules. The introduction's general talk of rules can thus obscure a central concern of *The division of labour*, as of earlier work. This is the lifting of the "yoke" of tradition and the passage from *mores* to modernity.

It is also worth asking about "norms", in the sense of the German moral science article's discussion of Wundt, which is not at all a discussion of them as detailed rules. Wundt, Durkheim indicates, sees norms as socially established, general maxims, embodying "moral ends ... which are conceived as obligatory" (1887c: 134–6; t.113–15). Durkheim himself, in insisting in the same article that there are "as many moralities as social types", stresses that they have their own "ends" and "ideals" (*ibid.*: 142; t.122). Passages earlier on in the article reveal his view of the norms – the obligatory ends and ideals – of our own, modern society as the "sentiment of human dignity" and "a more extensive personal freedom for everyone" (*ibid.*: 41; t.68).

Belief in this freedom and dignity involves attachment, not just to particular people but to everyone's status as a person, and to "the person" as a collective representation. Hence it is itself impersonal. Hence the aspirations of the modern human ideal, although not detailed rules, can pass almost all of Durkheim's tests of normal moral facts. They are moral, being impersonal (the 1885 Schaeffle test), and being shared, obligatory beliefs (the 1886 Spencer test). They are normal, because they are general throughout modern society but also because they are rooted in its dynamic (the 1890 Revolution test). They are facts, because, as beliefs rooted in our society and our very character, they are "things" resisting change at will (the 1887 German moral science and the 1892 Latin thesis test). They fail the 1893 introduction test, or they do if the introduction is taken as insisting on detailed rules, and, if it is, this emphasis can be discounted as too one-sided compared with the other moral concerns that run through *The division of labour* itself, as well as Durkheim's later *and* earlier work.

Let us now return to ideas versus structures, and a passage from *mores* to modernity. If we want an active, socially transformative role for ideas, it seems unpromising to look for it in *mores* and customs. What, anyway, does Durkheim mean when he says that *mores* "determine" structures? What, for that matter, does he mean when he says that the *conscience collective* "records" an underlying reality and does nothing more? He says the same in the lecture summarizing early work on his thesis on the division of labour, but expands on it in a way that is significant. *Mores* and law are "crystallizations" expressing only "already fixed and consolidated social changes"; they constitute "a legacy of the past which persists from sheer force of habit and conceals the present"; we must look elsewhere to get at "the movements of collective life" (1888c: 270–71).

He then goes into the empirical detective work of tracking such movements through signs of them, instead of jumping right away into discussion of their nature and causes. We can remark, even so, on a number of things. When he says that *mores* "determine" structures, this can mean that they fix, consolidate and crystallize them, rather than that they constitute fundamental, socially creative forces. But fixed, crystallized structures cannot constitute such forces either, unless to obstruct "the movements of collective life" and lock us into the past. It is thus vital to understand the "division" as a *dividing* of labour, as a *continuing process* – crystallizing, for a time, into a particular "division" in the sense of structure of labour, but then struggling to break free from this and to move on. It is also to struggle to break free from the *conscience collective*, in its aspect as a storehouse of beliefs, not just recording the past, but clinging obstinately to it. Such beliefs, like structures, can have an active role, in that it is actively conservative and backward looking. So it might again seem unpromising, in wanting ideas that are more socially dynamic, to go to religion. But this is to forget about the "new and audacious faith" of the Revolution.

Faith

By far the most important early texts in which Durkheim discusses religion are the reviews of Guyau and Spencer, in that order, although the review of Wundt in the German moral science article is of some interest too, as is, of course, the article on the Revolution. The Durkheimian line on religion will be gone into in more detail later. In the meantime, let us try to bring out a problem Durkheim struggled with all his life.

A standard view of religion is that it is both cognitive, involving a cosmological description of the world, and practical, helping to guide conduct. The question that then arises is what, if anything, is left once enlightenment replaces religion's practical side with secular ethics and its cognitive side with secular science and philosophy. Indeed, this is why Guyau argues for a "non-religion of the future". Durkheim wants to resist the conclusion. But how?

He accuses Guyau and Spencer of an "intellectualism" that sees religion as essentially cognitive, and insists, instead, that it is above all practical. Then this might save religion, if it is not essentially cognitive, from science. How can it save religion, if it is above all practical, from ethics? Or does his attack on intellectualist error contain the answer?

Intellectualism treats religion as some sort of debating society. It fails to understand that religion "dictates" ideas ([1886a] 1970a: 195; t.21), and that its beliefs are "obligatory" (1887b: 161–3; t.35–7). An intellectualist error is to think that a prejudice disappears because found irrational, when, on the contrary, "it is found irrational because it is already disappearing" ([1886a] 1970a: 194; t.20). A prejudice, Durkheim explains, is "not a false judgment" but a product of socially accumulated experience, a custom, a habit, and the greatest intellectualist error is to think that a society without prejudices would be a good thing, when, on the contrary, it would be like an organism without reflexes, "a monster incapable of living" (*ibid.*: 197; t.22). It is in this conservative-sounding context that he argues that the *conscience collective* simply records society and does nothing more. It is in the same conservative-sounding context that he says that "religion begins with faith, that is, with every belief accepted or submitted to without discussion" (*ibid.*: 195; t.21). It is also in the same context that he insists that there is no future without religion, whatever particular form it might take with the progress of modern society: "As long as men live together, there will be a faith held by them in common" (*ibid.*: 197; t.22).

Yet how, "without discussion", can a new secular humanist faith replace traditional religion, and how, without discussion, can it be part and parcel of enlightenment? If this is Durkheim's way of saving religion from ethics and modern demands for free thought and enquiry, it does not save it at all. In insisting on the obligatoriness of religious beliefs, he explains that it is because they are rooted in the social milieu and express vital, practical social concerns. But it is precisely his own point, in work on the division of labour, that modern demands for freedom are rooted in the social milieu and express vital, practical social concerns.

He is especially anxious to dissociate religion from metaphysics. If anything essential of religion remains it will not be an urge to construct "grandiose syntheses" and to ask and try to answer "insoluble questions". If anything is likely to disappear it is metaphysics itself. Its development "does not run parallel with the human mind". On the contrary, it is part of enlightenment that we see and recognize "the limits of our knowledge", and that recognition of such limits becomes "an integral element of the scientific outlook" (1887b: 311; t.38).

He is silent, on this occasion, about what we should do when we have to act beyond these limits. Yet his whole argument points firmly in the direction of practical faith. In fact it must, or concede Guyau's whole case for an enlightened non-religion of the future, getting away from dogma without discussion, embracing *anomie*, and coping with moral risk and doubt. He seems reluctant to address this case explicitly and directly. He plays up Guyau's interest in metaphysics, plays down his interest in practical ethics, and criticizes his failure to recognize the obligatoriness of religious beliefs, when his book is very much about the obligatory, not to be questioned beliefs of traditional religion and the impossibility of sustaining such dogmatism in modern society. But instead of just complaining about Durkheim's tactics, we need to follow him in his search for a more adequate response to the position represented by Guyau.

This is not least because Durkheim and Guyau are on the same republican side, and both agree that the Revolution, far from being over, is only beginning. Indeed, just as the article on the Revolution is the first time that Durkheim brings in collective creative ferment, it is also the first time that he definitely identifies modern secular ideals as a "faith". The principles of 1789 were "a religion, which has had its martyrs and apostles, which has profoundly moved the masses, and which, after all, has stirred up great things" ([1890a] 1970a: 216; t.35).

Liberty, equality, fraternity

The division of labour's new preface is famous for looking to the revival of occupational corporations. Durkheim mentions the ill of *anomie*, but does not just go on, vacuously, about it. The problems with which he is concerned are based in modern society's failure to respect and realize its own ideals. He sees in the occupational corporation a nexus of relationships that can entrench commitment to these ideals and the work of developing them. As the argument proceeds, the ideals he has in mind become clear. They are liberty, equality, fraternity.

Durkheim's first publication, as we have seen, also invokes corporatist reform. It reappears in a review of 1886, a lecture of 1892, the original edition of *The division of labour*, the lectures of 1895–6 on socialism, the lectures of the same period on professional and civic ethics, and *Suicide*. But the new preface to *The division of labour* is its fullest statement. Durkheim wants everyone to have a liberty that is real, rather than just a matter of formal rights that are no protection against the rich and powerful (1902b: iii–iv; t.3). He wants the equality of justice, in the distribution of wealth and social roles (*ibid.*: xxxiv; t.29). And to achieve these things he wants, through the occupational group, the fraternity of interlinking, solidary, moral milieux. In looking to an evolving system of self-governing, democratically organized groups, he goes through a list of functions, including the regulation of contracts and conditions of work, but also welfare provision, education and recreation, active participatory citizenship and, finally, the socialization of property (*ibid.*: xxx–xxxvi; t.26–31).

These are also all included, except education and recreation, in *Suicide* (1897a: 434–42, 448–51; t.378–84, 389–92). Though bringing in the socialization of property, the lectures on professional and civic ethics concentrate on the occupational group as the basis of citizenship ([1950a] 1969g: 128–41; t.95–109). The brief passage in the lectures on socialism concentrates on the occupational group as a moral milieu and a way to tackle "the social question" ([1928a] 1971d: 229–30; t.245–7). The original edition of *The division of labour* says even less, simply suggesting the need for occupational reform ([1893b] 1902b: 196–7; t.218–19). What do we find in earlier work?

A general theoretical basis is of course laid in the emphasis on the "real man", the need for particular relationships, and the modern dynamic of the division of labour and the human ideal. It has also been noted how the review of Schaeffle sees corporatist reform as the way to escape an oppressive, class-divided society and an oppressive, "despotic" state.

A review of Coste in the following year criticizes his utilitarianism, but agrees with his ideas for solidarity through a network of occupational groups, co-operative societies and other associations that are free and independent, since "the state enslaves all whom it protects" ([1886a] 1970a: 204–7). Indeed, the same review article very much attacks ideas of the state as "the supreme end" and as something that "soars invisibly above society" (*ibid.*: 199). Durkheim still insists on a role for the state, as an "organ" of society that is a focus and expression of its life (*ibid.*: 213), and he does so in going out of his way, on a number of occasions, to defend Schaeffle against French liberal critics. It is not necessarily a help to him that Schaeffle opposes "despotic" and supports "authoritarian" socialism (1888b: 4). He is free of the handicap in an article in which he develops his own account of socialism. It is essentially a movement to regulate and co-ordinate modern economic life, and to end the anarchy that prevails in it ([1893c] 1970a: 232–3). Or, as he says in the lectures on socialism, it is a "cry of pain, sometimes of anger" at "our collective malaise" ([1928a] 1971d: 37; t.41).

Tackling the malaise means tackling the massive inequalities of wealth in our society. Durkheim does not distance himself from Schaeffle's view that the way to do so is not to suppress but to "generalize" property, "to make economic life a social function and bring it under conscious, collective control" (1885a: 88). When he discusses how Fouillée also wants to reduce inequality, he criticizes him for a collection of piecemeal proposals that will do nothing to achieve this ([1885b] 1970a: 174–5, 181). In the 1892 lecture on the family he attacks the inequalities of undeserved, inherited wealth: "This injustice which seems to us more and more intolerable becomes more and more irreconcilable with the conditions of existence of our societies" (1921a: 10). He then argues for transmission, ownership and control of property via occupational groups (*ibid.*: 13).

In sum, Durkheim's early work contains his basic views on the need for occupational groups, in a movement towards realization of the modern human ideal and away from its state socialist and *laissez-faire* individualist subversion. As he himself says in *The division of labour*'s new preface, he had not gone into the question because he was intending and preparing a separate book on it (1902b: i; t.1).

So it is again misinformed to see some great change of view between the "early" and "late" Durkheim. We should look for tensions that continue throughout his work in an effort to sort out this or that problem. As good an example as any is the 1886 review article with its conservative talk about the need for prejudice and liberal talk about the need for social reform. A source of these tensions is that Durkheim develops his own views through criticism of all kinds of different positions, and sometimes plays one off against the other, as in his conservative-sounding attacks on philosophical radicalism.

He identifies this radicalism with "*raison raisonnante*". In the dictionary it means analytical, critical reasoning. With Durkheim, *raison raisonnante* becomes more like *folie raisonnante* – a reasoning that, with a mad crazed gleam in its eye, questions everything then answers everything, all by deduction from one or two principles. He first uses the term in the 1886 review, and again when he writes, looking forward to the progress of moral science:

> But, it is said, there are practical interests at stake. Will it not undermine moral beliefs if there is open discussion of causes so obscure? On the contrary, the conception of the science of morals that we have set out is traditional faith's best safeguard, for it protects it from *raison raisonnante*, its worst enemy. (1887c: 284; t.134)

Yet should conservatives really turn to Durkheim for protection from liberty, equality, fraternity, internationalism, humanism, socialism, the abolition of inherited wealth, etc.? Is it better to go under with *raison raisonnante* or the *science de la morale*? The 1886 review offers guidance.

Durkheim talks of the collapse of a multitude of traditional beliefs, "no longer adapted to the new conditions of social life". He makes no suggestion that moral science can or should save them. Rather, his argument is that, "amidst the ruins", *raison raisonnante* encourages the idea of a society without faith, and so arouses a monster incapable of living ([1886a] 1970a: 197; t.22). The implication is then that the need, in the changing conditions of life, is to ditch traditional faith and replace it with a new one.

The implication is also that "ideas", just because they are part of a complex underlying process, do active battle with one another. Durkheim's campaign for moral science, in ambivalence towards traditional faith, clearly involves worry about the power of *raison raisonnante*:

> If it is in fact thought that moral ideas are justiciable by dialectic, all is lost with them. Because they are very complex and the forms of logical reasoning are very simple, it is easy to prove that they are absurd. How many good and indeed great minds have taken pride in taking part in this work of dissolution! (1887c: 284; t.134)

Indeed, Durkheim comes close to seeing *raison raisonnante* as itself a fact, a powerful social and intellectual current of our time, sweeping minds along with it, and resistant to change at will.

He remarks in later lectures: "Individualism, like socialism, is above all a passion that asserts itself" ([1928a] 1971d: 37; t.41). And along with his positive talk of cults, faith and prejudice, there is also his negative talk about them – the "sometimes superstitious cult" of the economists ([1885b] 1970a: 177), English "faith" in the old liberalism ([1886a] 1970a: 205), Spencer's "prejudices" and Rousseau's "ferocious individualism" ([1888a] 1970a: 95). The tension is greatest in the article on the Revolution, and its "audacious faith" that "stirred up great things". After one of the longer passages on real man, there is an attack on doctrines of abstract man. These might concede that man is naturally social, yet do not accept anything resembling actual historical societies. They picture what we might call "abstract society", because Durkheim himself sees it as an idea of a way of life "where there would be no tradition, no past, where each would live within himself without concern for others" ([1890a] 1970a: 219; t.38). Abstract society seems like faithless society, a monstrosity incapable of living, and Durkheim had criticized Tönnies for taking it as a real account of the modern world (1889b: 421–2). It is nonetheless an entrenched part of the modern world, as Durkheim himself gives away when, in rallying to the Revolution's ideals and criticizing theorists of abstract man, he attacks their "shared faith", "intransigent individualism" and inveterate, not to be questioned "prejudices" ([1890a] 1970a: 221–3; t.39–41).

Durkheim's moral science is and has to be a critical, dialectical engagement with such ideas, even when he is at his slyest in insisting he is just approaching them as "facts". But the integrity of it is that he sees this science as the key to ethics and the way to try to sort out social and moral issues. Let us now turn to its development in his thesis on Montesquieu.

Chapter Two

Towards a new spirit of the laws

Durkheim's subsidiary thesis on Montesquieu is in a way far more important than *The rules*, because it is so important for the development of his internalist programme. He sees causality as necessary connexion. He looks for a rationale at work in things and as a type of society's essential, constitutive dynamic. He views such a dynamic in terms of both structures and ideas, and defines social facts as inclusive of ideas. They are will-independent rather than mind-independent, and resistant to change at will collectively rather than merely individually. He worries that his two sociological routes to the normal – generality and fit with a rationale – might diverge, and in *The division of labour* they do diverge. But, as in *The division of labour*, sociological holism clearly lets in moral individualism.

The Latin thesis collected dust, untranslated into French, and categorized as another interpretation of Montesquieu rather than as a seminal statement and development of Durkheim's own views.[1] It is of course *The rules* that helped to make his name, and that caused a stir when it first appeared as a series of articles in 1894–5. It has been a source of controversy ever since. The case for the defence is well put by Mike Gane (1988) and for the prosecution by Steven Lukes (1982), though without wanting to question its place in the sociological canon. This canonical status is why it is far more important, in a way, than the Latin thesis, apart from the other things that might be said for it.

A flaw, however, is that it concentrates so much on the limitations to individual action that it loses sight of the limitations to action collectively. It can also seem a collectivist manifesto that attacks not only methodological but moral individualism. Yet Durkheim's project is to defend moral individualism as a modern fact that cannot just be changed at will, even collectively. It is the Latin thesis, rather than *The rules*, that is more reflective of this, and that remains the real companion thesis to *The division of labour*, with its holist story of solidarity *and* freedom.

Social facts: mind-independent or will-independent?

After an acknowledgement to Montesquieu and his great book, *The spirit of the laws* (1748), the thesis begins by discussing the subject matter of social science. Durkheim sometimes talks of social facts (*civilia facta*), usually of social things (*res politicae*), and always interchangeably. He says there might not seem to be any problem: social science studies social things – "laws, *mores*, religions etc." (1892a: 11; tf.29; t.3).[2] But there is a problem. It is with belief in a power to create and change social institutions more or less at will. This fails to appreciate that they are indeed "things".

Durkheim first elaborates by saying that things "have their own characteristics and therefore require sciences that can describe and explain them" (*ibid.*: 11; tf.30; t.3–4). He then amplifies by saying that things "have their own stable nature and strength to resist human will" (*ibid.*: 20; tf.41; t.12). This is also how they were seen in the German moral science article (1887c: 44–5; t.72–3). It is again a way in which they are seen in *The rules* – the principal mark of a "thing" is that "it cannot be modified by a simple decree of the will". To be able to change it, if at all, "it is necessary not only to will it but to make a more or less strenuous effort" ([1895a] 1901c: 29; t.70).[3]

The Latin thesis connects belief in a power to shape the social world more or less at will with neglect of science and what is the case, and with preoccupation with "art" and what ought to be done. Durkheim concedes that art has always drawn on science to some extent. But he then criticizes philosophers who turn to science only to turn to psychology and human nature, and lack concern with social science and social things.

The author of *The spirit of the laws* is praised for initiating and developing just such a concern: "Montesquieu not only approaches social things as open to observation, but considers them distinct from those that other sciences investigate" (1892a: 26; tf.48; t.18). He explains social facts in terms of other social facts, in that he relates laws, *mores* and social conditions to one another. Although he describes laws as "natural" rather than conventional, he "deriv ⌣ them from the nature of society, not of man" (*ibid*.: 28; tf.52; t.21). Indeed, far from just taking the "nature of man" as a given, he sees people's very desires, habits of mind and character as varying between different societies (*ibid*.:27; tf.51; t.20).

Thus neither society nor character can be changed just by a decree of the will. Durkheim praises Montesquieu's respect for existing social institutions but also his readiness to point to the need for reform on the basis of understanding and accepting a society's essential nature, in contrast with those "who set out to reconstruct society from its foundations" (*ibid*.: 22–5; tf.43–8; t.15–18).

It is clear from Durkheim's first list of "social things" – laws, *mores*, religions, etc. – and from the whole argument of the thesis that they very much include "ideas" in some sense, and so cannot possibly be defined in any simple way as mind-independent. The essential point is that social things, even as ideas, are will-independent. Thus Durkheim insists that laws derive from *mores* rather than from the personal will of great men (*ibid*.: 19; tf.40; t.11), when, on the contrary, the functions of the legislator "consist simply in expressing more clearly what lies hidden and more obscure in other minds" (*ibid*.: 51; tf.84; t.42), and he agrees with Montesquieu about the grip religion can have over rulers and ruled alike (*ibid*.: 42–3; tf.71–2; t.34). If "things" in the form of our beliefs are resistant to change at will, it is to the will not just of political personages but of ourselves, individually *and* collectively. Why?

A basic reason concerns Durkheim's appeal, like Montesquieu, to a society's essential nature and rationale – the logic of the laws. Another, if also related, reason concerns Durkheim's repeated emphasis on things that are not obvious and apparent but hidden and obscure. They include "ideas" – beliefs, desires, sentiments, aspirations – that are "things" that lie hidden and obscure in the mind:

> We ordinarily believe that the only reasons for our actions are those whose influence on the will appears under the light of consciousness and we deny that there are others because we are unaware of them. (*ibid*.: 18; tf.39; t.11)[4]

Durkheim does not analyze "will". But if we have motives obscure to us, they resist an enlightened, conscious will. Could they not be governed by a will that is itself obscure? But the will is then a "thing" ᴵᴺᴰᴱᴾᴱᴺᴰᴱᴺᵀ?

)us control. In a debate many years later with the
ᵴeignobos, Durkheim keeps pressing on him the
᷂her or not he accepts the reality of the unconscious"
ℓ11). Seignobos wants a history that concentrates on
᷂ the ideas that individuals themselves have, and
Duᵣ. ⸍ insistent on the need to probe beyond the superficial
level of ᴄ᷂ ᴉscious, "clear" ideas.

A source of confusion is that in Durkheim's work talk of *conscience* and of the *conscience collective* standardly includes any level of activity in the mind, rather than just "clear" ideas, his standard way of referring to the conscious as against the hidden, vague and obscure. Nonetheless, an important way in which social things resist change at will is that they are ways of thinking, feeling and acting with deep, obscure roots within us, hidden from "consciousness".

Another reason, of course, is that they come from society, which puts down deep, strong roots in us in our very desires, habits of mind and character – however they surface as clear ideas – and as in the case of Montesquieu's "principles". These are a sociopolitical system's basic norms, such as "virtue" in a republic and "honour" in a monarchy, and take us back to a social rationale and reality that, individually or collectively, we cannot just change at will, indeed that helps to define and delimit the will.

They also take us back to the collectivist shortcomings of *The rules*. Durkheim writes in the preface to the new edition:

> It displeases man to renounce the unlimited power he has so long claimed over the social order . . . his dominion over things has not really begun until he recognizes that they have their own nature and is resigned to learning from them what they are. (1901c: xxii–xxiii; t.46)

This, as we shall see, echoes the moral education course's discussion of autonomy in relation not only to the social but to the natural world. The last way in which it should be interpreted is as a vision of an unlimited, instrumentalist power to use and control nature for human ends. It is the same in the case of the social world, and in that the new preface echoes the moral education lectures it is recognition of the limits even to collective action to change society at will, and even with enlightened knowledge of it.

But despite all the collectivist blare, the original edition of *The rules* drives out this more fundamentally collectivist point in an emphasis on the limits to our action as individuals. Thus its first official definition of a social fact is that it is *"capable of exercising an external constraint over the individual"*. The second, seen as equivalent, is that a social fact is *"general throughout a given society while having its own existence, independent of its individual manifestations"* ([1895a] 1901c: 14; t.59).

There has been much argument about the "external constraint" featuring in the first definition. But the second definition's talk of an "existence independent of its individual manifestations" is more significant. It marks a shift away from *The division of labour*'s *conscience collective*, with its beliefs and sentiments that individuals hold in common, to the view that these are never held in common, since our individual representations of a collective representation might draw on and even contribute to it but never adequately capture it. It has its own existence, "independent of its individual manifestations". If we ask where, unless in a metaphysical group mind, the Durkheimian answer that evolves brings in language itself, other symbolic systems, a body of knowledge, and a mode of thought itself in a collective tradition or process. In fact, as we shall also see, *The division of labour* already works along such lines, in tackling the implications of science as a body of knowledge that exists and develops, that individuals draw on and contribute to, but that is over and beyond everyone.

So social things can concern a collective, representational world that is "external" to individual consciousness in various ways. It depends on the existence of individual minds, but, given this brute fact, it is independent of its individual manifestations in them. Even in putting down deep, strong roots in individual minds, it can concern beliefs that, as in the Latin thesis and subsequently, are obscure to consciousness, or that, as in *The division of labour*'s official *conscience collective*, are held by us in common, or that, as in *The division of labour*'s modern *conscience collective*, and elsewhere, involve a multitude of disagreements around them.

But social things, in that they are to do with a representational world, are never mind-independent in a simple sense. They are always will-independent, or, more polemically and as in *The rules*, a "constraint". Alfred Fouillée grasps the point at issue in saying it is mistaken "to consider social facts, with MM. Durkheim and Lévy-Bruhl, as 'things' independent of individual wills" (Fouillée 1911a: 385). Some of Durkheim's modern critics seem less perceptive, in just going on about the social world as all idea and "meaning".

Are there any social things he definitely sees as mind-independent rather than will-independent? The answer, in brief, is that there are not, and the new preface to *The rules* insists that he had always seen social life as "entirely made up of representations" (1901c: xi; t.34). But the answer has to be worked out at two levels, and let us start with his insistence, in the original preface, that he is a "rationalist" rather than a "positivist" ([1895a] 1901c: ix; t.33).

This is obviously the case with the Latin thesis and the lectures on moral education, and is also the case with *The division of labour* and *The rules*, for it is to do with his subscription to causality as necessary connexion and with his search, through empirical detective work, for a logic and rationale in things. At this level all things – social or natural – are mind-dependent, since even the natural world, though existing will-independently "out there", is mind-dependent in our effort to discover an intelligible order through representations and signs of it. Thus at this level Newtonian gravity, say, is as real and as mind-dependent as may be.

Let us now move to another level and, for example, Durkheim's claim that Montesquieu sees population size as of especial explanatory importance (1892a: 47; tf.78; t.38). Or there is *The division of labour*'s explanatory emphasis on population size, population density, the way people are grouped, and, in a word, morphology. There is also concern with morphology in this sense in *The rules*. But it is also brought under talk of the "substratum" of social life to refer to all kinds of "crystallizations" of it, such as the way people are grouped, the distribution and design of habitations, networks of communication, and so on ([1895a] 1901c: 12–14; t.57–8). This particular discussion of the substratum, as the crystallization of ways of thinking, feeling and acting, clearly sees it as mind-dependent at the level not just of social scientific enquiry but of a sociocultural representational world itself. It might be wondered if the same is the case with discussions of morphology elsewhere, including in *The rules* itself. In fact it is the case, but with the complication, once more, of whether or not it is in the context of enquiry into all of human social evolution. If it is, Durkheim again abstracts morphology as an explanatory factor, and anti-materialist critics should again stand up and say if they believe, instead, in a World Spirit. It is perhaps true that it is not until his more detailed interest in emblems and other symbols that Durkheim really emphasizes how they are constitutive and part of a group's very description. It is still the case that abstracting a world-historical morphological factor from local representational worlds does not mean that how people are grouped can exist mind-independently of these. It just means that, being local, they cannot in themselves give us a world-historical factor, if we want one.

There is a point in the review of Antonio Labriola, one of the most original Marxist thinkers of the time, where Durkheim argues as if ideas must rest on a morphological "substratum" ([1897e] 1970a: 250; t.171). Peter Winch seizes on this to attack Durkheim and argue that ideas are on the contrary constitutive of relationships, as with the ideas of monks in a monastery (Winch 1958: 23–4). He could have read to the end of the review, where "in principle everything is religious" ([1897e] 1970a: 253; t.173). The fundamental problem, however, is that Winch works with a positivist idea of natural science and thinks Durkheim does too, but attacks the very idea of a positivist social science and Durkheim for subscribing to it. In fact Durkheim opposes positivism, in both natural and social science. In the case of social science, he is all for the empirical detective work needed to explore mind-dependent representational worlds and to discover necessary connexions and an underlying logic in such worlds as will-independent things.

Both in the Latin thesis and in *The rules* there are long passages hammering away at the need for empirical detective work. Is this to hammer away at the obvious? There is an attack on concentration on "clear" concepts as if these reveal the representational world, and thus on social theories that proceed "from ideas to things, not from things to ideas" ([1895a] 1901c: 16; t.60). The underlying worry is with disdain for "merely" empirical enquiry and with a tendency to see the social world, being mind-dependent, as accessible just through introspection.

The tendency might not be licensed by every idealist doctrine or by any, and it is difficult to pin down, yet it is there. According to Andrew Seth, Hegel "can only be interpreted to mean that thought out of its own abstract nature gives birth to the reality of things" (Seth [1887] 1893: 118). According to J. E. MacTaggart, criticizing Seth and writing in the *Revue de métaphysique et de morale*, "Hegel never . . . claimed to deduce all the givens of experience solely from the nature of pure thought" (MacTaggart 1893: 552). According to Dominique

Parodi, loosely connected with the Durkheimian circle, and commenting on trends in contemporary philosophy, "idealism claims to deduce thought, and through thought the world" (Parodi 1920: 431). Or, in Durkheim's own summing up of some such view, "The world is only a system of logically linked concepts" and so "thought, just by its powers, must be able to reconstruct it" (1897f: 287–8)

Durkheim's Latin thesis maintains *both* that things "have their own characteristics and therefore require sciences that can describe and explain them" *and* that things "have their own stable nature and strength to resist human will". His target is not only an anti-scientific voluntarism that would change the world at will but also an anti-scientific idealism that would deduce it from thought, and it remains relevant to insist, against forms of voluntarism and idealism that scuttle across the modern landscape, that social facts are things.

Social systems and the two routes to the normal

It is very much part of Durkheim's view that social science must be relational and comparative. It must understand "social things" in context and with reference not only to an individual society but to others of the same type. Moreover, comparative social science involves an idea of the normal, and the idea of the normal is in turn a key to ethics:

> Science, since it distinguishes different human societies by general class and type, necessarily describes the normal form of social life in each type in describing the type itself: for whatever pertains to the type is normal, and whatever is normal is healthy. (1892a: 15; tf.35; t.8)

There are two arguments in the Latin thesis for the need to distinguish social types. The first is brief, and runs as follows.

Science cannot describe individual entities, only types. It cannot describe individual entities, because their attributes are infinite and the infinite cannot be described. But it can describe types, because individuals (including individual societies) make up types through something definite that "constitutes their nature", through common characteristics that are limited and "reveal their essence" (*ibid.*: 16; tf.35–6; t.8–9) A similar argument appears in *The rules*, and again says that classification must be according to characteristics that are "essential" ([1895a] 1901c: 79–80; t.111).

In the thesis, as elsewhere, Durkheim criticizes the use of facts "arbitrarily and without method" (1892a: 14, 16; tf.33, 36; t.6, 8). The criticism links up with the second argument. This concerns the explanation of social facts, but also their interpretation in context. Durkheim insists on extensive, systematic comparison of sociohistorical data as the method by which social science can discover laws that explain these. He praises Montesquieu for his development through classification of just such a comparative science (*ibid.*: 60; tf.96–7; t.51). But in doing so he also praises Montesquieu for realizing how, in a particular society, different aspects of social life interconnect, so that each must be understood in the context of a whole. Durkheim attacks moralists who study morality and economists who study economics as if these are so separate from one another and from the rest of social life that they can be considered in complete abstraction from their specific, overall contexts (*ibid.*: 65–6; tf.102–4; t.55–7). Hence the second argument can be seen as both explanatory and interpretive. It is about the need for classification in order to compare like with like as the basis of explanatory laws. Yet it is also very much part of this that things must be placed in context, to identify them in terms of the same sorts of wholes, and to understand and explain them in terms of their interrelatedness within each of such wholes.

Durkheim says in *The rules*, after insisting on classification according to essential characteristics, that they cannot be known unless the explanation of facts is sufficiently advanced: *"These two parts of science are interdependent and progress through each other"* ([1895a] 1901c: 80; t.111; italics added). As he also says: "Comparative sociology is not a particular branch of sociology; it is sociology itself, in that it ceases to be purely descriptive and aspires to the explanation of facts" (*ibid.*: 137; t.157). Everything points to the classification of societies according to the essential causes of things in them, rather than just according to outward forms. The essential characteristics and explanatory interpretive arguments of the Latin thesis come together in this way too. *Suicide* also adopts an "aetiological" rather than "morphological" classification of the phenomena it studies – that is, a classification according to causes rather than according to forms (1897a: 143; t.147).

The only trouble is the long argument in *The rules* for a formal, morphological classification of societies. The charitable interpretation is that, true to Durkheimian method, it takes obvious phenomena to get comparative social science going but, as description and explanation develop "through one another", it looks forward to something better. The uncharitable interpretation is that, untrue to Durkheimian method, and after a few dialectical speculations, it offers morphological form as the real, definitive way to sort societies into types, because it is the cause of things in them. This interpretation seems correct when he sums up: "since the constitution of the social milieu results from the mode of composition of social aggregates, these two expressions even being at bottom synonymous, we now have proof that there are no more essential characteristics than those we have assigned as the basis of sociological classification" ([1895a] 1901c: 119; t.141). Such formalism is no doubt why one reviewer accused him, as we have seen, of constructing a "blind algebra" and others of emptying social life of "all its contents" (Brunschvicg & Halévy 1894: 567).

But the argument is again in the context of local versus world-historical stories, though this time not to look for something throughout evolution. Rather, the formalism is precisely to save the diversity of local worlds (complete with the contents of their own representations) from stories, driven by a single idea of the good life, of progress from "lower" to "higher" stages of a single human society – and, as in the 1887 inaugural lecture, Comte is the storyteller attacked.

How, on this issue, does Durkheim view Montesquieu? His classification distinguishes three types of government – republic, monarchy and despotism – and also recognizes peoples without government. It has often been seen as highly derivative. Durkheim sees it as highly original (1892a: 44; tf.73; t.35), as well as realistic: "perhaps nothing in the whole work will be found more truthful and penetrating than this classification, the principles of which can stand even now" (*ibid.*: 41; tf.70; t.33).

He considers it in fact a classification not of governments but of societies, bringing out how they systematically differ from one another in size, organization, social ties, law, morality, economic life, as well as politics, and how these interconnect in them as parts of a whole. But we need to introduce a contrast, not made by Durkheim himself, between "factorial" and "essentialist" theories of interconnectedness.

In a factorial theory, the tendency for a society to fit together as a system is just the product of the action and reaction on one another of all its different components. None has a special explanatory power. But in an essentialist theory the tendency towards system involves some sort of dynamic at the heart of things, pushing, pulling, shaping them to fit in with one another by fitting in with the pattern it contains. It is mistaken to see in *The spirit of the laws* a factorial theory of interconnectedness. Montesquieu works with an essentialist theory. Durkheim does too. His repeated talk of a society's "nature" or "essence" is not an empty form of words. It signifies recognition of Montesquieu's essentialist approach to interconnectedness and his own endorsement of some such approach.

Durkheim writes: "societies must have a certain nature which [1] results from the nature itself of the parts composing them and from their organization, and which [2] generates social facts" (*ibid.*: 20; tf.41; t.13; bracketed numbers added). This is consistent only with an essentialist theory. No cause is uncaused and, as in the first supporting argument, the nature of a society has to result from something. As in the second supporting argument it has an importance of its own, once formed, in generating social facts and institutions.

A complaint is made about Montesquieu's social types: "he distinguishes and names them, not according to the division of labour, or the nature of social ties, but on the basis simply of the supreme authority's constitution" (*ibid.*: 40; tf.69; t.32). In picking on the division of labour or the nature of social ties as the things to distinguish and name social types, Durkheim does not pick out just any factor. He says Montesquieu chooses government because at first sight "nothing is more striking in public life; nothing more draws to itself everyone's attention", but also because it is necessary "to distinguish each type by its most important property, from which the others derive" (*ibid.*: 40–41; tf.69; t.32).

So Durkheim disagrees that government is the "most important property, from which the others derive", but agrees on picking out such a property – in his case, the division of labour and the nature of social ties – and again we are dealing with an essentialist theory of interconnectedness.

How are we to get at the underlying, essential realities from which other social facts derive? Durkheim worries:

Things are so diverse that what they have in common lies, as if veiled, out of sight; so changeable that they seem to escape the observer. Moreover, causes and effects are so interwoven that every care must be taken not to confuse them. (1892a: 21; tf.42; t.13)

Or again:

In that which particularly concerns social science, there were certain special difficulties deriving from the very nature of social life. For it is so changeable, so diverse and multiform as not to seem reducible to fixed and definite laws. (*ibid.*: 73; tf.111–12; t.63).[5]

In enquiring how social things interconnect, Durkheim counts "ideas" amongst "things". Indeed, he gives them a fundamental role in arguing that *mores* are the source of laws. This is part of his campaign against exaggerations of the influence of government. A difficulty for him, therefore, is not with "ideas" but with government itself.

Durkheim does not just exclude government from a society's essential nature. He even denies it is a reliable sign of this. He repeats the point that the same form of government can be found in different types of society, and that, when its form of government changes, a society's nature need not change (*ibid.*: 16–17, 41; tf.36–7, 69; t.9, 33). Yet how does the point square with an essentialist theory of interconnectedness? Government, though not all important, seems important enough that any social dynamic that counts for much must influence or determine it. Is there a way round the problem?

In viewing Montesquieu's "governments" as societies, Durkheim associates the republic with ancient Greek and Italian city states, monarchy with the large nations of modern Europe, and despotism with Asiatic empires (*ibid.*: 32–3; tf.57–8; t.25–6). He also views them as ideal-types, in which, for example, Montesquieu exaggerates equality in a republic and commitment to the common good. But he still insists on their realism and, for example, sees a great difference between republican demands for commitment to community and modern individualistic demands for a large and important sphere of private life (*ibid.*: 41–2; tf.70–71; t.33–4). He even remarks that if Montesquieu had known about modern France he would not have counted it a republic (*ibid.*: 32; tf.57; t.25). This carefully avoids saying that Third Republican France is therefore a monarchy, and in the lectures on occupational and civic ethics Durkheim insists that modern society demands – but does not always get – democratic government ([1950a] 1969g: 123–5; t.89–91). As in the Schaeffle review, it can get a highly authoritarian regime instead. Then a way round our problem is that each type of society generates its own appropriate form of government (or a limited range of forms of government). But this real, underlying tendency is not to the exclusion of "abnormal" cases.

Yet how can there be "abnormal" cases, in conflict with what is entailed by a society's essential nature? As in the article on the Revolution, the thesis on Montesquieu maps out two routes to the normal – generality and fit with an underlying rationale. Durkheim is very much worried by the possibility that the two routes might diverge, in very much wanting to insist, against Montesquieu, that they rarely if ever do. Thus he points out that slavery was general throughout ancient city states and attacks Montesquieu for nonetheless seeing it as in conflict with the nature of a republic (1892a: 57; tf.92; t.48). Indeed, Durkheim comes close to insisting that something *must* express a social type's underlying rationale if it is general throughout it – which, apart from anything else, still does not tell us how there can be unusual, "abnormal" cases in conflict with the rationale.

To tackle these problems, we must do some empirical detective work of our own and bring out Durkheim's views on explanation. How does he understand causality? What does he think of Montesquieu's idea of "accidental" causes? What does he make of "final" as against "efficient" explanation?

Social explanation, necessary connexion and the internalist programme

Durkheim agrees with Montesquieu: "Laws are necessary connexions which follow from the nature of things" (1892a: 45; tf.75; t.36).[6]

It is clear that he agrees with this because he complains that Montesquieu nonetheless fails to realize how, as in the slavery case, "something cannot be almost universal in an entire species unless it corresponds with definite necessities" (*ibid.*: 57; tf.92; t.48). Similarly, he complains that Montesquieu "attributes to human societies I know not what power to deviate from their own nature", bringing into social life "a *contingency* which, at least at first sight, seems incompatible with a definite order . . . [and] which it is to be feared may undermine the very foundations of social science" (*ibid.*: 53–4; tf.87; t.44). It might prove only a limited threat, since for Montesquieu "wherever things are appropriate [*justae*] they follow necessary laws, and this necessity ceases only when there is a deviation from the normal state" (*ibid.*: 56–7; tf.91; t.47). But Durkheim remains worried by times when necessity ceases, and when Montesquieu brings in "accidental" causes (*ibid.*: 55; tf.89; t.45).

Although all the fuss over other issues has distracted attention from it, the same fundamental idea of causality shows up in *The rules.* Durkheim attacks John Stuart Mill's view that "cause and effect are absolutely heterogeneous, that there is no logical connexion between them". He maintains, against Mill, that the causal link is "intelligible" and "consists of a relationship which results from the nature of things". He continues:

> it is only the philosophers who have ever cast doubt on the intelligibility of the causal relationship. For the scientist it is not in question; it is assumed by the very method of science. How can one otherwise explain both the role of deduction, so important in experimental reasoning, and the basic principle of the proportionality between cause and effect? ([1895a] 1901c: 126; t.149)

Durkheim explains the role of deduction in science in going on to see in "the method of concomitant variations the supreme instrument of sociological research" (*ibid.*: 131; t.153). He wonders in general what experimental method gives mechanical access to a causal relationship, "without the facts which it establishes calling for elaboration by the mind". But a crucial point in the case of concomitant, regular connexion between two phenomena is that it can occur, not because one is the cause of the other, but "because they are both effects of the same cause, or indeed because there exists a third phenomenon . . . which is the effect of the first and cause of the second". Hence the facts always "need to be interpreted" (*ibid.*: 130; t.152). It is possible to attempt a positivist account of all this. But, far from doing so, Durkheim takes it as further proof of science's commitment to the search for necessary, intelligible connexion.

It is instructive to compare Durkheim on the issue with his teacher, Emile Boutroux. Standard, almost ritual, talk of his influence on Durkheim concerns his ideas on the specific characters of the different sciences.[7] These ideas are set out in his lecture course of 1892–3, just at the time of his examination of Durkheim's two theses (Boutroux 1895b). But his work is very much about causality itself and the issue of necessity versus contingency.

A view often seen as Humean – and taken up by Charles Renouvier, someone also seen as influential on Durkheim[8] – is that "science can establish nothing more than certain regular successions of phenomena, which are and remain discontinuous and heterogeneous" (Parodi 1920: 165–6). Boutroux, in a lecture course of 1896–7, corrects such an interpretation. Hume argues *both* that we can observe only regularities *and* that it is a regularity, a habit of human life, that we work with an idea of necessary connexion in nature:

> The notion of causality, as necessary connexion, thus rests on a sentiment (*feeling*), but on a natural sentiment, and therefore entirely worthy of trust. (Boutroux 1926: 100)

Boutroux then goes over Kant's attempt, in response to Hume, to secure necessity on rational, *a priori* grounds. He also goes over subsequent philosophical debate, and moves towards his own position, appealing to the development of science itself. Kant was impressed by a Newtonian science that united "necessity" and "fact", and we should be similarly impressed if science had remained like this. But it has not. We can move away from "absolute necessity in things", since science has outgrown it (*ibid.*: 105, 129–31). This is itself a move away from the *a priori* critique of necessity in his highly regarded thesis, *The contingency of the laws of nature* (Boutroux [1874] 1895a). Instead, his new, more empirical approach is to study science as actually practised and to see how it has given up working with causality just as necessary connexion. He was already taking this line in the lecture course of 1892–3, to emphasize in mathematics as in other sciences "the often contingent determination and often artificial construction accepted above all because it succeeds" (Boutroux 1895b: 138; t.209).

Durkheim argues, in the conclusion to *The rules*, for letting sociology develop like other sciences:

All that it asks is for the application of the principle of causality to social phenomena. Moreover, this principle is posed by it, not as a rational necessity, but only as an empirical postulate, the product of a legitimate induction. Since the law of causality has been verified in the other realms of nature and has progressively extended its domain . . ., one is entitled to accept it as equally true of the social world; and it is possible to add today that research undertaken on the basis of this postulate tends to confirm it. But this is not to decide the question of knowing if the causal link excludes all contingency. ([1895a] 1901c: 139–40; t.159).

The research he might have in mind concerns causes that "*necessitate* a growing division of labour" ([1893b] 1902b: 244; t.262). Durkheim is *not* asking us to reject the necessitarian principle of causality. He is asking us to accept it, but empirically, through the "legitimate induction" that since it works in the natural sciences it should be tried in the social sciences, and without excluding contingency altogether. In a way this brackets his other arguments, and means that if Durkheim and Boutroux agree on an "empirical" test of principles of causality they disagree on its outcome. Durkheim sees necessity as remaining central, and does not accept that modern science works with contingency to the far-reaching extent Boutroux seems to suggest.

Let us now return to the Latin thesis and to the point where Durkheim criticizes Montesquieu's introduction of "accidental" causes. He refers to, but does not quote, a passage about these.[9] On looking it up we read:

> The principle of despotic government is endlessly corrupted because it is corrupt by nature. Other governments are destroyed because particular accidents violate their nature; this one is destroyed by its internal vice if accidental causes do not prevent its principle from becoming corrupt. (Montesquieu 1748: VIII.10)

It is clear that the causes Montesquieu describes as accidental are causes he sees as external to a sociopolitical system. In monarchies and republics such causes can work against and destroy the system. In despotisms they can work against and yet support it, in helping to prevent its internal, self-generated collapse. In every case they are "accidental" and "contingent" in that they lie outside a particular social type's dynamic. It need not be that they lie outside an order of necessarily connected things in the social world in general, and are irreducible to explanation of the form "whenever X occurs in a situation Y it brings about or tends to bring about Z". Indeed, external causes offer a relatively straightforward explanation of a society's "deviation" from its nature. Unless Durkheim just misunderstands Montesquieu, or rejects the very idea of external causes, his worry is with a failure to look for any explanation of social problems in terms of internal social processes. This in fact seems to be his worry, since he immediately goes on to insist that "disease is no less inherent in the nature of living things than health". They are part of the same type, "so that they can be compared, and the comparison helps to explain both" (1892a: 55; tf.89; t.46).

He again insists in *The rules* that disease, like health, is inherent in "the nature of creatures". It is just that it is not inherent in "their normal nature", in that an entire species cannot be diseased "in itself and through its own basic constitution" ([1895a] 1901c: 58; t.93). Thus Montesquieu in fact works with an internalist account of the problems existing in despotism, yet Durkheim does not give him any credit for doing so, and instead attacks him for considering a whole social type corrupt (1892a: 57; tf.92–3; t.48). Perhaps this contradicts or perhaps it is consistent with Durkheim's agreement that despotism is a sociological monstrosity, "in which only the head is alive, having absorbed all the energies of the body" (*ibid.*: 39–40; tf.67–8; t.31). The more fundamental point is that in Montesquieu's account of despotism the same dynamic tends to the same result: internal, self-generated collapse. Hence Durkheim's problem is how, without bringing external causes into an account of a social world, there can be a same dynamic and yet different results – "health" and "disease", the "general" and the "exceptional", "equilibrium" and "crisis", or, in a word, the "normal" and "abnormal".

It is not much help to develop, as in *The rules*, the distinction between normal and abnormal patterns of crime and other "deviations" (such as, in *Suicide*, individualism's pathological forms). It only transposes on to another level the problem of how the same dynamic has different results, in this case normal and abnormal patterns of "deviation". But it is of help to return to *The rules* and Durkheim's insistence that the intelligibility of things means that "the same effect can sustain this relationship only with a single cause, since it can express only a single nature" ([1895a] 1901c: 126; t.149). This means we can rule out a dynamic that has very different effects yet consists of only a single, monolithic cause. The internalist programme requires a dynamic that can have different effects because it consists of a complex of interdependent yet different elements.

Durkheim develops this, as we shall see, in taking over Montesquieu's ideas of a social system's "structure" and "principle". There is still a lot of work to do to sort out how, as he says in *The division of labour*, "in comparing the normal type with itself . . . we can discover what is not wholly in accord with it, which contains contradictions" ([1893b] 1902b: xl; t.34). In the meantime it also helps to move on from the issue of internalist versus externalist explanation, to tackle discussion, in the Latin thesis, of the relationship between efficient, original, functional and final explanation.

Durkheim is all for efficient explanation, and quite happy with functional explanation as a form of it. A social institution's usefulness can be an efficient cause that explains its continuing existence. It is just that it does not explain why a "useful" institution comes about in the first place (1892a: 53; tf.86; t.43). Durkheim wants a historical, developmental sociology that investigates the origins rather than simply the functions of things. But he is all against appeal, in doing so, to final explanation in terms of conscious design.

This comes across in repeated criticism of Montesquieu for exaggerating the role of the lawgiver. But a theory need not bring in conscious design to bring in conscious action. It can explain society, to some extent, in terms of the unintended or unforeseen consequences of such action. Durkheim is again quite happy with this. He approves of Montesquieu's holistic account of monarchy as a system turning on the private, individual pursuit of "honour" (*ibid.*: 38; tf.65–6; t.30–31). He also recognizes how for Montesquieu the lawgiver's role is based precisely on such understanding and acceptance of how a system works, so that the role is limited (*ibid.*: 51; tf.83–4; t.42). He recognizes that it is precisely not about a power to change things completely (*ibid.*: 22; tf.44; t.15). The criticism of Montesquieu's lawgiver fizzles out. But the hostility to conscious design stays in place. It is one and the same as hostility to the idealism and voluntarism that would change the world at will, and construct a new social order unrooted in an existing reality.

Durkheim is ambivalent about Montesquieu in another way. He praises his interest in original efficient causes (*ibid.*: 46; tf.76; t.37), yet a few pages on accuses him of not even suspecting the possibility of such causes (*ibid.*: 51; tf.83; t.41). But, for example, Montesquieu devotes most of the last part of *The spirit of the laws* to the "origins" and "revolutions" of the French monarchy. The criticism of his inattention to long-term change is wholly unjustified, as Georges Davy remarks (Durkheim 1953a: 22–3; t.154), and also Luc Fraisse, in an interesting discussion of Durkheimian and other contemporary sociological interpretations of Montesquieu (Fraisse 1989: 213–14). It is true that Durkheim criticizes Montesquieu's inattention to "progress". Yet he makes this point in a curious way.

He says that Montesquieu, "in discussing particular peoples, does not deny that their principle can grow or be corrupted", and then accuses him of thinking this principle "is fixed and definite from the very beginning, remaining intact throughout their entire history" (1892a: 68; tf.107; t.59). He offers a note in support, which quotes from *The spirit of the laws* as follows:

If it [the state] has preserved its principles and its constitution changes, the latter corrects itself; if it has lost its principles when its constitution starts to change, the constitution is corrupted. (Montesquieu 1748: XI.13)[10]

How can principles remain intact and go on forever if, as in this passage, they can be "lost"?

Montesquieu, Durkheim adds, "does not realize that the nature of societies contains opposites, which struggle with one another, just because it frees itself from an earlier form only little by little and moves little by little to one born out of this" (1892a: 68–9; tf.107; t.59).[11] Yet Montesquieu writes, a few sentences on from the passage quoted by Durkheim:

States are often more flourishing during the imperceptible shift from one constitution to another than they are under either constitution. At that time all the springs of government are stretched ... and there is a noble rivalry between those who defend the declining constitution and those who put forward the one that prevails. (Montesquieu 1748: XI.13)

But it is not just a question of catching Durkheim out.

We can now see a way in which, in the thesis, Durkheim brings contradiction and conflict into social life – so much so that "the nature of societies" always contains them. They can be part of the evolution of a new social type. They are also built into a social type itself. The unfolding of its dynamic through different stages of development entails a conflict, at any one time, between these. In fact, such conflict seems so normal that we need to ask how it might be abnormal, and *The division of labour* attempts some sort of answer.

Another issue arises over his interest in ever-present change versus his praise of Montesquieu's interest in tendencies towards system, in how, as parts of a social whole, things "influence and harmonize with one another" (1892a: 65; tf.103–4; t.56). But these are complementary interests in a dynamic that crystallizes, for a time, in a particular stage of development, and still has an impetus to move on. Durkheim does not confuse tendency towards system with stationariness. Indeed, just as he is wrong to emphasize Montesquieu's interest in tendency towards system and to deny his concern with conflict and change, it is wrong to impose the same one-sidedness on Durkheim. Like Montesquieu, he combines both concerns.

It is in this context that we can return to the insufficiency of functional explanation and reopen the case for final explanation. We can just agree with Durkheim about the limitations of functional explanation, yet suggest that his discussion misses the power and point of final explanation.

Final explanation concerns "the means which the nature of a society requires to realize itself, that is, to achieve its end; *but it is possible that these are lacking*" (*ibid.*: 51; tf.83; t.41; italics added).[12] This misses the point that a self-realizing dynamic works to supply such "means". It helps to fill the explanatory gap in simple functionalism between the "usefulness" of institutions and their efficient causes, since its pressure to make things fit the pattern it contains is a pressure to develop and bring about these institutions. Indeed, in helping to bring about the "useful", it works to identify things as this in the first place. A dynamic crucially explains what happens in such and such societies because it constitutes their nature and self-realizing *telos*, and it constitutes their nature and self-realizing *telos* because it crucially explains what happens in them. Durkheim himself almost says as much when, in asking what Montesquieu means by something's

"nature", he says that "he designates by this term, not all the properties of a thing, but only those which *contain the others within them*
and make it a member of such and such a type, that is, its essence"
(*ibid.*: 55; tf.88–9; t.45; italics added).

A society's self-realizing dynamic can contain ideas, including local
ideas of the *telos* for man, that are nonetheless continually evolving
aspirations rather than very "clear", completely fixed conceptions.
Nor need it completely fill the explanatory gap of simple functionalism. A dynamic can be resisted, slowed down, distorted, even
destroyed by "accidental" causes, or by internal "contradictions" and
"crises", or by a combination of these. There is plenty of room here
for an insufficiency of "means" – yet also for an understanding of a
society's development in terms of a dynamic, and so in terms of efficient original causation as a continuous process. It still involves a historical perspective. However, it does not have to peer all the way back
into ancient, misty beginnings, or convert, as Durkheim worries in
The rules, into a Comtean world-historical progress of "man".

The "spirit" of the laws

Montesquieu emphasizes his intention to examine laws, not just in
their relation with each one in a series of things, but taking all these
relations together, which is when he talks of the "SPIRIT OF THE LAWS"
(Montesquieu 1748: I.3). Durkheim never discusses the term's meaning, and does not give anything away with the book's title, since he does
not translate it into Latin. But it was translated, during the theological
dispute over it at publication, as *Mens Legum*.[13] This is to interpret it as
the mind, intelligence, logic or rationale of the laws. Durkheim, for his
part, very much discusses and accepts Montesquieu's theory as about
an underlying, dynamic rationale in things.

But what in their theories emerges as a social dynamic, and especially as modern society's dynamic? Does Durkheim conduct a campaign to play up Montesquieu's interest in "structures" and play
down his interest in "principles"?

He discusses virtue in a republic, honour in a monarchy and fear in a
despotism without making clear that Montesquieu describes them as
the "principles" of these systems (1892a: 33–44; tf.58–73; t.26–35).
He worries about the idea that societies can deviate from their own

nature, again without making clear that the main case Montesquieu considers is the corruption of their principles (1748: VIII). He asks what Montesquieu means by something's "nature", says it concerns essential properties containing and determining the others, and quotes Montesquieu as follows:

> There is this difference between the nature of the government and its principle, that its nature is that which makes it what it is. (1892a: 55, n.1; tf.89, n.29)[14]

On checking up on the passage we read:

> There is this difference between the nature of the government and its principle, that its nature is that which makes it what it is, and its principle that which makes it act. The one is its particular structure, and the other the human passions which set it in motion. (Montesquieu 1748: III.1)

The message we seem to get from Durkheim is that in Montesquieu's theory a society's nature *qua* essence is its nature *qua* structure. The message we get from Montesquieu is that the heart of a system consists not just of its structure but also of its principle. Principles bring a vital dimension to the idea of the "spirit" of the laws. They animate structures and constitutions and are if anything more important to Montesquieu. This is the implication of his claim: "The corruption of each government almost always begins with that of its principles" (1748: VIII.1). It is also the implication of his claim that if the state "has preserved its principles and its constitution changes, the latter corrects itself; if it has lost its principles when the constitution starts to change, the constitution is corrupted". Durkheim himself draws on the passage, but to allege that for Montesquieu the principles are fixed from the outset and forever.

At least the principles get a mention. Yet that is the point. In general, when we do encounter the principles, we encounter them unexplained and in passing, or in quotations from Montesquieu himself in the notes. If Durkheim obscures them, is it to praise Montesquieu for his insight into the overriding importance of social structure? Or is it to criticize Montesquieu for working with an oversimple idea of a social dynamic? Or perhaps Durkheim just takes knowledge of the famous principles for granted.

Let us consider the note in which they make their main appearance. Durkheim praises Montesquieu, in the chapter on classification, for the empirical foundation and truthfulness of his social types. He repeats this praise at the end of the chapter on explanation, but the very next chapter, on method, attacks Montesquieu as unscientific because of the way he relies on definition and deduction. This is supported in a long note, starring the principles (1892a: 61, n.3; tf.98, n.4; t.52, n.12). Durkheim complains that Montesquieu first defines his three types of society, then deduces their principles from these definitions, then deduces one thing after another from the principles. Montesquieu – who has just summed up each government's structure – is quoted and condemned out of his own mouth: "Nothing more is needed for me to find their three principles; they derive naturally from this" (1748: III.2).

Does Durkheim's use of the passage confuse a logic of discovery with a logic of society? Montesquieu's logic of discovery goes from structures to look for principles, seeing in the first a sign of the second. It is not at all the same as a logic of society in which structures are all-determining. Indeed, a logic of discovery might seem thoroughly Durkheimian that starts with formal political structures as relatively obvious phenomena, then uses them to track other things – the "principles" – that are more fundamental and important.

But as the discussion in the main text proceeds, it is evident that Durkheim is not so much confusing as weaving together concerns with a logic of discovery and a logic of society in a concerted criticism of Montesquieu's approach. One concern is that we might rely too much on deduction, as against empirical social investigation. The other is that we might assume that a formal, school logic is also the logic at work in society. In criticizing the assumption, Durkheim writes:

We are not asserting that social things are in themselves irrational. But if a certain logic underlies these, it is different from the one we use in deduction; it does not have the same simplicity; perhaps it even follows other laws. It is thus necessary for us to learn it from things themselves. (1892a: 64; tf.101; t.54)

So Durkheim is protesting at reduction of a social rationale to a sort of social algebra. He is not protesting at the very idea of such a rationale and of necessary connexions between social things, not least as ideas. The collective norms constituting Montesquieu's principles are prime examples of ideas that qualify as "social things", resisting change at will and requiring empirical enquiry to understand them. A social rationale involving them requires this too, to track meanings and their implications that, far from being transparent, are complex and obscure. Yet if an underlying rationale is as troublesome to get at as Durkheim suggests, why see generality as a simple, surefire sign of it? In *The division of labour* he accepts that this test is not always reliable (1893b: 36–7; t.434–5), and does the same in *The rules* ([1895a] 1901c: 60–61; t.94–5). Even in the Latin thesis he might do so, in praising Montesquieu's understanding that "it is only in rare cases that something can be universal which is not healthy and rational at the same time" (1892a: 58; tf.93; t.48–9). But it is Durkheim's commitment to search for a rationale in things that, perhaps, matters most.[15]

It is as part of this that he argues as if readers of his thesis are already familiar with Montesquieu's talk of "principles". In discussing each of Montesquieu's social types he first goes into its structure. He then goes into its principle, only he renames it as its "social tie" (*sociale vinculum*). Members of these different societies "are not organized according to the same structure or united by the same ties" (*ibid.*: 34: tf.59; t.27). Moreover, even though departing from Montesquieu's terminology, his discussion takes the two elements at the core of each of Montesquieu's systems and, far from trying to emphasize one at the expense of the other, brings out their importance and interdependence. This is not so surprising if we turn to his main thesis – his own new *Spirit of the laws*. Its dynamic of modern society also involves two interdependent elements, a "structure" and a "principle" – the division of labour and the human ideal.

The Latin thesis associates Montesquieu's "monarchy" with the modern social world, and characterizes its structure in terms of an extensive division of labour (*ibid.*: 37; tf.63; t.29).[16] What is its social tie?

"Not country but class is the idea preoccupying people" (*ibid.*: 37–8; tf.64–5; t.30).[17] Or this is how Durkheim first discusses things, and it captures an essential feature of Montesquieu's contrast of monarchy with republican virtue and patriotism. Each *social order* strives to advance itself rather than the common good.

It is only afterwards that Durkheim identifies honour as a "private ambition, of individuals or classes" (*ibid.*: 38; tf.66; t.31). His discussion of collective norms of honour follows Montesquieu in including the "private interest" of ambition for wealth and power, and in the view that "honour easily falls into vice, since it can generate an excessive self-love". Like honour itself, its pathological, egoistic forms lie in the nature of modern society and "arise just because private life has grown and individuals enjoy a greater freedom to pursue their own interest" (*ibid.*: 39; tf.66–7; t.31). But none of this is to reduce honour to mere self-interest. Honour, whatever else it is, is an ethic of esteem and self-esteem, dependent on a concern for "character and freedom and dignity" (*ibid.*: 39; tf.66; t.31).[18]

Durkheim seems attracted by Montesquieu's holistic account of a certain kind of moral individualism, and to go along with the view that collective norms of private honour can be a genuine social tie: people "bring about the common good unconsciously, while believing that they act only for their own", and "the very conflict between different parts of society effects their union" (*ibid.*: 38; tf.65–6; 30–1). Later on, however, a shift is apparent both in his interpretation of modern individualism and in his attitude to it as a genuine social tie:

Each of us has his own personality, opinions, morals, religion, and sets himself and his affairs more thoroughly apart from society and public affairs. Therefore social cohesion cannot be the same or come from the same source, but depends on a division of labour. (*ibid.*: 42; tf.70–71; t.33–4)

This reads more like an account of the individualism not of old regime honour but of a liberal new era's human ideal. The Latin thesis thus contains the germs of an internalist account of individualism's pathological forms, which lie in the nature of modern society itself, giving individuals "greater freedom to pursue their own interest". But it also contains the germs of a problem, surfacing in *The division of labour*, about individualism in its normal, new era form. It does not read, in the passage quoted, like a Durkheimian "social tie". It clearly involves, even so, a route from methodological holism to moral individualism, and can remain a Montesquieuan "principle" at the heart of the modern *conscience collective*.

Chapter Three

The division of labour

Durkheim's book has a passage from Aristotle on the title page:

> A city is not made up of people who are the same: it is different from an alliance.[1]

A contemporary edition of Aristotle comments on the passage and explains that a state is "an organism", whereas an alliance is "an aggregate of homogeneous members" (Susemihl & Hicks 1894: 216). Durkheim expresses his essential thesis in similar terms. Modern society coheres through the difference of a division of labour and is an "organism". Traditional society coheres through likeness and is an aggregate of "homogeneous members".

The division of labour and its limits

The division of labour must be understood as a dividing of labour, as a continuing process rather than just as a crystallized structure. It must still be understood as a basic social pattern that is contained in the process and crystallizes from time to time into particular structures.

Durkheim sees it as a more or less generalizable pattern. It is not confined to economic life, but extends to politics, law, administration, science, the arts . . . ([1893b] 1902b: 2; t.40). The full title of his book, after all, is *The division of social labour* rather than *The social division of labour*.

Yet are there not important limits to such a pattern of relationships in our society, and are there not other patterns that are just as important? Let us tackle this question first. It opens up a whole range of issues – to do with gender, locality, politics and religion, education, culture, and personal developing and flourishing.

Is Durkheim's talk about *la personne humaine* more about the individual as man than about the individual as woman? The pioneering study of his sociology of women is by Philippe Besnard (1973). It is a brilliant piece of detective work in an area of great concern to Durkheim, yet where he seems to have gone out of his way to cover his tracks. Others who have since contributed to the subject include Mike Gane (1983) and Jennifer Lehmann (1994). Here, let us just try to discover Durkheim's response to the following question: is a gendered division of labour compatible with the modern human ideal?

In the mainstream liberal emphasis on everyone as a person, the answer is "no". In what can be a liberal emphasis on men's and women's difference but equality, the answer can be "yes". Since Durkheim fails to deliver any obvious, consistent agreement with either answer, does he come out, in his ideas on woman, as a liberal at all?

It is easy to pillory him in reading in *The division of labour* about the decreasing average size of modern women's brains compared with men's ([1893b] 1902b: 20–21, 24; t.57–8, 69). But it is not an attempt at biological reductionism. It is in fact the reverse. It is part of his continuing concern with the interaction, in "life", of social, psychic and physical factors, and an interest in the impact of social evolution and culture on the body itself. He argues that in early societies "feminine and masculine functions are not sharply distinguished" and "the two sexes lead almost the same existence" (*ibid.*: 21; t.58). He then sees a growing division of labour between men and women, which also involves growing physical differences between them. He concedes that "in certain classes" in modern society women cultivate literature and the arts just like men, so that there appears to be a return to homogeneity. But he insists that the appearance is deceptive: "woman fulfils her own nature" and "art and literature become feminine", while men increasingly turn to science (*ibid.*: 23; t.60). Given Durkheim's views generally, and of early society in particular, it cannot be that woman fulfils "her own nature" in the sense of something immutably fixed in the genes. It can only be "her nature" in the sense of a character that has become deeply engrained through social evolution and culture. So is modern society, with its ideals of freedom, equality and *la personne humaine*, supposed just to perpetuate the past? Durkheim does not usually think so. Indeed, there is a contrast between the young, up and coming sociologist's insistence on a division of labour based on gender and his readiness to dismiss one based on age. He sees in older generations "the force of tradition"; respect for them is nowadays reduced "to a few polite practices, inspired by a sort of pity"; and "all men who have reached maturity are treated almost as equals" (*ibid.*: 280–81; t.294–5). A mystery that remains is why modernity does not demand this for all persons and reduce gender-based discrimination to "a few polite practices" too.

Suicide involves the view that men are more "social" in that they are more active in public collective life than women, yet eventually sees men and women becoming "equally socialized, but in different ways" (1897a: 443; t.385). Champions of equal rights for women with men "forget that the work of centuries cannot be instantly abolished; that legal equality cannot be legitimate as long as psychological inequality is so flagrant". In immediately urging efforts to reduce such inequality, Durkheim argues that men and women need to develop "the same nature" (*ibid.*: 444; t.386). So another mystery is how modern man and woman can become equal "but in different ways" and also in developing "the same nature".

Durkheim is similarly ambivalent in a later article. He appears to suggest in one sentence that there must be a change away from the extensive, traditional differentiation of the sexes, only to take this back in the next sentence ([1898a(ii)] 1969c: 99, n.1). There is also wavering and uncertainty in a series of reviews about the feminist movement. He again insists, in one, that "woman should seek equality in the functions commensurate with her nature" (1900a(30): 391). He attacks, in another, an author arguing on just these lines. This fails to address "the great difficulty":

> the equality of the two sexes cannot increase unless woman becomes more involved in public life; but then how will the family have to be transformed? Profound changes will be necessary, which we perhaps cannot avoid, but must anticipate. (1901a(iii) (28): 364)

He later criticizes others who do seem to address and anticipate them. A review of Charles Letourneau says the problem is "more complex" than just seeing women's subordination as a product of history and then seeking a greater equality between the two sexes in education, domestic life and the wider society (1904a(18): 434). A review of Gaston Richard reports his argument that the modern individualist ethic tends towards "the increasingly complete assimilation of both sexes from the moral, legal and political points of view" (1910a(iii) (20): 369). There is then a complaint that the author's history of the family is "too simple". But that is all. Durkheim is silent on the main argument about the demands of modern individualism, coming out neither to agree nor to disagree with it. There is in the end the same silence in an immediately preceding review of Marianne Weber. Durkheim objects to talk of woman's complete subordination in the traditional "patriarchal family" and asks: "who does not feel that whatever may contribute to the weakening of the organic unity of the family and of marriage must necessarily result in drying up this source of feminine greatness?" He especially worries that the "religion" of hearth and home cannot survive, and that women will in fact lose out, if the family is reduced to "a precarious alliance of two beings who, at any instant, can separate at will, and each of whom, while the association lasts, has their own circle of interests and preoccupations". Again, however, instead of coming out for or against individualism's egalitarian demands, he just ends by saying the problem is more complex than often thought, which is all he wants to establish (1910a(iii) (19): 368–9).

A contribution to a debate on divorce by mutual consent expresses "disquiet" at the idea, and Durkheim sets out to oppose it – without rigidifying marriage by opposing divorce altogether – on the grounds that it threatens both men and women as individuals, as well as the institution of marriage itself and society generally (1906d: 549). There then follows a long statistical analysis relating ease of divorce to suicide. It is in going over this and other analyses that Besnard argues that Durkheim's practical concerns led him to play down the malaise he diagnosed as "fatalism" (Besnard 1973, 1993c: 171–9). Part of the picture is that, for married relative to single people, ease of divorce lowers men's protection from anomic suicide yet is beneficial to women in increasing their protection from fatalistic suicide. But it is also part of the picture, it should be stressed, that the family, for Durkheim, is no ordinary institution. It is at the heart of his concern with particular connexions and attachments, a source of moral life that introduces, along with friendship, the whole argument of *The division of labour.* Hence his long-standing "disquiet" at *échangiste* and other forms of individualism that, whatever their benefits here or there, threaten the dissolution of deep, strong, particular attachments. The family is an institution where we can not only form but learn to form these attachments. It is in this context that it is necessary to understand his ambivalence about the far-reaching impact of the modern human ideal's abstract egalitarian demands. Indeed, it is a recognition of the ambivalent power of the demands themselves. They are nonetheless demands of the modern *conscience collective* that place definite limits on the generalizability of the division of labour as a pattern of relationships, and so also mean that the human ideal must be an active, constitutive part of modern society's dynamic, shaping the division of labour through beliefs that attack its far-reaching organization of our lives through "extraneous" considerations such as gender.

But the division of labour runs into limits both with the human ideal and with other patterns of relationships.

Pluralism is when, either as individuals or as groups, we go our separate ways and coexist in pursuit of different and otherwise conflicting ideas about things. As in the Latin thesis, "each of us has his own personality, opinions, morals, religion and sets himself and his affairs more thoroughly apart from society and public affairs".

Factionalism is when we form opposing groups but then come together to dispute our way by due process to a collective line on an issue, in a readiness to accept it as legitimate even if still seeing it as wrong. In the Latin thesis Montesquieu's ideal-typical republic has no "opposing parties" (1892a: 35; tf.61; t.28). In contrast his ideal-typical monarchy runs on a distribution of power and a rivalry in which "none can rise above the others and reduce them to nothing" (*ibid.*: 37; tf.64; t.30) – although Durkheim skips the chapter on liberty and party politics in England (Montesquieu 1748: XI.6).

Segmentariness is a division into groups that are essentially similar in their organization and beliefs, even if ready, like rival clans, to cut each other's throats. Durkheim especially associates it, of course, with traditional society. But it also features, in the note in *The division of labour*, in his own observations on England ([1893b] 1902b: 266, n.4; 282, n.30).

Let us briefly comment on all this, beginning with pluralism and religious coexistence as an example.

It can be seen as a basic, background assumption of the analysis, in *Suicide*, of Catholics, Protestants and Jews. But it is also basic to *Suicide*, as to Durkheim's other work, that modern enlarged society has and must have the division of socio-economic labour as a central institution, with the market as part of it. Then, as in his case for a growing role for the state, this necessarily demands the evolution of collective lines on a whole range of issues. Hence, with other pressures for these, it necessarily limits the scope for going, pluralistically, our separate ways, even if pluralism, as part of the human ideal, in turn limits the division of labour as a completely generalizable pattern. The only question, given the demand for all kinds of collective lines, is the process through which to evolve them.

This connects with Durkheim's concern with meaningful participatory citizenship, and with the concern, here, with factionalism. The factions of liberal moral politics can and do include religious groups, so that it is mistaken just to see them in terms of pluralism. Moreover, a kind of division of labour can be seen at work in the conflicts between different tendencies and parties, and again this might be so even with religious groups. It is at any rate important to understand religious, political or other groups in terms of a mix of patterns, rather than only the one. Doing so still allows, of course, for cases of the pre-eminence of a particular pattern, and still presupposes different ideal-typical patterns.

Indeed, if we now apply one of Durkheim's favourite arguments – the argument by elimination – we can knock out pluralism and factionalism as fundamental ideal-typical patterns of modern society. Pluralism is perhaps less important than factionalism, because of the need for collective lines. But both are necessary and limit the division of labour's generalizability. Even so, if they are not to collapse into out-and-out conflict, social dissolution, or an authoritarian coercive state, both depend on norms of tolerance and a basic cohesion that must come from somewhere else. It must be the division of labour and its intermediate interlocking groups, or the human ideal of the modern *conscience collective*, or a combination of these.

What about segmentariness?

It is ironic that Durkheim sees England as abnormal because of the continuing vitality of its local institutions. If England is nowadays a pathological case it is partly because local self-government has been suppressed.[2] Durkheim's campaign against the modern importance of locality and segmentariness in a way contradicts other concerns, and has various motives. One is just a preoccupation with the division of labour. Another is that he does not see how locality can be a basis of wider, active and informed citizenship. Another is that segmentary communities unite and divide us in the wrong way, in loyalty to our own group and indifference or outright hostility to others. Indeed, this is why he is so much against an aggressive "blind patriotism". Yet it is also where contradictoriness comes in, once we see national identity as itself a form of local identity. Durkheim is all for national identity, but as part of the evolution of a human *patrie*, and as a particular, anchoring link between the identities of individual and man. This is the reason, despite any protests from him, for seeing it as a local identity in a system of modern political societies as more or less segmentary groups, with a similar organization and commitment to the human ideal, even though, as in *The division of labour*, each develops its own particular expression of this ([1893b] 1902b: 392; t.397). Moreover, Durkheim does not stick with the existing nation-state but looks to the emergence, as in *The division of labour*, of Europe (*ibid.*: 401–2; t.405), and generally, as in *Suicide*, of much larger societies (1897a: 430, n.1; t.375, n.13). This only underlines the case for a cluster of local-cum-segmentary identities important to each of us. Looking around the modern world – as at America, where no one is just American – it in fact seems the normal pattern. It is the idea of a homogeneous, single-tier national identity, such as "British", that is abnormal, and increasingly so.

Local-cum-segmentary identities still cannot constitute a fundamental ideal-typical pattern of modern society, even as one and many, and a vast complex society of societies. If they are not to collapse into a "blind patriotism", they again depend on sentiments and a cohesion that must come from elsewhere, either the division of labour or the human ideal or their combination. So although pluralism, factionalism and segmentariness are all necessary and important limits to the division of labour's generalizability, the most fundamental limit to it emerges as the human ideal of the modern *conscience collective* itself, as in the particular case, with which our discussion began, of gender. Let us now consider the case of citizenship.

In the review of Schaeffle it is the *involvement* with one another in a conflict of egoisms that can usher in an authoritarian coercive state. In *The division of labour*'s new preface it is the *withdrawal* from one another, into atomized, pluralist little worlds, that can do this. These may be two sides of the same problematic. They are nonetheless different sides, and let us pursue the concern, not only in *The division of labour* but in the thesis on Montesquieu, with an individualism in which everyone "sets himself and his affairs more thoroughly apart from society and public affairs". It is a concern rooted in the French liberal tradition and perhaps its first clearest expression – by someone else indebted to Montesquieu – is in Constant's *Ancient and modern liberty* (1819). Modern liberty is about freedom both as individual and as citizen. Yet freedom as an individual both depends on and tends to undermine freedom as a citizen, leading to its own internal, self-generated collapse. We can become so absorbed in our own private lives that, instead of attending to public affairs, we leave them to others and so risk letting in an authoritarian state that does not just stop at trampling on our rights as citizens but also seeks to suppress individual freedom itself. Constant ends with an appeal to a general sense of public spiritedness, in which everyone, "emerging from the sphere of their usual labours", instead of giving up freedom either as an individual or as citizen, "learns to combine the two together" ([1819] 1980: 514; t.327). Does this just beg the question of how, with individualism, there can be public spiritedness? Or is it to seize on something essential?

Durkheim increasingly moves to the second view. But at first, in a review of Fouillée, he ridicules the liberal republican "dream" in which the individual emerges from the limited horizons of the modern division of labour to convert, on election day, into a generally concerned, active and informed citizen ([1885b] 1970a: 181–2). He is more alive to the issues by the time of the lectures on occupational and civic ethics. He still seems suspicious of orthodox liberal republicanism and its *régime des partis*, associating it with "our political malaise", but now presses for active citizenship through autonomous occupational groups as the real road to democracy and away from the risk of an authoritarian state ([1950a] 1969g: 128–30; t.95–7). It is the same in *The division of labour*'s new preface, except that he is even more insistent on the need for intermediate groups that stop individualism letting in authoritarianism, that foster public spiritedness and that draw us into "the general torrent of social life" (1902b: xxxiii; t.28). Another difference, however, involves his idea that the occupational group can also be a centre for continuing education, recreation and the arts (*ibid*.: xxxi; t.26–7). The concern is clearest in his inaugural lecture at the Sorbonne in the same year, where he argues that "only a broad human culture can give modern societies the citizens they need" ([1903b] 1922a: 116; t.121). He re-emphasizes the point in his own report of the lecture, saying it is about how "only a truly human culture can give European peoples the citizens they need" (1904a(40): 684).

The original edition of *The division of labour* is all against "dilettantism" ([1893b] 1902b: 397; t.402), and also pours cold water on suggestions for offsetting the crampingness of specialization with a general education and culture that interest the worker in "art, literature etc.". This is incompatible with modern conditions and would raise people's sights too much, making specialization "intolerable" (*ibid*.: 364; t.372). Durkheim goes on to say that he opposes a "premature", narrowly vocational training, but supports an education that encourages a liking for "circumscribed tasks" (*ibid*.: 398, n.1; 402, n.3). There is nonetheless a considerable evolution of his views on this issue, beginning, perhaps, with an article on the teaching of philosophy (1895b), but already clear in the lectures on moral education, which, as has been noted, can be dated to 1898–9. His ideas are taken further not only in the inaugural lecture but in the course on the history of educational thought in France. Durkheim makes a powerful case in this for a "new humanism". Modern society and its citizens need an education that spans the sciences, history, literature and the arts. This is not to aim at an impossible encyclopaedism. But it must involve particular, detailed studies in the sciences, etc., and at the same time teach the distinctive, generalizable forms of argument that inform these, so equipping us both to draw on and to contribute to them. It is concerned, Durkheim concludes, with "the development of the whole man" (1938a, vol. 2: 226; t.348).

The whole man is the citizen envisaged in both the 1902 lecture and the 1902 preface. But the whole man is also connected with a distinctive "philosophy of life" that runs through Durkheim's work, including *The division of labour*, and that is first emphasized by W. S. F. Pickering (1984: 352–61). It is discussed by him in terms of Durkheim's commitment to the *vie sérieuse* but in recognition of the need for the *vie légère*. The *vie sérieuse* is life in earnest. It is about the division of *labour*, the struggle for existence, the family, citizenship, duty, knowledge of the world, science. But we need release in the *vie légère*, in the recreation of the game, the free-play of the imagination, the enjoyment of art and the "aesthetic" of something done just for the sake of it. Thus the original introduction to *The division of labour* insists on the need, as part of life in earnest, for a morality of duty and obligation. But there is also need for an "aesthetic of the moral", a supererogation that takes us beyond duty and obligation to pursue an ideal of the good completely spontaneously (1893b: 32; t.431). The lectures on moral education make the point that the free-play of art and the game loses its *raison d'être* if, in relating to life for real, it becomes life for real (1925a: 312–13; t.272–30). It destroys the distinction between the *vie sérieuse* and the *vie légère* and the balance we must each work out between them, though with the centre of gravity always in the *vie sérieuse*. This concern with the whole man is consistent with *The division of labour*'s disapproval of the dilettante, but inconsistent with its suspicion of a general culture and education. These come to have value for Durkheim as a basis, for the individual, of flourishing in a whole life, and not just because of society's need for informed, public spirited citizens. But there is this need, which cannot be met without a broad, truly human culture.

A modern or a world-historical dynamic?

The division of labour very much remains in the ring, even in discussing the limits to it as a generalizable pattern of relationships. It remains in the ring as something constitutive of modern society and its dynamic. To qualify as this it has to have far-reaching consequences, and Durkheim certainly sees it as having these. The division of labour helps to generate our ideals. It transforms social structures and institutions. It affects law, government, economic life, science and the arts, the family, even our personalities. It is a fundamental source of cohesion.

Yet no cause is uncaused – not even a society's dynamic – and Durkheim accordingly offers us an explanation of the division of labour itself. But this is above all from the point of view of evolutionary world history. This dominates and distorts interest in it, not as something with origins in the remote past, but as a dynamic of the modern social world, continuously at work and gathering force in it.

Durkheim's explanation begins in *The division of labour*, Book II. He ignores, on this occasion, appeals to an unfolding World Spirit, but concentrates on the homelier notion of everyone's pursuit of happiness. In its essentials, his attack on the notion is like Kant's in the third *Critique*. Man formulates the idea of happiness so diversely and changes it so often that it is a "wavering concept" (Kant [1790] 1913: 430; t.317). But Kant is looking for something qualifying as man's end and *telos*. Durkheim is not. He explicitly dissociates himself from accounts that are "teleological" ([1893b] 1902b: 330, n.1; t.339, n.1). He describes his own account as "mechanical": "Everything happens mechanically" (*ibid.*: 253; t.270); "All these changes are thus produced mechanically by necessary causes" (*ibid.*: 257; t.273).

In the context, however, "everything" and "all these changes" concern an account of world-historical evolution, and the same is true of the "teleological"/"mechanical" opposition itself. Just as Kant is after a world-historical teleological story, Durkheim is after a world-historical mechanical one. On the other hand, as we shall see, Kant does not mean it must be a story of man's *telos* as man's always conscious end. Durkheim just assumes teleology has to be such a story, and so a terminological difference masks an important agreement between them. It is in any case clear that, in keeping out world-historical conscious Ideas, Durkheim can still let in an active role for humbler, local social sentiments and beliefs. He in fact does exactly this, in his account's explanatory core. It involves the three following main claims:

(a) The division of labour faces an "insurmountable obstacle" in the very nature of traditional communities, and so cannot develop by itself but only if the communities are already changing from within (*ibid.*: 237; t.256).

(b) The change is morphological, involving increases in a society's "volume" and "density" (*ibid.*: 237–44; t.256–62).

(c) These increases do not simply permit but *"necessitate"* the development of the division of labour (*ibid.*: 244; t.262).

Claim (a) implies some sort of role for the shared sentiments and beliefs of the traditional *conscience collective* in obstructing the changes described in claims (b) and (c). Claim (b) involves the "break in equilibrium" described just after talk of everything happening mechanically (*ibid.*: 253; t.270). Claim (c), putting everything down to this morphological break in equilibrium, simplifies and misrepresents the arguments that follow in support, as is obvious from inspecting them:

(ci) It is because members of a traditional homogeneous society seek the same things that, with increasing size and density, people "find themselves in rivalry everywhere" and "the struggle for existence" is intensified to breaking-point (*ibid.*: 248; t.266).

(cii) The division of labour is a way of coping with the situation; in developing different functions, needs, values, and objectives, people can both coexist and co-operate, contain the conflicts between them, and live together in "the new conditions of existence" (*ibid.*: 248–59; t.266–75).

(ciii) The division of labour prevails over other solutions because it "can come into effect only amongst members of an already constituted society" (*ibid.*: 259; t.275), because it thus depends on a pre-existing "cohesion", "community of beliefs" and "pressure of sentiments" (*ibid.*: 261; t.277), and because, in this context and as already argued, it constitutes the best, "mitigated resolution" of the struggle for existence (*ibid.*: 253; t.270).

(civ) The other, in general less attractive, solutions are "emigration, colonization, resignation to a precarious, more contested existence, and finally the total elimination of the weakest through suicide or in other ways" (*ibid.*: 270–71 ; t.286).[3]

Boutroux, it has been noted, insists that the division of labour is not "mechanical" but is driven by an "end", the ideal of the cessation of the struggle for existence; there are, after all, other solutions to the struggle, "the simplest of which is eating one another" (Boutroux 1895b: 131; t.199). He may or may not have in mind Durkheim's point about the "elimination of the weakest through suicide or in other ways". But does he or does he not undermine Durkheim's thesis?

This cannot be that the division of labour is "mechanical" in the sense that it is necessitated, as in an understandable interpretation of claim (c), by morphology alone. It is necessitated, as in the claim's supporting arguments, by morphology plus pre-existing solidary beliefs and sentiments (the very things at first working against its emergence). But the division of labour might remain mechanical in that it is necessitated, as in a more consistent interpretation of claim (c), by morphology as the only specifiable world-historical factor plus a pre-existing solidariness that is unspecifiable in this way, since related to beliefs that are local in their nature and content. This is not undermined by the universality Boutroux sees both in the idea of a struggle for existence and in the ideal of its cessation. Durkheim's argument goes through without such a universality in the pre-existing solidary beliefs, and as though ideas of the struggle for existence and its cessation are the same amongst hunter-gatherers as in modern Paris. Instead, a necessary condition of his argument is that they are near enough the same in the type or types of society in which "original" breaks in equilibrium occur; otherwise the pre-existing beliefs might let in other solutions, such as emigration, colonization, etc. Is it a sufficient condition?

The point of the question is that breaks in equilibrium might fail to occur in some, many or most such societies, so failing to trigger the morphological motor of world evolution, and so failing it, not as such a motor, but as a world-historical force in every society. A long note reads:

> We do not have to inquire here if the fact which determines the progress of the division of labour and of civilization, that is, the increase in social mass and density, has a mechanistic explanation . . . We content ourselves with stating this law of gravitation of the social world, without going any further. But a teleological explanation does not seem any more imperative here than elsewhere. The walls separating the different parts of society are bit by bit worn away by the force of things, through a sort of natural attrition, the effect of which can also be reinforced by the impact of violent causes . . . Thus social density grows, and growth in volume is due to causes of the same kind. ([1893b] 1902b: 330, n.1; 339, n.8)

Apart from ruling out a universal conscious End, Durkheim should have contented himself with uninterest in *any* explanation of the break in equilibrium. Even if this occurs through accidental causes, external to the dynamics of the societies concerned, it is consistent with his thesis that *once* there is the break the division of labour is off and away.

The note comes in the concluding chapter to Book II, and is immediately followed by a remark in the main text:

> even while an effect of necessary causes, civilization can become an end, a desired objective, in a word, an ideal. (*ibid.*: 330; t.339)

We are thus exactly at the point in the book as a whole where Durkheim has wrapped up all he wants to say about the division of labour as a world-historical dynamic, starts to concentrate on it as modernity's dynamic and, in doing so, emphasizes the part in this of the human ideal.

But it is also important to reread or rework his world-historical story as an account of a continuous process in modern society itself. A skeletal version is that growth in the division of labour stimulates growth in social size and density, which stimulates growth in the division of labour, and so on. As he himself puts it:

> If society, in concentrating, determines the division of labour, this in turn develops the concentration of society. (*ibid.*: 241; t.260)

He immediately insists that the division of labour remains "the derived fact", and so he is still stuck in the German woods. Once out of these we must address the question: what can help to explain the division of labour as modernity's dynamic such that it is not itself modernity's dynamic?

But the question posed, it is not so difficult to find Durkheim's answer. It is just that it is not in Book II, dealing with the division of labour's "causes". It is in Book I, dealing with its "functions". It is true that Book II helps to explain modernity's division of labour through a developing historical process such as, skeletally, a growing division of labour due to growing volume and density due to a growing division of labour due to growing volume and density, etc. But it is Book I that explains why, from processes like this, we should pick out the division of labour as modernity's constitutive dynamic. It is the division of labour, rather than volume or density, that contains a basic, generalizable pattern of relationships, even though, as already discussed, there are limits to this built into modernity's dynamic itself. It is also the division of labour, rather than volume or density, that is a source of modern cohesion, modern morals and modern character. Let us start with investigation of it as a source of modern cohesion.

Cohesion versus consensus

The division of labour's story of organic cohesion met with disbelief from the beginning. Gabriel Tarde reviewed the original edition along with two other books, on social and racial conflict:

M. Durkheim spares us these frightful scenes. With him, nothing of wars, massacres, brutal annexations. It seems to the reader that the river of progress's flow has been on a mossy bed without raging torrents, and that humanity, always tranquil, has passed gently in the course of the ages from one state of uniform peace based on the juxtaposition of similar and inoffensive tribes or clans, to a state of multiform and even more profound peace, secured by the reciprocity of services between categories of workers who are more and more specialized and solidary at the same time. The passage from a sort of paradisic to a sort of phalanstarian regime. (Tarde 1893: 625)[4]

Albion Small reviewed the second edition, and concentrated on its argument for reviving the occupational corporation:

Corporations are the creatures of interests . . . Incorporating an interest primarily stimulates all the predatory and domineering traits of the persons conscious of the interest. Their very incorporation makes opposing interests relatively weaker. If the latter incorporate, the struggle between the interests is fiercer than ever, till one corporation submits to the other, or both are subordinated to a third. M. Durkheim is undoubtedly correct that incorporation of interests does facilitate the process of adjusting them, just as a pitched battle between armies is more decisive than desultory guerilla warfare. (Small 1902: 568)

Such criticisms have a point. But, unless it is supposed that modern society can run just on conflict or coercion, where are we going to find a basic source of modern cohesion? Not in pluralism. Not in factionalism. Not in segmentariness. They all presuppose it. There is another candidate still to be disqualified: belief in interest itself as a social and moral cement. This done, the choice is between cohesion through the division of labour and consensus around the modern *conscience collective*'s human ideal.

Let us first take an argument that works against a number of things, not least reliance on pluralism. It is Durkheim's argument against reliance on "negative" rights. Negative rights entitle people to enjoy their own property, manage their own lives, go their own ways. They essentially protect them from one another's interference. They "mark cleanly the barriers which separate them". But they do not constitute "a positive social link" ([1893b] 1902b: 88; t.119). They nonetheless depend on such a link:

> In reality, for men to recognize and mutually guarantee rights, it must first of all be that they love each other, that for whatever reason they are attached to each other and to the society of which they are part. Justice is full of charity – or, to return to our expressions, negative solidarity is only an emanation of another solidarity that is of a positive nature. (*ibid.*: 90–91; t.121–2)

The liberalism that just goes on about negative rights is often shallow and irresponsible in its inattention to the basis of effective respect for such rights. It forgets, as Durkheim puts it, that "justice is full of charity". Indeed, it forgets virtue. It is preoccupied with only one of the great questions of ethics – how to define the right, or, in its case, rights. It is as uninterested in what to do with one's rights as it is in the issues of moral character, motive and milieu tied up with ethical respect for them.

But the communitarianism that just denounces the "liberal individual" and goes on about a return to fellow-feeling and consensus is shallow too, in its inattention to the individualist aspirations of the human ideal as facts rooted in the modern milieu and character. There can be no return, in Durkheim's view, to the traditional small-scale homogeneous community as something that most of us could or would want to live in. This has been swept away by the division of labour itself and all the factors interacting with it – the continuing enlargement of modern society, its increasing density, pace of life, movement, communication and, not least, aspirations to freedom.

These are the general causes that in the original edition of his book "diminish the force of tradition" (1893b: 337). In the second edition and more famously they "lift the collective yoke" (1902b: 290; t.303).

The individual thus becomes "a source of spontaneous activity" ([1893b] 1902b: 144; t.169). The division of labour "pushes us into forming a distinct personality" (*ibid.*: 268; t.283). The "sphere of action of each individual extends in fact, and little by little the fact becomes a right" (*ibid.*: 285; t.299). We each become an "autonomous source of action" and centre of thought in which "the very materials of consciousness have a personal character" (*ibid.*: 399; t.403–4). Just as in the thesis on Montesquieu each of us has "his own personality, opinions, morals, religion", so in *The division of labour* each of us has and keeps to "his own opinions, beliefs, aspirations", as well as "personal character" and "turn of mind" (*ibid.*: 175–6; t.198). There is a modern *conscience collective*, with the human ideal at its core, but in its very nature consensus around it opens the way to a "multitude of individual disagreements" (*ibid.*: 147; t.172).

The meaning of Durkheim's whole argument about modern society is clear. There is no freedom without cohesion but no cohesion without freedom, which rules out the cohesion of an extensive consensus. Despite changes and developments in his view of the modern *conscience collective*'s human ideal, he never gave up this basic position. As he states it in the preface to *The division of labour*, "the individual, while becoming more autonomous, depends more closely on society", "these two movements, however contradictory in appearance, take place in parallel", and their combination is possible through "a transformation of social solidarity due to the ever-increasing development of the division of labour" (*ibid.*: xliii–xliv; t.37–8).

The fundamental thought about the division of labour is that it is a pattern of different yet complementary and interlocking activities that, even as it individualizes us, generates attachment to one another. Durkheim also wants attachment to society as such, and again looks to the division of labour for this, in giving us a sense of our part in a whole. But the sense of a whole takes on an importance of its own, once formed. Nor can it just be the division of labour that generates it. The division of labour evolves within an already constituted society and he still looks, as we have seen, to a pre-existing solidariness. It also evolves within the society, in process of formation, of a human *patrie*, and he looks to emerging solidariness with it too. *The division of labour* refers only in passing to times of collective ferment, in discussing the strength of feeling "in large assemblies" (*ibid.*: 67; t.99). Durkheim emphasizes the long march of individualism, "that does not date from our own day, or from 1789, or from the Reformation . . ." (*ibid.*: 146: t.171). His concern is again with a world-historical story, but is consistent with his list of dates as a list of especially formative periods of collective creative ferment. So in switching focus on to the modern world itself we can bring in the collective creative ferment of the article on the Revolution, and how it helped to usher in the ideals of a new era. The upshot of all this is that there is no way in which Durkheim's modern dynamic can just consist of the division of labour. Ideals such as of freedom, justice and everyone's status as a person have both their own importance once formed and their own relatively autonomous sources of formation. It is the same with feelings of identity with a society – such as, say, France – which are so central to Durkheim's view of solidariness. As a modern dynamic, the division of labour can be a fundamental, but not the only source of cohesion.

Let us now move on to his argument against appeals to interest as a social and moral cement. At one level it is part of his lifelong campaign against methodological individualism. It is not of course just this, and again at one level it is part of his basic ethical view, insisting that at its core ethical life means an attachment, integrated into our character, to one another and to society as ends. Ethical life, in other words, depends on such cohesion and solidarity. At another level, following from this, his argument against appeals to interest is to defend moral individualism as a genuine ethic against utilitarian, economistic and other versions of it that he believes cannot be ethical at all. He is moved to describe them, in rallying to the human ideal during the Dreyfus Affair, as a "sordid commercialism" ([1898c] 1970a: 262; t.60).[5] The attack on a focus on interest is in fact also an attack on a focus on the market and market-exchange. The development of the division of labour involves the development of the market, which is a central modern institution. But it is the division of labour, not the market, that can be a source of social and moral cohesion.

Thus one of the passages in *The division of labour* expressing Durkheim's basic ethical view runs:

> if interest relates men, it is never for more than a few instants; it can create between them only an external link. In the act of exchange, the different agents remain outside of each other, and, their business over, withdraw and retreat entirely into themselves. Consciences are only superficially in contact; they do not permeate or become strongly attached to one another. ([1893b] 1902b: 180–81; t.203)

Let us leave this for the moment, and concentrate on the argument, where it occurs, that "all in the contract is not contractual".

This is an intellectual *tour de force*, one of the book's showpieces. It is directed against Herbert Spencer, and another intellectual *tour de force* is the discussion of Durkheim's whole reading of Spencer by Massimo Borlandi (1993). But Durkheim's criticism of Spencer, on this occasion, is of the view that modern cohesion is based on the division of labour through "a co-operation automatically produced by everyone's pursuit of their own interests" ([1893b] 1902b: 177; t.200). He makes clear that Spencer rejects theories of a "contract" in which individuals agree to join together to form society itself, but that he instead sees an evolution towards a society in which individuals co-operate with one another through "private, freely made agreements". Then solidarity would just be the accord, expressed in contracts, of individual interests, and "society would just be the gathering-place where individuals exchanged the products of their labour, without any properly social action coming in to regulate this exchange" (*ibid.*: 180; t.203).

Durkheim insists, in contrast, on the active role of society and its collective experience, ideas and institutions. His criticism develops arguments in earlier work and takes two main forms. One emphasizes that the growth of social activity brings both increasing freedom *and* increasing regulation, that this regulation concerns all kinds of relationships in no way contractual, and that an important function of the state is to sustain in us "the sentiment of common solidarity" (*ibid.*: 207; t.227). The other criticism addresses exchange and the contract itself. It includes the passage, already noted, expressing Durkheim's basic ethical view and opposition to *échangisme*. It also concentrates on the contract, to insist it cannot be completely "contractual", in the sense of involving only explicit inter-individual agreement and consent.

Contracts necessarily involve the wider society. They necessarily involve the wider society to interpret, regulate or, indeed, create the terms of the contract, and they necessarily involve it to decide whether or not to enforce a contract, or in what ways, precisely, to do so.

Thus a basic point is that it is for society rather than the contracting parties themselves to decide who, in the first place, are persons competent to enter into a contract (*ibid.*: 189; t.211). Underlying this (though Durkheim does not, here, say so) is the idea of the person as itself an essentially social, collective representation. Another basic point is that a contract inevitably contains implicit, background terms, and so inevitably requires social interpretation of these according to equity, usage and the law (*ibid.*: 190; t.212). But Durkheim also

91

insists on the inevitability of social interpretation and regulation *even in the case of explicit terms.*

Individuals rely on the development, through collective experience and the law, of standard forms of contract. These include implicit terms, with the background understandings and conventions for interpreting them. They also of course include explicit terms, with the conventions for interpreting these. Moreover, they constitute the basis on which contracts may be revised and on which certain contracts may be rendered void because exceptional, flawed, unjust, etc. Individuals rely on collective experience's standard forms of contract because they cannot create, on their own and from scratch, agreements that are detailed and comprehensive in their coverage of different possible eventualities. Why do contracts need such coverage? Although "the division of labour renders interests solidary, it does not confuse them; it leaves them rival and distinct", letting in searches "to acquire as many rights as possible, in exchange for as few obligations as possible". A contract is thus "a compromise between the rivalry of interests and their solidarity" (*ibid.*: 191; t.213). It would be wrecked by an indeterminacy letting in endless disputes and continuing battles over the basis of a relationship. Contracts work because they are "non-contractual", in that they involve collectively developed standard forms of contract and conventions of interpretation on which, as individuals, we depend in going about our affairs and in entering into reasonably stable and equitable agreements and relationships with one another.

Durkheim concedes so far, as the "contractual" core of the contract, a naïve notion of the individual's free, voluntary acceptance of it. He still concedes such a notion, in beginning to question if it is the "contractual" core, when he argues: "The agreement of parties cannot render a clause just which inherently is not, and there are rules of justice whose violation social justice should prevent, even if those interested have consented to it" (*ibid.*: 194; t.216). He then discusses how "revolutions" take a long time to accomplish, and that in the meanwhile "unjust contracts, unsocial by definition, have been executed with the agreement of society" (*ibid.*: 194–5; t.216). This appeal to the unfolding of social ideals is to rescue the contract from ossification in a *status quo* and from the belief that the experience of "experience" is that there is never a need for change. It is at the same time to ask about consent itself. Indeed, it is to transform consent into a *contractual and non-contractual* core of the contract. Individuals "agree" and "consent" in terms of collective ideas of agreement and consent, evolving in collective processes, and debated and decided on through them.

There is thus a long discussion, in the lectures on occupational and civic ethics, of consent and the contract as evolving collective ideas ([1950a] 1969g: chs.15–18). But there is also a discussion along these lines in *The division of labour* itself, in the chapter in Book III on the division of labour's constrained, abnormal form. Durkheim condemns "leonine", "exploitative" contracts based on a socially reactionary and subversive conception of consent. The cohesion of modern society depends on contracts in accord with its developing ideals and the division of labour's dynamic and rationale. Accordingly, "a contract is fully consented to only if the services exchanged have an a equivalent social value" ([1893b] 1902b: 376; t.386).

This, it must be stressed, is not to replace the consensual core of the contract with something else. On the contrary, it is to insist on a consensual core of the contract. It is also to complete the argument that all in the contract is not contractual with the point that the very notions of consent, interest and the person at the contract's contractual core are themselves socially evolving collective representations. This leaves plenty of room for individual freedom since, again, it is all about individual freedom and what, in modern society, it means. What does it do for the division of labour as a source of cohesion? It leaves it in place as a basic source of this, but necessarily in combination with the modern *conscience collective*'s human ideal. Indeed, it is necessarily the two together that make clear that Durkheim's argument can rule out ethical life's reduction to interest even while letting in a place for the play of interest, within the framework of ethical ideals, relationships and identities. The search in the contract "to acquire as many rights as possible, in exchange for as few obligations as possible" must occur, after all, within just such a framework if there is to be anything like contractual legitimacy and through it solidarity.

Chapter Four

The organic self

The division of labour, as a modern dynamic, is a source both of our ideals and of our character. Let us now turn to this aspect of things, though the issue of cohesion rumbles on.

Individualism and individuality

Durkheim is concerned not just with individualism but with individuality. This is something rightly stressed, in discussing the Durkheimian "birth of the individual", by François-André Isambert (1993a,b). Let us start, even so, with individualism.

The individualism that Durkheim sees and defends as the ethic of our time is an ethic not just of the individual but of the individual as man. This is an absolutely fundamental point, and not as obvious and straightforward as, at first sight, it might seem. It involves a dualism, in which an ideal of individuality is part and parcel of the ideal of humanity. The dualism's Durkheimian explanation concerns the development of the division of labour, such that there are increasingly only two fundamental identities we can have, the identity of the distinct "individual" and the identity in common of "man". But it also concerns the development of modern society such that it demands a universalist ethic of "the person".

This means, amongst other things, insistence on every individual's same basic moral status and rights to respect and regard. Indeed, an ethic of the person is the only way to extend this status to every individual, and to oppose reactionary individualisms that withhold it. The modern individualist ideal is and has to be, for Durkheim, humanist and republican. Its aspirations find expression in 1789's "liberty, equality, fraternity".

Georges Gurvitch has also remarked on how Durkheim sees in the modern ideal "all the values to which he adheres most: equality, liberty, justice, fraternity" (Gurvitch 1963, vol. 2: 17). Moreover, it is important to emphasize, he sees them as coming together in an inseparable package. It will not do to insist on a definition of freedom that in effect writes off other modern ideals, and that camouflages, behind a lot of philosophical talk, a recipe for a minimalist police state and an anomic and oppressive class-divided society. It is a recipe for such things if only because the other ideals, which the libertarian state has to trample on, will not go away but are part and parcel of the modern world. Similarly, it will not do to insist on conceptions of equality and community that in effect write off freedom, in a recipe for a "despotic socialism". Durkheim's project is a commitment to a continuing, developing search to work and rework the human ideal's different aspirations, which, whatever the tensions between them, must combine into a whole.

It is bound to be a dispute-filled search, if only because of the nature of the human ideal, with its commitment to individualism and free thought, but also, in Durkheim's account, because of the nature of modern individuality itself. However, his appeal to the division of labour as a basic source of our individuality can at the same time obscure the point about individuality itself as a source of differences and disputes.

Thus he says, summarizing the argument of Book I, that it is through the development of the division of labour that the individual "while having a personal character and activity distinguishing him from others, depends on them to the very extent that he is distinct, and in consequence on the society that results from their union" ([1893b] 1902b: 205; t.226). A little later on he is heavily collectivistic:

> Since the individual is not self-sufficient, it is from society that he receives everything necessary to him, just as it is for society that he works. There thus forms a very strong sense of the state of dependence in which he finds himself: he becomes used to taking proper measure of himself, that is, to seeing himself as only part of a whole, an organ of an organism.

This is immediately balanced with more individualistic concerns:

> On its side, society learns to regard the members composing it, no longer as objects over which it has rights, but as people working together whom it cannot do without and towards whom it has duties . . . [It] develops to the extent that individual personality becomes stronger. (*ibid.*: 207–8; t.228)

But the general picture is of a diversity and cohesion that are two sides of the same thing, the division of labour. It is the organic diversity and organic cohesion of differences that are nonetheless complementary and interlocking.

The picture is seriously misleading. Durkheim has just wrapped up his case against Spencer. It includes an argument about egoism and altruism, which is of interest and in a way original. This criticizes the view that "egoism is humanity's starting-point and altruism only a recent conquest" (*ibid.*: 173; t.196). Altruism exists in every society, and in traditional societies, where the *conscience collective* so dominates people's lives, it is found in "a truly intemperate form" (*ibid.*: 174; t.197). Egoism always exists too, but especially develops with modern society. Egoism is equated, in this passage, with individualism. Durkheim defines it in terms of "sentiments and representations which are exclusively personal", and indeed just talks of it as "individuality" (*ibid.*: 175; t.197–8). It is also in this passage that he observes how, in modern society, each of us has and holds on to "his own opinions, beliefs, aspirations". Then an argument that is in a way original is how altruism becomes part and parcel of "egoism", that is, of individualism and our individuality. It does so because "we have our own way of being altruistic, which comes from our personal character and turn of mind" (*ibid.*: 176; t.198). That is, we each have our own ideas of good causes, and so have our own ways of being altruistic in terms, as he has just said, of our own "opinions, beliefs, aspirations".

The individualization of altruism thus connects with all the emphasis, already noted, on how we each become an "autonomous source of action" and a centre of thought in which "the very materials of consciousness have a personal character".

This does not sound as if it can just be a matter of *organic* diversity, of differences that are complementary and cohesive rather than conflicting. Nor is it. The crucial passage comes earlier on, when

Durkheim discusses the nature of the modern *conscience collective* and of the human ideal at its core. It increasingly involves, around this "common faith", ways of thinking and feeling that are "very general and indefinite" and that let in "a growing multitude of individual disagreements [*dissidences*]" (*ibid.*: 147; t.172). *Dissidences*, even if including the differences of organic cohesion, must also refer to the conflicts involved in pluralism, factionalism and the freedom in which we each have our own "opinions, beliefs, aspirations".

It is a failure to grasp the Durkheimian problematic to appeal, in this situation, just to the division of labour or to a substantive consensus around the human ideal. The division of labour and the very nature of the human ideal constitute a basic source of freedom's conflicting substantive opinions around it. It is essential to appeal to other things, even though these also have their basic source in the division of labour and the human ideal. They are procedural norms of tolerance and due process, and, sustaining them, feelings of attachment to one another and of a shared identity. Without such things there cannot be the pluralism that, tolerantly, lets us go separate ways, or the factionalism that, patiently, argues over and tries to negotiate an acceptable collective line. Factionalism, as has been seen, is more important than pluralism. We cannot simply go our separate ways on issues such as justice, equality or, indeed, freedom itself. They are collective issues on which, through all our disagreements, we need to decide for a time, and in a moving agenda, collective policies and lines.

But if it is the nature of the modern personality that, through "a growing multitude of disagreements", is part of the problem, it is also where we must look for the mutual attachment – amidst the disputes – that is part of any solution. Then we can rule out one kind of character right away. This is the abstract atomistic man attacked in Durkheim's early writings, and who reappears in *The division of labour* in the Leibnizian philosophical guise of "the monad":

> Collective life is not born from individual life, but it is, on the contrary, the second which is born from the first. It is only on this condition that it is possible to explain how, without the disintegration of society, the individual personality of its members could form and grow . . . It is not the absolute personality of the monad, self-sufficient and able to do without the rest of the world, but that of an organ or part of an organ with its own definite func-

tion, yet unable, without endangering its own existence, to separate itself from the rest of the organism. (*ibid*.: 264; t.279–80)

If we now look for Durkheim's own positive account of the modern
self, let us baptize it, in light of this and other passages, as the organic
self. It has to be a source *both* of different, disagreed beliefs and opinions *and* of mutual attachment.

The organic self

The nature of the self became a central issue in the "liberal–
communitarian" debate of Durkheim's time, just as it has become this
in the corresponding debate nowadays. He was by no means alone in
the search for an alternative, at once liberal and communitarian, to
the self as asocial atom. Thus there is the neo-Hegelian account developed by Bernard Bosanquet in *The philosophical theory of the state*
(1899), which includes various references to Durkheim.[1] Or there is
James Seth's *Study of ethical principles* (1894). This went through
innumerable editions, and rediscovers and reconstructs Aristotelian
virtue ethics for the modern world.[2]

The current liberal–communitarian debate goes over old ground,
often as if it is new. But the importance for it of Durkheim's general
position has begun to be recognized, for example by Mimi Bik
(1987).[3] There have since been contributions by R. T. Hall (1991) and
Mark Cladis (1992), amongst others (Watts Miller 1993b).

It helps, if we return to Durkheim's account of the self, to pick out
three elements that are universal yet that are transformed by modernity. They concern opacity, embodiedness and the situated identity and
self-constitutive ends of the "real man".

A major Durkheimian theme is the opacity of sentiments that lie
hidden in the self, as if out of sight from the conscious will. This
surfaces in his criticism of atomistic, libertarian ideas of morality:

> It consists, instead, of a state of dependence. Far from serving to
> emancipate the individual and detach him from his surrounding
> milieu, its essential function is, on the contrary, to make him an
> integral part of a whole, and in consequence to curtail some of his
> liberty of action.

He at once accepts how some people might find recognition of such dependence intolerable:

> But this is because they are unaware of the sources from which their own morality flows, since these sources are very deep. Consciousness is a bad judge of what goes on in the depths of our being, since it does not penetrate there. ([1893b] 1902b: 394; t.398–9)

The implication, in the context, is that it is our own modern ideals of individual freedom that make for difficulty in seeing and stomaching their collective basis, and it is also the implication of his earlier, despairing remarks about the inveterate, not to be questioned prejudices of an "intransigent individualism". The autonomy of the lectures on moral education is a struggle to emancipate the will through self-knowledge, which is necessarily a collectively developed self-knowledge and a struggle towards an unrealizable ideal. It is of interest to note Onora O'Neill's comment: "Kant insists, in ways that some contemporary 'Kantians' do not, that human beings have quite limited capacities to enact their autonomy" since, amongst other things, "he holds that our maxims of action are obscure to ourselves and to others" (O'Neill 1992: 219).

Another major Durkheimian theme is the interaction in "life" of the physical, psychic and social aspects of our being. Durkheim always insists on the self's embodiedness, but believes in the modern individual's increasing "spiritualization", and *The division of labour* mounts a powerful argument against racist, reactionary theories of biological reduction. The argument is that social processes break up isolated, local genetic pools. They therefore so transform the influence of heredity that "man" becomes the general type, genetic distinctness is essentially between individuals, culture becomes more important, and "the individual is less strongly chained to his past" ([1893b] 1902b: 317; t.328).

But perhaps one of Durkheim's most fascinating discussions concerns the nature and ambivalence of modern sexuality. It comes some time after *The division of labour*, when he had become interested in the dualism of the sacred, as something both negative and positive. It is nonetheless a continuation of his interest in a similar dualism in ethical life. Thus he talks of the sentiment, at the basis of our morality, of respect for the person, and how this surrounds the body with moral barriers against its invasion. The sexual act, in the intensity of its contact, so breaks through these that it can be desecrating and defiling. Yet it can be so positive a union that through it two persons together form "a new personality". It is if this does not happen, and it is just an exchange between individuals who then go their separate ways, that the act's intimate physical nature means a moral loss of respect and of status and dignity as a person. Durkheim is adamant that "free consent" cannot wipe away the meaning, in our ethical culture of the person, of such casualness towards the embodied self (1911a: 45–7; t.145–7).

In fact, the argument is a development of the way Durkheim begins his whole thesis on the division of labour, in the first chapter of Book I, where he considers the cases of friendship and marriage, introduces the organic self and attacks *échangisme*.

When friendship is based not on likeness but on difference, it is on complementary difference:

> However richly endowed we may be, we always lack something, and the best of us are aware of our insufficiency. That is why we seek in our friends the qualities we do not have, since in uniting with them we participate in some way in their nature, and so feel less incomplete. ([1893b] 1902b: 18–19: t.55–6)

There thus arise small groups of friends "in which each has a role in keeping with his character, in which there is a true exchange of services", but in a division of labour that, far from just being "economic", is above all moral in its impact on people and creation amongst them of a "sentiment of solidarity" (*ibid*.: 19; t.56).

A long discussion follows on sex, love and marriage, the sources of "perhaps the strongest of all the unselfish inclinations" (*ibid*.: 20; t.56). It is where he argues that the evolution of social differences between men and women, in a gendered division of labour, explains many of the physical differences that have arisen between them and that become part of men's and women's "nature" in the sense of characteristics deeply engrained in culture and *mores*, rather than immutably fixed in the genes. It is accordingly completely consistent with the general argument, later in the book, against biological reduction, and indeed is part of a republican anthropology that is necessary both for men's and women's equality and for everyone's equality as persons. Nor does the problem, for men's and women's equality, really lie in Durkheim's sociological sense of "nature" as culturally engrained characteristics, "the work of centuries", as he says in *Suicide*. He is quite ready, when he sees the need, to argue against "the work of centuries". The problem instead lies, as already seen, in his deep attachment to marriage and its particular connexions, and in his worry at its destruction by individualism's abstract programmatic demands. But we can now see clearly that it is a deep attachment to marriage's particular connexions both as a division of labour *per se* and as a gendered division of labour. Without this, marriage would again become a loose, unstable relationship between separate individuals (*ibid.*: 24; t.61). Because of it, "the union of two spouses ... is no longer an external contact, temporary and partial, but an intimate, lasting association, often indissoluble over the two people's lifetimes" (*ibid.*: 23; t.59).

Can appeal to Durkheim's view of friendship allow some reworking of his view of marriage? He is committed to the love that forms, in a kind of division of labour, between friends, whether or not he especially has in mind friendship between men, and whether or not he disapproved of homosexual love. Indeed, his argument that sexuality demands a social and moral union between persons if it is not to violate respect and self-respect can apply as much to homosexual as to heterosexual bodily initimacy (again, not that he himself might have admitted this). But a Durkheimian sociology of the homosexual as of the heterosexual couple, and as of friendship itself, would still look for some sort of division of labour, as an essential part of interdependence and solidarity.

Let us now move on to his general argument for this, which introduces the organic self in an attack on *échangisme*. Friendship, marriage and other relationships based on the interdependence of a division of labour necessarily involve some kind of exchange. But they do not reduce to exchange:

> it just translates this mutual dependence outwardly. It is thus only a superficial expression of an internal, very deep state. Precisely because this state is constant, it gives rise to a whole mechanism of images which function with a continuity that exchange lacks. The image of the one who completes us becomes inseparable in us

from our own, not only because it is frequently associated with it, but above all because it is its natural complement; hence it becomes an integral and permanent part of our consciousness, to the point that we can no longer do without it and seek everything that can increase its energy. (*ibid.*: 25; t.61–2)

So, in a general opposition to the self-sufficient "monad", Durkheim places a general emphasis on our incompleteness.

This takes him to the division of labour, to insistence that it is *not* just the other side of exchange, and to discovery of the organic self. The division of labour is not and cannot be just the other side of exchange. In a generalized system of exchange we go to the market, do our business and leave, so that it is a superficial, transient business, abstracted from other, particular, more continuous and enduring relationships. The division of labour necessarily involves, in our actual activities and roles, particular, more continuous and enduring relationships. It is in these particular connexions, and in the paradigmatic cases of friendship and the family, that there forms an "internal, very deep state", involving representations constituting the very material of our consciousness, and in which "the image" of the other becomes an integral, permanent part of our being, of the "I" rather than just the "me".

This, then, is the organic self, attaching us to others and to society as ends that are constitutive of our own selves, and deeply rooted in our consciousness and character. It has nothing to do with an *échangisme* in which individuals simply use one another as instruments of their own separate interests and purposes. It has everything to do with ethical life, in which there is mutual respect, concern, attraction and commitment to one another, rather than just usefulness to one another. So it also has to do with the socially situated identity and attachments of "the real man". But how can the organic self emerge from "the real man" to become both a communitarian and a liberal self?

We can still develop the individuality of distinct centres of thought and action, even in the attachment to others as ends, integration of images of them in our own consciousness, joining of our lives together and formation, as in marriage, of "a new personality". We need not, indeed cannot, become attached to everyone as an end in the same way, or integrate the same images of the same others into our consciousness, or join our lives together in the same particular connexions, or form, as in marriage, the same complex "new personalities".

All the processes of individuation that Durkheim sees in the division of labour as modernity's dynamic can go ahead.

Nor is it just the individuation of organic diversity. It is also the individuation of *dissidences*. Then a basic point about the organic self is that the attachment to one another as ends which is part and parcel of it helps to take the strain of the disagreements which are part and parcel of it too. If we think through Durkheim's apparent romanticization of friendship, marriage and "organic solidarity", it has to involve something like this. Love is not love if it cannot cope with our hurts and disputes.

In the case of the wider society, it is again because of our disputes that we need an attachment to one another that precisely does not just depend on ideological agreement. Yet how, in the case of the wider society, does the organic self work and become attached not just to the particular but to the generalized other? We run into the Humean problem of how an extensive human sympathy develops that transcends not simply self-interest but the particular connexions of family and friends, and overrides the communitarian norms in which MacDonalds and Campbells happily murder one other. For some reason, English commentators tend to concentrate on the difficulties presented by self-interest. This is to see MacDonalds and Campbells as London stockbrockers in disguise. French commentators are more alive to the importance of the Humean *homme de clan*.[4] Durkheim, for his part, articulates the problem through his lectures of the 1890s on Rousseau.

He seeks to reconcile Rousseau's claims that sympathy is a natural moral sentiment and yet that it might not extend very far. In Rousseau's view:

> in order to see a man, a fellow creature, in every human being, whoever he may be, it is necessary to have powers of abstraction and reflection that primitives lack. For them, mankind is confined to their immediate entourage, to the little circle of individuals to whom they are related. "They have the idea of a father, a son, a brother, and not of man. Their hut contained all their fellows . . . beyond these and their family the universe was nothing to them." Compassion could therefore be activated only within this little milieu. "Hence the apparent contradictions seen amongst the brothers of the nations . . . so fierce in their manners

and so tender in their hearts; such love for their family and such hatred of their kind." ([1918b] 1953a: 124–5; t.72–3)[5]

In Durkheim's own view, though morality is driven by sentiment rather than just by reason, there cannot be a change towards more general, humanitarian ways of *feeling* without a change towards more general, abstract ways of *thinking*. This cannot happen by itself. It depends on all the social processes that, as in *The division of labour*'s original edition, "diminish the force of tradition", and, as in the new edition, "lift the collective yoke". It also involves the times of creative collective ferment that, as in the article on the Revolution, usher in a new and audacious faith. The new, audacious faith of the human ideal overcomes particularism and attaches organic selves more extensively to one another through integration, in the consciousness, of a universalist abstract idea of the person. This is what a change towards more general ways of thinking and feeling is about.

"The person" as a collective representation

The article on the revolution is the first time that Durkheim really identifies the modern secular ideal as a "faith". The next time is in a much discussed passage, in Book I of *The division of labour*, on the nature of the modern *conscience collective*: "the individual has become the object of a sort of religion"; "We make the dignity of the person into a cult"; "it is, if one likes, a common faith" ([1893b] 1902b: 147; t.172). It is something of a problematic passage because of what Durkheim says, in the middle of it, about our new ethic-cum-religion:

> If it turns all wills towards the same end, this end is not social. It thus occupies a completely exceptional place in the *conscience collective*. It is from society that it draws all its force, but it is not to society that it attaches us; it is to ourselves. Hence it does not constitute a true social link. (*ibid.*)

Can he be serious?
A cult that attaches us to ourselves is going to attach us to one another and to society, given that it is attachment to organic selves. Durkheim seems to throw away the whole point of his account of the

organic self, introduced at the beginning of Book I and reasserted in its conclusion:

> even where society rests most completely on the division of labour, it does not decompose into so many juxtaposed atoms, between which it can establish only external, transient contacts. Its members are instead united by ties which extend far beyond the short moments in which exchange takes place. (*ibid.*: 207; t.227)

Of course, a cult that attached us to ourselves as "so many juxtaposed atoms" would not attach us to one another or society. But it is hard to believe that Durkheim has momentarily adopted the idea of the atomistic self – attacked throughout his work, and throughout *The division of labour*.

An explanation, perhaps, is that he is using one of his favourite rhetorical devices – overstatement and emphatic contrast – to drive a message home. The message, in this case, is that the cohesion of the division of labour is more important than any coming from consensus around the modern *conscience collective*'s human ideal. After some more rhetoric to the same effect, Durkheim wraps up the passage and the chapter as a whole just by saying that the division of labour is the force that "principally" makes for modern cohesion (*ibid.*: 148; t.173).

A passage in *Suicide* is almost the reverse of the passage in *The division of labour*:

> The cult of man is hence something completely different from the egoistic individualism ... which leads to suicide. Far from detaching individuals from society and from every end which goes beyond them, it unites them in the same thought and makes them servants of the same work. For the man thus held up to collective love and respect is not the sensible, empirical individual that we each are; it is man in general, ideal humanity, as conceived by each people at each moment of its history. (1897a: 382; t.336–7)[6]

We can take this literally if we like and see great somersaults in Durkheim's position, except that, if taken literally, it again works against the overall argument of which it is part.

Durkheim rightly wants to emphasize the centrality of "the person" as a collective representation. It is constitutive of everyone's status as a person, underwrites the Kantian imperative to respect the humanity in anyone's person, and so also underwrites duties both to others and to oneself. It thus leads on to the Kantian conclusion of Durkheim's argument, that the ethic of the person is violated not just by murder, but by self-murder:

> From the moment that the human person is and must be considered something sacred, over which neither the individual nor the group has free disposal, any attack must be forbidden . . . If, in itself and in a general way, the violent destruction of a human life shocks us as a sacrilege, we cannot tolerate it in any circumstances. (*ibid.*: 383; t.337)

To get to his conclusion, however, Durkheim has to shift the meaning of "the person". He has to shift from it as an abstract collective idea to its reference to the individual embodied person – as in the Kantian imperative, but also as in police reports and, say, having something on one's "person". The flesh and blood person is no doubt a symbol – *the* symbol – of the human person, and the violent destruction of this flesh and blood symbol's life is no doubt a sacrilegious outrage against the cult of the human person. But it is the flesh and blood person who actually gets killed, whose death provokes the shock, and whose life is protected by the cult. Indeed, that is the point of the cult – to protect, respect and regard everyone as a person – and it makes nonsense of this if it is only the abstract idea of the person that is held sacred, not the empirical individuals that embody and represent it.

This is not just the point underlying Durkheim's particular argument that the human ethic condemns suicide. It also underlies his defence of individualism in the intervention, a year later, in the Dreyfus Affair. Given the nature of the piece and the circumstances – the social and political crisis surrounding a Jewish army captain's alleged treason – it is perhaps understandable that it is where, of all Durkheim's work, he most talks up the human ideal. A passage reads:

> Whoever attacks the life of a man, the liberty of a man, the honour of a man stirs up in us a sentiment of horror in every way analogous with that felt by the believer who sees his idol

profaned. A morality like this is not just a hygienic regime or a judicious economic management of existence. It is a religion in which man is at the same time worshipper and God. ([1898c] 1970a: 265; t.62)

But this is to go on to insist that utilitarian doctrines can easily accept "all kinds of compromises", whereas the individual, sacralized in a cult of man, cannot be "more jealously protected" (ibid.).

Jean-Claude Filloux is unhappy that Durkheim defends "individualism", and suggests a revival of Charles Renouvier's talk of "personalism" (Filloux 1990: 48). The suggestion has something in it, but still does not capture the issues at stake. Renouvier, like Durkheim, drew on Kant, and Boutroux, in his lectures on Kant, helps to bring out the issues.

Boutroux wants both to socialize and to individualize Kantianism. He emphasizes Kant's search for a "moral community" (Boutroux 1926: 280). He then asks if Kant is an "individualist", to answer that he is not at all: the universality of the person is precisely a liberation from the empirical sensibility and particularity of the individual (ibid.: 351). He goes on to ask if this will do, and to answer that it will not. The modern social and moral world involves increasing concern with "the particular, the specific, the individual", and so involves a "need for diversity, for individuality at the same time as for universality and likeness". Then how can we just make do with Kantian universal reason? How can persons be distinct, rather than homogeneous, without bringing the empirical individual back in? Indeed, reason cannot just cut itself off from the human empirical world, but "is in reality linked with nature and inseparable from it, even logically". Modern ethics must find a way of combining rather than opting between the particular and the universal, although – which is where the lectures conclude – "the problem is immense" (ibid.: 373–4).

It is of course a problem that The division of labour sets out to solve. Durkheim continues to wrestle with it, as in a passage on "the individual" and "the person" in The elementary forms (1912a: 386–90; t.305–8). This includes more of Durkheim's own thoughts on Kant. They involve a basic agreement with Boutroux:

For [Kant] the keystone of the personality is the will. The will is the faculty of acting in conformity with reason, and reason is that which is most impersonal in us. For reason is not my reason; it is human reason in general. It is the power the mind has to rise above the particular, the contingent, the individual, to think under the form of the universal. So it can be said from this point of view that what makes a man a person is that whereby he is identical with other men, that which makes him a man, and not a certain man. The senses, the body, in a word everything that individualizes is on the contrary considered by Kant as the antagonist of the personality. (*ibid.*: 388; t.306)

The passage continues as if on the Kantian side – for the person and against the individual – but then finishes with the following note:

We nonetheless do not deny the importance of the individual factor . . . there can be no social life unless distinct individuals are associated, and it is all the richer the more numerous they are and the more different from one another. The individual factor is thus the condition of the impersonal factor. The converse is no less true, since society itself is an important source of individual differentiation (see *The division of labour*). (*ibid.*: 390, n.1; t.308, n.128)

Paul Ladrière draws attention to the passage and its importance. It is perhaps the only one where Durkheim really analyzes the notion of the person; it involves his emphasis on it, which he does not owe to Kant, as an abstract collective representation; it brings home to us an issue, about the contrast yet interrelationship between "the person" and "the individual", that is often just lost nowadays (Ladrière 1990: 147–50). It can be added both that Durkheim takes us far beyond Boutroux in tackling the issue, and that he does so in his work as a whole, including *The division of labour* and *Suicide*, problematic passages and all.

Or consider a brief observation in the lectures on Rousseau:

Rousseau sees only two poles of human reality, the abstract, general individual, who is the agent and object of social life, and the concrete, empirical individual, who is the antagonist of all collective existence. These two poles are in a sense at odds, and yet the first without the second is merely a logical entity. ([1918b] 1953a: 191; t.131)

This brings out the nature of Durkheim's commitment to the individual as man. It is a commitment to "personalism", but to individualism too.

The organic self plays an essential part in all this. It is necessarily embodied, involved in particular attachments, constituted through organic diversity, and a source of the *dissidences* that it itself helps to cope with. At the same time it must incorporate and integrate into the consciousness an abstract idea of the person, attaching us to the humanity of the generalized other as well as in ourselves. These are two interrelated sets of conditions for the resolution of two interrelated modern problematics that Durkheim's work, centrally, addresses – the self's attachment not only to others but to a wider society as ends, and the self's combination of the person's universality and the individual's particularity and distinctness.

Individualism's pathologies: the case of suicide

Suicide, as everyone knows, is not just about suicide. But what is it about? One of the answers must be that it is an exploration of the pathologies of the modern world, above all of the pathological forms of the individualism and individuality that Durkheim sees as such central, constitutive features of our society. Let us approach it in this way and make some preliminary comments.[7]

Durkheim looks for real, underlying suicidogenic currents that sweep people away to their deaths. We can just set aside criticisms of this that are inspired by a positivism or whatever that Durkheim's basic, rationalist conception of science rejects. Let us instead notice a problem that arises within his approach itself. He takes suicide rates as the main starting point for getting at and detecting suicidogenic currents. Yet a main concern is with detecting individualism's wider pathogenic currents, which show up not just in suicide but in other ways. So what is the relationship between suicidogenic and these wider currents, and their different manifestations? Durkheim is well aware of the problem – as we shall see in discussing his account of the relationship between suicide and murder.

It is in any case evident that he develops and offers us a sociology of risk. This obviously includes the risks to us as individuals of being swept away to our deaths or affected in other ways by real, powerful yet often obscure social forces that we hardly understand. But, more importantly, it is about risks to our wider society itself. Just as importantly, it is an internalist sociology of risk. It is about systemic risks, both to us as individuals and to our wider society, inherent in the very nature of our society, in a dynamic at work in it that is a source of our ills as well as of our ideals. Thus individualism's pathological forms will not go away, even with increasing realization of individualism's human ideal in a republic of persons. They are part and parcel of the ideal, so that even a republic risks derailment by them in some or other crisis, just as there remain risks of suicide and so on for its individual members. What we may and should hope is that the pathologies, and so the risks from them, are contained.

A question arises if it is here that Durkheim falters in what is otherwise one of the great achievements of his internalist programme. *Suicide* is a sustained, determined effort at an internalist explanation of modern risks and pathologies. The problem occurs when he draws on the distinction developed in *The rules* to ask if the existing patterns of suicide are normal and contained, or abnormal and symptomatic of some worrying malaise. He concludes that the rate is abnormally high, "a pathological phenomenon that is all the time becoming more menacing" (1897a: 424; t.370). He goes on to see it as symptomatic of a malaise, indeed "an alarming moral poverty", to do with "a profound change in our social structure" (*ibid.*: 445–6; t.387).

Is he offering a clearly internalist account to do with the end result of the change, a menace built into the "structure" of modernity itself? Or is he emphasizing something in a way external to modernity, belonging to the change towards it? But let us leave such questions until discussion of Book III of *The division of labour*, which is on the division of labour's abnormal forms, and where the problem is fundamental.

A final preliminary point has to do with the course on moral education. Philippe Besnard dates it to 1898–99, that is, to just after *Suicide*. He emphasizes, in doing so, the use of a similar, very basic conceptual scheme. *Suicide*'s concerns with regulation and integration correspond with the lecture course's concerns with discipline and attachment, morality's two universal elements (Besnard 1993b: 127). The concern with these two elements goes back, as has been seen, to Durkheim's earliest writings on morality. But it is transformed in the lectures into a rich, complex account that involves, amongst other things, a dualism of reason and sentiment. We do our duty through respect for an imperative moral authority and in disciplining a crowd of desires. We pursue the good through positive social sentiments, idealistic impulses and fellow-feeling.

Suicide's four categories and two oppositions are: egoism versus altruism, and *anomie* versus fatalism. It helps to understand them in terms of the moral education course's moral elements, and to start with things at their most formal. Egoism is underattachment, altruism overattachment. *Anomie* is underdiscipline, fatalism overdiscipline.

Since we are on the lookout for individualism's pathologies, there is obviously egoistic as well as anomic individualism. But what about fatalistic individualism? Or, and again as a pathology, altruistic individualism?

We must anyway inject the dualism of reason and sentiment. Let us start with the cases of egoism and *anomie*, and come to fatalism and altruism later. Egoism is underemotive and overintellectual, a retreat from the social sentiments of attachment, a numbing of them in a withdrawal into a private little intellectual world of one's own – an apathy. *Anomie* is overemotive and underintellectual, an unfettering of desires from discipline, an enslavement to compulsive, limitless wants that can as much turn against oneself as drive an instrumentalism turned against others – an antipathy.

Durkheim writes:

> But society cannot disintegrate unless, to the same extent, the individual detaches himself from social life, unless his own ends become more important than common ends, unless, in a word, his personality tends to place itself above the collective personality . . . If we agree to call egoism this state in which the individual self is asserted to excess against the social self and at its expense, we can call egoistic the particular type of suicide which results from inordinate individuation. (1897a: 223; t.229)[8]

He then goes on to say why egoism risks suicide. His explanation, at bottom, is that in retreating from the social into the individual self we retreat from everything that can give our lives meaning, anchorage and a definite, "objective foundation":

> All that remains is an artificial combination of illusory images, a phantasmagoria which the least reflection is sufficient to dissolve;

nothing, therefore, which can serve as an end of our actions . . . nothing our efforts can lay hold of, and we feel them lost in empti-ness. (*ibid*.: 228; t.213)

Egoism is a real tendency in our individualistic society to try to become monads. We withdraw from people around us and from feel-ings of attachment to them. We seek our innermost "authentic" self, and instead fall into an intellectual vertigo. One version is the *raison raisonnante* that sets out to question everything, finds answers to nothing, and falls into extreme scepticism. It is discussed in many ways nowadays, even, despite its long history, as postmodernism. Hume suffered from something of the sort as an adolescent. He called it, after an ancient Greek philosopher, Pyrrhonian scepticism, and turned to post-Pyrrhonian scepticism. This grounds enquiries about the world in its basic, commonsense acceptance, and there is a similar-ity with Durkheimian enlightened acceptance of basic, given realities. Durkheim has extreme, egoistic scepticism in mind when talking of metaphysical systems that set out "to prove to men the senselessness of life" (*ibid*.: 229; t.214).

Let us now go from egoism to *anomie*. Durkheim writes:

Both types of people committing suicide suffer from what has been called the disease of the infinite. But the disease does not assume the same form in the two cases. In one, it is the reflective mind that is affected and hypertrophied beyond measure; in the other, it is the sensibility that is overaroused and out of control. In one, thought, through retreat into itself, no longer has an object; in the other, passion, ceasing to recognize limits, no longer has a goal. The first is lost in the infinity of imagination, the second in the infinity of desire. (*ibid*.: 324; t.287)

So, where egoism is underattached, underemotive and overintellec-tual, *anomie* is underdisciplined, underintellectual and overemotive. How does it risk suicide, and why see in it an antipathy in contrast with egoism's apathy?

Durkheim, obviously, sets up ideal-types, explores various combi-nations and overlaps between them, and sees a "special affinity" between egoism and *anomie*: it is "almost inevitable that the egoist should have some disposition towards non-restraint; for, since he is detached from society, it has not enough hold to govern him" (*ibid*.:

113

THE ORGANIC SELF

325; t.288). But one way of insisting they are nonetheless different is through comparison of suicide and murder. Egoism turns away from others to focus on oneself, in an "apathy produced by exaggerated individuation" (*ibid.*: 406; t.356). So it protects individuals from one another through the very way in which it does not protect them from themselves. It contributes to suicide, but not to murder. In contrast, *anomie*'s emotiveness can erupt into a violence directed against one-self or against others and unconstrained by the ethic of respect for the person. So with *anomie*, and especially in the great centres of modern life, "murder and suicide develop in parallel" (*ibid.*: 408–9: t.358).

The case of exploitation is of direct interest here, and again involves the issue of difference and overlap. Exploitation is seen as a "variant of *anomie*" in an interpretation of Durkheim by Dominick LaCapra (1972: 161). It is brought "within the province of fatalism" in a criticism of this interpretation by Philippe Besnard (1993c: 188). Might it not, in some or many cases, involve both? It looks like a variant of *anomie* if uncontained, self-interested desires impose on others a relationship that is "exploitative" in terms of a Durkheimian appeal to the modern ethic's aspirations to justice and demands for respect for persons. It comes within the province of fatalism if the relationship is just accepted in a dispirited, crushed resignation – the repression of desires by an excessive discipline, which is how Durkheim sees fatalism in his brief note on it (1897a: 311, n.1; t.276, n.25).

Besnard has done most to uncover fatalism, and it resurfaces in the moral education lectures both in an attack on a repressive asceticism and in Durkheim's anxiety to argue that enlightened acceptance is not passive acceptance. But something else needs to be uncovered – altruism. *Suicide*'s discussion of this concentrates on contexts, such as the army, that reproduce a traditional, highly collective communitarianism in the middle of modernity. Nor is it just that Durkheim forgets about *The division of labour*'s altruism, as something very much involving the individual personality and the pursuit, in our own way, of good causes of especial concern to us. As with fatalism, he seems to want to play it down in insisting that it is only in exceptional cases that modern individuals "renounce life . . . for something they love better than themselves" (*ibid.*: 246–7; t.228). He immediately adds a note on the Revolution:

The frequent suicides of the men of the Revolution were probably due, at least in part, to an altruistic state of mind. In these times of internal struggles and of collective enthusiasm the individual personality had lost some of its value. The interests of country or of party came before everything. The many executions sprang, no doubt, from the same cause. One killed others as readily as oneself. (*ibid*.: 247, n.1; 228, n.34)

The note is interesting for at least two reasons. One is the widening out of the issue of modern altruism, and away just from suicide. The other is the basic mistake Durkheim makes in it about the modern ethic of "the individual personality". In effect he emphasizes only its expression in norms of moderation. He suppresses its expression in intense, core convictions about the human ideal and this or that cause taken up as an essential part of it – whether women's liberation, racial equality, the campaign over the innocence of Dreyfus, etc. Liberalism, as a morality, would be nothing without such core, often intolerant, even fanatical convictions – Durkheim's own point in the article on the Dreyfus Affair: "A religion that tolerates sacrileges abdicates all dominion over consciences", and the same is true of the "religion of the individual" ([1898c] 1970a: 274; t.68). But even as a religion, liberalism must somehow combine tolerance and intolerance, moderation and conviction. The necessary tension between these can be broken in a zealous altruistic individualism, killing others or oneself in one's own particular, favourite good cause, so that it is an expression of the individual personality though also, as Durkheim says, a devaluation of it. Altruism can thus emerge as an individualistic pathology too.

Suicide is deceptive because of the way, in the early chapters on egoistic individualism, it can so easily come across as a hymn to the highly integrated, traditional homogeneous community. Groups such as the Catholic Church have "beneficent", "salutary", "protective" effects on their members, in contrast with the free-thinking, suicidogenic ways of Protestants. If we read on, however, Durkheim makes it clear that it is hopeless to look to a revival of the traditional, dogmatically religious community. There can be no viable religion of the future unless it accepts free thought and concedes to "the right of criticism and inquiry, to individual initiative, a much greater place than even the most liberal Protestant sects" (1897a: 431; t.375). Then it is this

115

aspect of modern society's human ideal that is the basic source of two of individualism's pathological forms – the apathetic egoism that *Suicide* brings out and the sympathetic altruism that it obscures. It is not the basic source of the other pathological forms, the antipathetic *anomie* that is again brought out, and the emotively repressive or, to invent a term, "hypopathetic" fatalism that is again obscured. We have to look for the basic sources of such pathologies, and especially of *anomie*, elsewhere – not in individualism as free thought but in the aspect of it that, as in the Latin thesis, has to do with how, by the very nature of modern society, "private life has grown and individuals enjoy a greater freedom to pursue their own interest". This accordingly returns us to *The division of labour*, since it also has to do with Book III's discussion of the division of labour's abnormal forms – not least the exploitation and oppression of the constrained form.

Chapter Five

Modern ills and modern ideals

Book III of *The division of labour* discusses the "anomic", then the "constrained", then "another" unnamed abnormal form of the division of labour. The discussion of the constrained form sets up, in opposition to it, the ideal of the "spontaneous" division of labour. But let us use this term in opposition to *all* of the division of labour's abnormal forms.

The spontaneous division of labour

Durkheim switches concern, by the end of Book II, from evolution to modernity, and in doing so is ready to bring in ideals. A "mechanistic conception of society does not exclude the ideal" ([1893b] 1902b: 331; t.340). On the contrary, it "not only does not deprive us of ideals, but allows us to believe that we shall never lack them"; there is and will always be "a free field open to our efforts" (*ibid*.: 336: t.344).

So this can prepare the way for the human ideal as an active element of modernity's dynamic, interdependent with and helping to guide the division of labour – "reflection intervenes to direct the course" (*ibid*.: 331; t.339).

It certainly prepares the way for Book III's discussion of the division of labour's abnormal forms. Thought's intervention, "to direct the course", is to help to overcome them. This, however, is part of a set of three basic concerns. Endorsing the human ideal as the modern social ideal is a matter of ethics. Evaluating our actual society in terms of it is a matter of critique. Getting from the actual to the ideal is a matter of reform.

The process is not just an affair of clear ideas. It involves "obscure", "awakening" aspirations, giving people a sense of "something lacking" and of "where they must channel their efforts" (*ibid.*: 331; t.340). It remains the case that thought – clear or obscure – needs to channel efforts just because all need not be going "normally" and unworryingly.

But it also remains the case that Durkheim insists, as in the Latin thesis, that if "health is natural, so is sickness" (*ibid.*: 330; t.339). Everything seems set, in Book II's run-up to Book III, for internalism. We can look forward to an appeal to our society's own dynamic to understand modern ideals, modern ills, and spontaneous movements for reform.

Yet as soon as Book III begins Durkheim worries that the division of labour might be suspected of "logically implying" its abnormal forms (*ibid.*: 343; t.353), and that these have been seen as its "necessary effect" beyond a certain stage of development (*ibid.*: 348; t.357). This does not read like an internalist introduction at all.

In sum, we must look out for a number of things in Book III: the human ideal's relationship with the division of labour, the interplay of ethics, critique and reform, and what becomes of internalism. But the place to start is with the "spontaneous" division of labour itself.

– *Developing and flourishing*. Durkheim's main thesis, as stated in the preface, is that the modern world promises both increasing individual freedom and increasing social cohesion owing to the division of labour. But this, he eventually explains in Book III, has to be the spontaneous division of labour: "the division of labour produces solidarity only if it is spontaneous and to the degree that it is spontaneous." And this, he at once explains, means the absence "of everything that can shackle, even indirectly, the free unfolding of the social power each carries within him" (*ibid.*: 370; t.377). It is an ideal, in other words, of a society in which everyone can develop and flourish as a person. It is the ideal that drives Durkheim's vision of things, and means that the human ideal becomes part and parcel of the "spontaneous" division of labour as his modern social dynamic.

– *Isomorphism*. He next insists on a situation in which "social inequalities exactly express natural inequalities" (*ibid.*: 370; t.377). Is such isomorphism either necessary or sufficient for everyone's developing and flourishing? It may be necessary for everyone's equal degree of development of their potential. It may be insufficient for everyone's flourishing fully up to their potential – a pattern and distribution of social roles could parallel, but fall below, the pattern and distribution of natural capacities. It is in any case problematic to tie the ideal of developing and flourishing so closely to moral geometry. This is not to criticize the very idea of natural potential as "unDurkheimian". On the contrary, the argument that everyone is qualified to develop and flourish as a person in a society of persons requires a republican, anti-reactionary anthropology.

- *Equal opportunity*. In looking to isomorphism, Durkheim also looks to "absolute equality in the external conditions of struggle" as its "necessary and sufficient" condition (*ibid*.: 370–71; t.377). It is obviously not a sufficient condition. There could be too many able people chasing too few suitable roles. It might not even be a necessary condition.

- *Contractual justice*. This, as already seen, means that "a contract is fully consented to only if the services exchanged have an equivalent social value" (*ibid*.: 376; t.383). But Durkheim now casts doubt on moral geometry. Equivalent social value cannot be "calculated mathematically", and we must rely on general notions of it in the "public conscience" (*ibid*.: 376; t.382). Equivalent exchange still has an "objective foundation", again in external equality as a "necessary and sufficient condition" (*ibid*.: 377; t.383).[1] Whatever might be made of this, an underlying point is correct. We cannot appeal to "free" contracts or the "free" market without an idea of justice that is already contained in our idea of freedom in the first place. It is mistaken to argue, as some *laissez-faire* liberals seem to do, that any exchange is equivalent and hence just if it is a transaction of the "free" market – but as if such "freedom" is a pure primitive term. The negative rights standardly determining their conceptions of a free market already carry within them a conception of justice. The only question is which package of interacting ideas of freedom and justice to work with, and this cannot be decided just by pulling stipulative definitions out of a hat. It involves us, like Durkheim, in wider theoretical argument.

Thus his approach to contractual justice invokes the "public conscience", which "demands in an ever more pressing manner exact reciprocity in services exchanged" (*ibid*.: 379–80; t.386). Similarly, he goes to the "public conscience" to see in its demands for equality a demand for equal opportunity (*ibid.*: 372–3; t.379).

In these and other cases there may be a need to clarify or rework developing ideals. In all cases there is a need to understand them in terms of a dynamic reality. But they themselves can form part of this reality, and it is important to notice the activism forming part of Durkheim's language, a language of struggle and striving, a free field always open to our efforts, etc. Modern societies "strive and must strive to eliminate external inequalities as far as possible" (*ibid.*: 374; t.380). The development of the modern ideal is "a work of justice", and the progress already made in it, however important, "might well give only a small idea of what will be achieved" (*ibid.*: 374; t.381). The "task" set for us is "to bring increasingly greater equity into our social relationships, in order to ensure the free unfolding of all socially useful powers" (*ibid.*: 381; t.387).

It is a "task", unmistakably, of the human ideal. This is consistent with it as a reality that is engrained in the modern situation and character, and that we cannot just change at will, indeed that helps to constitute the will. It is consistent with the world-evolutionary argument running through the thesis as a whole, that everything happens mechanically. And it is consistent with insistence on reform such that the division of labour "is itself, that nothing comes from outside to distort it" (*ibid.*: 364; t.372) – if we assume, as we are entitled to do, that this refers to the spontaneous division of labour.

So we now have in place two interdependent elements of Durkheim's modern dynamic: the relationships and processes of the division of labour as a Montesquieuan "structure" and the unfolding aspirations of the human ideal as a Montesquieuan "principle". What we do not appear to have is any room for an internalist account of abnormalities arising from within the dynamic itself. Despite criticism, in the Latin thesis, of Montesquieu's reliance on external, "accidental" causes, it looks as if, in the main thesis, Durkheim wants to rely on them himself to explain abnormal forms of the division of labour. He again asserts that it "does not produce these consequences through a necessity of its nature, but only in exceptional and abnormal circumstances", which is when he insists that, to tackle the ills, it "is itself, that nothing comes from outside to distort it".

It is nonetheless possible to keep looking for an internalist account from him. In fact a kind of internalism is involved in what we might just discuss as his "Book III" strategy. This combines, but in an unsatisfactory way, what we might again just discuss as "logical" and "developmental" strategies. A logical strategy focuses on the nature and implications of the spontaneous division of labour's ideal-typical rationale. As a logical internalism, it looks for pathologies built into the rationale itself – something the Book III strategy rejects, in favour of a logical purism. A developmental strategy explores the actual division of labour's evolution through various stages of modern society with their own internal, characteristic circumstances and problems, and asks questions that Book III's developmentalism suppresses.

Is the "abnormal" division of labour abnormal?

One view is that Durkheim has to accept something as normal if it is general. The criticism is then made that he contradicts himself in seeing the division of labour's "abnormal" forms as abnormal, when, as he more or less concedes, they are general in our existing society. The criticism is mistaken, since it disregards the second route to the normal and the search for fit with a rationale. It nonetheless prompts the question of how to explain a lack of fit, and whether or not Book III has an adequate answer.

The second route to the normal is set out in various places, starting with the article on the Revolution, but mainly getting going with the search, in the Latin thesis, for the real and its rationale – the concern, again, of the moral education lectures and of debates in the 1900s. The concern is banalized in *The rules*, with talk of fit with a social type's "general conditions" ([1895a] 1901c: 64; t.97). It is obscured in *The division of labour*'s original introduction, in a formula designed to establish the division of labour as *the* fundamental modern moral fact, on the universalist grounds that it "serves the same ends and depends on the same causes" as facts already known as moral (1893b: 37–8; t.434–5). Once so installed, it can work as a dynamic explaining other things.

The introduction also defines the normal in terms of different stages of a society's development (*ibid.*: 35–8; t.433–5). The Latin thesis involves a similar interest in stages of development, and the definition carries through to *The rules*. We can now return to Book III. Durkheim writes:

It could thus seem that we do not have the right to consider as normal a character which the division of labour never presents in a pure state, if it is not on the other hand noted that the more there is social advance . . . the more these inequalities tend to be completely levelled. ([1893b] 1902b: 372; t.378) [2]

He also writes:

When, nonetheless, it is considered that over the centuries men have been content with a much less perfect justice, the question arises if these aspirations are not perhaps due to an unreasonable impatience, if they do not represent a deviation from the normal state rather than an anticipation of the coming normal state. (*ibid.*: 381; t.387)

Both passages help to bring out the Book III strategy.

Durkheim invokes the modern era as a whole to do one job, and its different stages of development to do another. The whole-era job is to identify and condemn existing forms of the division of labour that, though general, are out of fit with a long-term rationale. The developmentalist job is to say how they come about, in an explanation that keeps the rationale clean. Thus the division of labour does not so much explain them as explain their withering away. In becoming spontaneous and "itself", it sheds things that it does not "logically imply", but that belong to the circumstances of earlier stages (including the present) and of transition between them.

How is the strategy put to work? Most of the discussion of the constrained division of labour concerns economic life, so does much of the discussion of the anomic form, and one basic line blames the rapidity of change. But let us concentrate on the other, which blames institutions and outlooks rooted in our society's past.

Thus the division of labour has become less constrained in that social role, rank and public office are no longer inherited, and "the regime of castes has disappeared in law". But it survives "in *mores*, through the persistence of certain prejudices, a certain credit attaching to some, a certain discredit to others, which is independent of their merits" (*ibid.*: 371; t.378). There is the survival, too, of inherited wealth. There remain "careers which are wholly closed or more inaccessible to people without inherited money" (*ibid.*: 372; t.378), while there must be unjust contracts as long as there are "rich and poor at birth" (*ibid.*: 378; t.384).

So Durkheim appeals to a kind of developmentalism to explain the continuing strength of caste-like beliefs and institutions, and appeals to whole-era ethics to anticipate and explain their withering away, but also to condemn them as abnormal in the here and now. Let us first consider this from the point of view of a developmental strategy.

In such a strategy something must be normal if it is an integral part, at a particular stage, of the modern dynamic's own development. The Book III strategy's developmentalism involves Durkheim either in a blindness to the point or in a determination not to ask about and address it. It will not do just to see something as abnormal because, in the existing stage, it is not what it should become in succeeding stages. We have to fix on it as it actually is in the existing stage, and ask about its normality or abnormality in this context. This leaves open all kinds of possibilities, but also raises all kinds of questions. One is whether a period of very rapid change is or is not an integral, normal part of the modern dynamic's development. Another, in concerning a pattern of different, conflicting beliefs, then affects critique of institutions.

The division of labour's original introduction talks of an opposition in which "different moral practices moderate one another and their antagonism produces their equilibrium" (1893b: 41).[3] The new introduction revises this to how moral life "responds to different and even contradictory necessities" and so is naturally made up, in part, of "antagonistic elements limiting and balancing each other" (1902b: 7; t.44). But in both passages, and as in the Latin thesis, it is an important general feature of Durkheim's approach that there are always built-in conflicts in society between different movements, tendencies and factions. It is thus not just whole-era ethics to criticize things at particular stages of modernity in terms of its own unfolding human ideal. It is part of the ethics of these stages themselves. For it is part of the normal process of conflict in them that aspirations arise that criticize the *status quo*, demand reform, and help to move debate and disputes on to a new agenda.

Book III is about doing all these things. Yet what is the basis on which Durkheim sides, here as elsewhere, with the party of a radical future? All the different tendencies – conservative, moderate, radical – might be normal and part of the same rationale, at this or that stage of development. Both the original and the revised introductions seem almost pure expressions of liberal moral politics as a kind of division of labour in which the "antagonistic elements" contribute to the stability and movement of society as a whole in "limiting and balancing each other". So, again, on what basis can Durkheim take sides?

This is a rather worrying, even fundamental, problem for his ethical position. Although there is a solution, the Book III strategy remains in trouble. Suppose that on enquiry we see an existing institution as normal in its historical, developmental context. Then we cannot criticize it as abnormal in its context. But we can still criticize it as in need of reform. We can do so as part of the very process of keeping the modern dynamic going, and in a more radical commitment to its "work of justice". Perhaps this is still to criticize it in a Book III way, except that it is now both normal and abnormal. Indeed, it might be to avoid such complexity and confusion that Durkheim suppresses questions that a developmental strategy ought to consider. It still does not justify their suppression, if a proper exploration of the developmental strategy necessarily results in complexity.

A proper exploration of the logical strategy also results in complexity. Developmentalism is essential for understanding how, in the actual world, a dynamic emerges, makes headway, runs into obstacles or is distorted, even destroyed. Indeed, the logical strategy lies at the core of developmentalism and its interest in the nature and implications of the dynamic itself. But the Book III strategy takes refuge in a kind of logical purism – one that blames abnormalities on developmental problems and refuses to enquire if it is the rationale itself that might be a continuing source of them.

Thus a standard complaint is that Durkheim has little or no interest in how class can be a continuing, built-in obstruction in our society to realization of the human ideal. The complaint is double-edged. One reason is that it does not explain how there comes to be the human ideal and appeal to it to criticize actual society. Another reason is that it offers little or no account either of a viable republic or of how, through reform, to get there.

It may be right that "Durkheim did not attribute to the phenomenon of *social classes* the importance which it merits" (Cuvillier 1948: 79). Perhaps we should look to the independent-minded, quasi-Durkheimian Maurice Halbwachs for greater insight (Gurvitch 1963, vol. 1: 367–81). Even Jean-Claude Filloux, who has done most to develop Durkheim's views on the subject and is ready to ascribe to him a theory of class, emphasizes its equivocal nature and "lack of firmness" (Filloux 1977: 205). Charles-Henry Cuin is more damning, but in an interesting and instructive way (Cuin 1987, 1991). Let us now turn to issues involving class, amongst other things.

Class, the market and technology

We read in *The division of labour* that the "farmworker, if in harmony with his conditions of existence, is and must be closed to the aesthetic pleasures normal amongst the educated" ([1893b] 1902b: 219; t.240). This is not just a passing remark. In *Suicide*, the "identity of origin, of culture and of tasks makes occupational activity the richest material for a common life" (1897a: 435; t.378). In *The division of labour*'s new preface, the practice of the same occupation readily produces "a certain intellectual and moral homogeneity" (1902b: xxx; t.26). In a subsequent debate:

> The worker reduced to a producer is an abstraction. There exists an intellectual and moral life in which he participates. It is as impossible for him not to take part in this as not to breathe the air around him. To say that the worker is only a producer is to make the mistake of the old economists, to resurrect the old notion of *homo economicus*. ([1905e] 1970a: 286)

Durkheim is concerned, in saying this, with a wider society and *patrie* in which "bourgeois and workers" share the same ideas. He still insists that "these ideas take on a different coloration according to class" (*ibid.*: 291). A later article argues on similar lines.

There is a need for a general, shared culture and education. It is still the case that each occupation constitutes a milieu ruled by "certain ideas, certain usages, certain ways of seeing things" ([1911c] 1922a: 45; t.68). Education is thus about preparing the individual for participation in "the political society as a whole and the special milieu for which he is particularly destined" (*ibid.*: 49; t.71). Both passages are quoted by Cuin (1987: 50), who tends to play down the importance to Durkheim of an education that, through a human culture, prepares the citizen and the "whole man". But he is undoubtedly right to play up the importance to Durkheim of occupation as a particular milieu –

even, despite all the Book III talk about equal opportunity, as a milieu to which the individual is "particularly destined".

For Durkheim, in sum, class is mediated by occupation, and both occupation and class very much involve groups constituting distinct sociocultural milieux, with a sense of their own identity. This is important in at least two ways. The first concerns inherited wealth. Even with its complete abolition, a republic would still not be a classless society. Classes in some sense would remain, through the occupational groups and sociocultural milieux of the division of labour. The hope must instead be for a republic that is not a class-divided society, riven by deep, antagonistic conflicts. Durkheim never proposes, anyway, the complete abolition of inherited wealth. His ideas on the subject are vague, and seem deliberately so. He avoids blueprints such as John Stuart Mill's idea of a system of worker-owned co-operatives, and does not go into distinctions between, say, "personal wealth" and "the means of production". He certainly insists on some sort of change from wealth organized and inherited through the family to its organization and distribution through the occupational group, and is always against its concentration in the state. But his intention seems more to identify such a change as a catalyst, opening the way, as occupational groups themselves develop, to the exploration of various possibilities. These might include, though he never mentions it, the worker-owned co-operative. They still need not mean a classless society, given his view of class as something that is not just economic.

Indeed, this takes us to the second point. This concerns what has been discussed as "social inheritance", for example by Jean-Claude Filloux (1977: 207) and François Cardi (1993: 40).[4] It is about the transmission, not of wealth, but of all kinds of other things – social abilities, knowledge, contacts, outlooks, values, motivations and aspirations themselves – through all kinds of particular connexions, whether the family, the school, the peer group or occupation. An interesting study of it is Paul Willis's *Learning to labour: how working class kids get working class jobs* (1977).[5] Durkheim, given his sociocultural line on occupation and class, must have been aware of the importance of social inheritance – to the extent that he talks, as Cuin notes, and in a way in line with Willis, of the milieu to which the individual is "particularly destined". The importance of social inheritance is, not least, that it rules out equal life chances on anything on a Book III scale.

A choice might still be made between equal life chances and particular connexions, with their involvement of social inheritance. But it is difficult to imagine a Durkheimian campaign to suppress particular connexions. They are central to his whole social and moral theory.

The choice, anyway, is more complex. It is mistaken to think that Book III's demand for a match of natural potential and social role forgets about socially developed and acquired abilities. It instead requires a translation of natural potential into socially acquired abilities into social roles, and an isomorphism in the patterns of all three. Let us lump together socially acquired abilities – whether or not through social inheritance, and including aspirations – and just talk of them as merit. We then now have a three-way choice, involving particular connexions, equal opportunity and merit. Put at its starkest, the relationship between them is such that we can combine any two but not all three.

If we combine particular connexions with roles filled according to merit, we rule out equal opportunity. If we combine merit and equal opportunity, we must make war on particular connexions. If we combine particular connexions with roles filled to ensure equal opportunity, we bury merit.

James Fishkin sets this up as a modern "trilemma", but in a discussion that concentrates on the particular connexions just of the family. In settling for a compromise that involves all the values, he complains that "we live in a moral culture imbued with absolutist expectations" and argues that we should jettison these (Fishkin 1987: 47–8). This is not necessarily a realistic or sensible suggestion, as can be seen by turning to a debate on equality between Durkheim and Parodi.

Durkheim insists, against Parodi, that our "egalitarian practices" do not depend on any need we have for logical consistency, since they in fact rest on two contradictory conceptions. One demands equal treatment according to merit, while the other demands an equal treatment despite inequalities in value or worth (1910b: 62; t.67–8). One, through differentials according to the relative importance of tasks, implies hierarchy, while the other implies a complete levelling (*ibid.*: 69; t.75). Moreover, the two conceptions are so contradictory that they form the basis of two opposing theories. One is the favourite principle of orthodox economists, the other of moralists and ascetics. Yet, far from having to choose between them and sacrifice one to the other, society can and does combine them in practice: "Each has its place in moral reality" (*ibid.*: 66; t.72).

This is precisely not an argument that we all ought to join the party of moderation and jettison every "absolutist" ideal – even though it is not an argument against the imperativeness, in a liberal moral culture, of fudge and mudge. Rather, it is an argument against reduction of ethical life to this, when even liberalism must be driven by passions and involve the ideals and convictions of a religion. Again, it is not just a passing argument. It echoes talk, in *The division of labour*'s introductions, of some sort of practical settlement in moral life, but between distinct "antagonistic elements" that express its different demands and aspirations. It is also reflected in *Ethics*, which contrasts *morale* with *moeurs* to contrast our ideals with the compromises of moral life at its more "mediocre" (1920a: 76; t.92).

Equality remains one of the great ideals Durkheim sees at work in the modern world, even in its contradictory conceptions. It is a necessary, inspirational *mystique*, even in the inevitable accommodation and mediocrity of *politique*. But does there remain a place for attachment to it as a *mystique* of equal opportunity?

Book III combines two quite plausible premises with an invalid if in a way quite plausible conclusion. The first premiss is that the modern world involves a belief in equality, and the second premiss is that it involves, in fact, an increasing inequality. The conclusion is that the belief can only be in equality of opportunity ([1893b] 1902b: 372–3; t.379). This is invalid because, for example, the belief could instead be in equality of treatment according to merit, or in the same basic status as persons. It becomes plausible if taken as a claim that the belief must be a belief in, amongst other things, equality of opportunity.

But let us begin with a focus on the second premiss, to ask why there may be an increasing inequality. Let us imagine Year I of a future republic in which there are the particular connexions of family, etc., there is a spontaneous division of labour such that inherited wealth has disappeared to the point of irrelevance, there is a market system of worker-owned co-operatives, and there is an isomorphism – in which everyone is more or less equal – of natural abilities, merit and roles. There is, more or less, equality of conditions.[6]

How, in line with an internal logic of things, might the situation develop? A repetitive pattern will emerge in which, as a result of one round of exchange, there are always individuals and co-operatives at a relative advantage in going into the next round. A cumulative pattern will also emerge in which relative advantage carries through successive rounds, to build on itself and increase. There are at least two reasons for the repetitive pattern. One concerns merit. Even if it is more or less equal, it is still different, bringing, even in an accommodation of values, different rewards. The other concerns luck. Playing the market may involve more skill than playing roulette, but nonetheless involves an ineliminable element of luck, in which some do very well while others lose out, including co-operatives that must close down and leave members jobless and bankrupt. There are various reasons – through someone's continuous gain or another's irrecoverable loss – for a transformation of repetitive relative advantage into a cumulative pattern. It is virtually certain there will be cases in which this occurs. Then in themselves, and in triggering things such as social inheritance, they entail the emergence in society as a whole of inequality of conditions.

A criticism of Durkheimian appeal to equality of opportunity is that it is not this that matters but equality of conditions. The criticism loses force if even a republic that starts with a reasonably strict equality of conditions must move towards inequality in them. The same applies to criticism of Durkheim's attempt to blame exploitative contracts on inherited wealth, rather than simply on unequal wealth.

- *There must be unjust contracts if there are rich and poor at birth* – the epigram of Durkheim.
- *There must be unjust contracts if there are rich and poor* – the revision suggested by Cuin (1991: 25).
- *There must be unjust contracts* – the revision it boils down to.

This new version assumes the modern inevitability *both* of inequality of conditions *and* of systematic, exploitative abuse of it. Durkheim accepts the first assumption, and critics disguise their own failure to challenge it by going for easier meat instead, such as his focus on equal opportunity or on inherited wealth. So, if we leave the first assumption in place, the key to things is to ask about the second: must there be systematic, exploitative abuse of inequality of conditions?

But this is not just a matter of exploitative contracts. It concerns the nature of work itself and relationships within it. Durkheim writes, describing the modern industrial worker:

> Every day, he repeats the same movements with a monotonous regularity, neither interested in nor understanding them . . . he is

no more than a lifeless mechanism that an external force sets in operation and that always proceeds in the same direction and in the same way. Clearly, whatever our representation of the moral ideal, there cannot remain indifference to such a debasement of human nature. ([1893b] 1902b: 363; t.371)

This obviously goes beyond exchange in an abstract labour market to focus on actual technology and production in the labour process itself. Philippe Besnard argues that it constitutes a fourth Durkheimian "abnormal" form of the division of labour (Besnard 1987: 36–40; 1993a: 205–7). He calls it *travail en miettes*, in doing so drawing on Georges Friedmann (1964: 135–54). This is fragmented, minutely parcelled up and, by implication, robotic work. But it is also, from Durkheim's description, overdisciplined, crushing work. It thus seems the very opposite – the fatalistic opposite – of *anomie* and its undisciplined unfettering of desires. Yet Durkheim brings it into the anomic division of labour – in fact into the end of his chapter on this, Book III's opening chapter, and before all the talk of equality, justice and the republic to come, which never mentions it again. Besnard suggests it is another example of Durkheim's burial of an issue he could not or did not want to handle, just as he buries fatalism itself in *Suicide* (Besnard 1993a: 207).

It can certainly seem like tears and sympathy, followed by a sell-out. A life spent making the eighteenth part of a pin does not matter, provided work is reorganized so that there is mutual contact, understanding of how functions fit in with another and a sense of an overall aim. Nobody is then "a machine . . ., however specialized, however uniform their activity might be" ([1893b] 1902b: 365; t.373).[7]

Durkheim's tears are at a "debasement" of human nature. Let us therefore talk of degraded, debased labour. This no doubt involves desocialized labour. So it can come into a chapter on *anomie* calling for resocialization through mutual contact, a sense of an overall aim, etc. But degraded labour must also be about deskilled labour – which wastes people's abilities and indeed crushes them as persons. A deskilled job is still a deskilled job, even if we get good wages, think of the social contribution we are making, and in other ways try to keep up our self-respect and self-esteem. It has already been discussed how exploitation might combine both *anomie* and fatalism. Durkheim can seem to sell out, of all things, to *anomie*, to the ethically unfettered desires that are ready, in the pursuit of self-interest, to reduce others to a "lifeless mechanism that an external force sets in operation and that always proceeds in the same direction and in the same way". At the same time he can seem to recommend, to people at the receiving end, the fatalism of just accepting this repression and instrumentalization. It is to lose sight, in both cases, of the modern human ideal and how it demands respect for everyone as a person – a duty to respect others, as well as a duty to oneself of self-respect and pride.

Durkheim is either unable or unwilling to address the challenge presented by deskilled, not just desocialized, work to the aspiration he himself sees at the very core of the spontaneous division of labour and the human ideal – the aspiration to a society of everyone's developing and flourishing as a person. It is the way, after all, in which he introduces and defines the spontaneous division of labour: the absence "of everything that can shackle, even indirectly, the free unfolding of the social power each carries within him" (*ibid*.: 370; t.377).

Or consider Book III's last chapter, on the division of labour's "other", unnamed, abnormal form. It involves one thing and another, and could be called the "bureaucratic" division of labour, as suggested by Philippe Besnard (1987: 43–6). It certainly worries about a proliferation of jobs that underoccupy people. But a basic concern, here, seems to be with roles that are genuine, in that they stretch, extend and fully engage us. It is with such a concern that the chapter ends. It is with a division of labour that creates solidarity "not only because it limits everyone's activity, but also because it increases it" ([1893b] 1902b: 389–90; t.395).

This immediately leads on to *The division of labour*'s overall conclusion, where Durkheim again talks of a "more specialized, but more intense life" (398; t.403). The point supports a larger argument, central to the conclusion and to the thesis as a whole. Durkheim is anxious to defend the division of labour in terms of an ethic of developing and flourishing, and very much criticizes the view that, "in making each of us an incomplete being", it "diminishes the individual personality" (*ibid*.: 398: t.402). On the contrary, he insists, we flourish through a more specialized, but more intense life, and – as in the idea of the organic self – through "our association with other beings who have what we lack and who complete us". Far from being diminished by the division of labour, the individual personality develops through it, since "to be a person is to be an autonomous source of action" and to become a distinct centre of thought in which "the very materials of consciousness have a personal character" (*ibid.*: 399; 403–4).

Durkheim goes to Aristotle for the motto of *The division of labour* – "A city is not made up of people who are the same" – and returns to him in the conclusion: "We start from the principle that man must realize his own nature and fulfil, as Aristotle said, his own *ergon*" (*ibid.*: 399; t.403). This avoids mention of the other side of man's function and *ergon*, man's end and *telos*. But the argument, in effect, is that modern man's *telos* is both as a distinct individual personality and as an organic part of a wider society and "city". In starting from principles he so closely associates with Aristotle, Durkheim's concern with the good life for man is with an ethic of human developing, flourishing and self-realization.

Developing and flourishing

If equal opportunity is important, we need to remember what it is about. Durkheim tends to forget, in all Book III's moral mathematics, what it is about – "the free unfolding of the social power each carries within him". He certainly fails to explore other routes to this. There are good reasons for wanting another route. His approach in Book III goes against his whole view of society, the ethical life and developing and flourishing.

A kind of rational madness underlies the liberalism that seeks a sweeping equality of opportunity and a social system in which, whatever our point of entry to it, all positions are completely open and accessible to us. The madness is that we should each sit down and decide on a "life plan", which, thanks to equal life chances, we are free to pursue and can be any we choose. It is not just that it might already be too late if we postpone doing so until the age of, say, five. It is that the very idea reeks of an "abstract society" made up of "abstract individuals", free to draw up life plans but with no life history.

How can we draw up life plans unless we have a life history? Yet how, given a life history, can we be completely free to draw up and choose life plans? Or how, given life histories with an anchorage in particular connexions that are varied and diverse rather than just the same, can there be equal life chances?

Durkheim sees egoism as a disease of the intellect, withdrawing us

132

into a "phantasmagoric" self and away from attachment to others and a milieu. It cannot be a form of developing and flourishing, even though its source lies in an individualism that is. This, with its cult of free thought, involves a whole range of different conceptions of developing and flourishing. In doing so, it looks to a whole range of different milieux, identities and groups. Together, they form a web of different particular connexions that rules out, as a "sociological monstrosity", a city made up of people who are the same, and in which anywhere leads everywhere.

Nor is *anomie* about developing and flourishing, even though its source again lies in an individualism that is. This, with its concern with interests, might include very different conceptions of these and so of developing and flourishing in terms of them. But *anomie* goes beyond any, and again feeds the sociological monstrosity of abstract society in eating away at definite commitments and connexions. It involves an instrumentalist separation from one another in which we go to market, get what we can get, and make off, an estrangement that guarantees systematic, exploitative abuse of unequal power, wealth and conditions. Durkheim's epigram can be revised, yet again: *There must be unjust contracts if there is pervasive anomie.* This is another reason for doubt about the Book III liberalism of equal life chances. Its abstract individuals can look forward not to these but to the conflict of unfettered egoisms and the oppressive, class-divided society of the Schaeffle review.

So let us now try to construct a Durkheimian alternative Book III, around the ideal of a republic in which all of us can develop and flourish.

The starting place must be with occupational groups. A basic point, of course, is that they are interlocking, intermediate groups that, in attaching us to particular connexions, attach us to a wider society. But it is also part of this that they constitute distinct sociocultural and moral milieux. Hence a basic condition of the republic is not that there has to be a sweeping equality of opportunity but that all of these milieux, though different, are ways of developing and flourishing.

One of the ways is that they are self-governing groups, fostering participation in their own affairs and citizenship in the wider society. Durkheim argues as if they can become the sole basis of politics. But they cannot keep out factions, parties and other wider movements of opinion. One of the reasons is that they themselves are concerned, as a basis of citizenship, with the freedom to express and organize around our different opinions.[8]

This has to do with the liberalism of free thought. But it also brings in the liberalism of freedom to pursue, as well as organize around, our interests. So it returns us to questions about inequality, the market, and just versus unjust contracts and relationships. Durkheim does not denounce the market as such, the play of interests in it, or unequal wealth. His target is the separation from one another that generates instrumentalism through the market and takes unjust advantage of unequal wealth. His essential line is that it is the modern humanist ethic that defines man's exploitation of man in the first place, and that is also how to overcome it – through the organic self, the moral milieux of interlocking intermediate groups, and a cult and culture of man.

How is justice tied up with developing and flourishing? The injustice of exploitation is not simply an affair of material interests. It involves an intrinsic moral damage, on both sides. The lack of respect that instrumentalizes others is a lack of self-discipline, an unfettering of desires that enslaves oneself as well as others to them. The fatalism that crushes desires in its acceptance of instrumentalization crushes pride, in a loss of self-respect and the will to defend it. As Parodi complains, Durkheim's emphasis on completely contradictory conceptions of equality is a simplification. The justice of exchange of services of "equivalent social value" has to do with merit, but also with everyone's dignity. Its recognition of what is one another's due is a part – though not the only part – of the esteem and self-esteem involved in everyone's dignity as a person. Material interests matter and demand justice because moral interests matter and demand justice.

This is a constitutive argument about morality's concern with interests and definitions of them. It is different from the regulatory argument, found, for example, in *Suicide*. Durkheim discusses the "almost infinite extension of the market", attacks the reduction of social life to interest, and sees this as the "dogma of economic materialism" (1897a: 283–4; t.255–6). On the other hand, just as he attacks the idea that traditional religion can stem modern demands for free thought, he emphasizes its powerlessness against modern concern with "earthly interests". The regulation and discipline these interests need must come "by giving them an organization in accord with their importance" (441; t.383).

Book I of *The division of labour* mobilizes both the constitutive and

134

regulatory arguments in its general critique of the reduction of social and moral life to interest, and in its particular emphasis on the non-contractual element of contract. But Book III's attack on inherited wealth might involve an assumption that forgets all this. It is that people will necessarily take advantage of greater wealth to pursue their interests in a way that instrumentalizes and oppresses others. There must be unjust contracts if there are rich and poor at birth, since "one class of society is obliged, in order to live, to take any price for its services, while the other need not to do so because of the resources at its disposal" ([1893b] 1902b: 378; t.384). Does it matter that Durkheim adds the qualification that if such resources are unmerited they form an "unjust advantage"? Does he not still assume that unequal wealth, however coming about, will be exploited to the full? Even "just" advantage will be systematically abused.

It is important, in considering this, to go to *The division of labour*'s new preface. Durkheim attacks the freedom of "nominal" rights as a protection against the rich and powerful, and insists on a real freedom for everyone that depends on a complex "regulation" (1902b: iii–iv; t.3). It is not a regulation, through physical force, by a hypertrophied state. It is a regulation, through moral force, by autonomous, interlocking groups. An implication is that appeal to the regulation of interests must combine with a constitutive argument about them. How can a moral force get a grip on and regulate interests without an internal determination of them, and how are they going to be constrained, especially in the case of the rich and powerful, just by an external physical force? But there is another implication, working, in a sense, the other way. If autonomous, interlocking groups are moral forces, it seems part of this that they are also countervailing groups in a system in which, as in the thesis on Montesquieu, there are checks and balances and power is spread around.

A first conclusion of a Durkheimian reconstruction of Book III is that a republic of everyone's developing and flourishing excludes completely equal life chances, with their liberalism of the abstract society. A second conclusion is that it excludes an inequality of conditions that is without limits – and not just because the need for limits is a constant Durkheimian theme, but again because of his critique of abstract society. His insistence on integration through the division of labour, intermediate groups and the organic self is an attack on a world of separation and estrangement, the "sordid" world of economic man – *échangiste*, materialistic and market driven. It might be mistaken to see inherited wealth as a basic source of modern inequality. It may still combine with marketeering liberalism to create the society of "rich and poor" that Durkheim so obviously opposes. An ethical republic is impossible with an inequality of this kind, which, with its gulfs, systematically secretes instrumentalism through the market. A republic can have inequality and can have the market, yet without such instrumentalism. It can do so through moral force, but necessarily conjoined with the physical force of a spread of power, and groups that are at the same time intermediate, interlocking *and* countervailing groups.

A third conclusion is that a republic of everyone's developing and flourishing as a person must have a human culture and an education that lets in, amongst other things, some sort of freedom of opportunity and movement. The republic's distinct sociocultural and moral milieux entail different conceptions of developing and flourishing. So, on the one hand, it can be a kind of imperialism to use the conception of a particular group (or class) to criticize the lack of developing and flourishing in another. On the other hand, without a general, collective ideal of this, indifference and apologetics could recruit relativism to count anything as "flourishing".

A human culture is in any case necessary, both to entrench the human ideal as a real social ideal and for the education needed by the citizen and "the whole man". Durkheim is certainly concerned with education for this, even if, as Cuin suggests, he is not especially concerned with it as a vehicle of social mobility and opportunity. A human culture's education for citizenship and "the whole man", even if for flourishing in the particular milieux to which we are attached and "destined", must nonetheless enable some sort of mobility, whether between milieux or between roles within them. This is just as well, given the whole Durkheimian approach to the modern world and emphasis on individual differences around collective conceptions (in a group, as in the wider society). A republic must recognize and accommodate aspirations of some individuals in a particular situation to move out of it, just because such aspirations, far from being abstract life-plan choices, are rooted in a milieu and in the diversity that is part of it.

Therefore an ideal of equal opportunity remains essential. But the opportunity that counts most is that every milieu, whether we stay in it or move to another, offers a way of developing and flourishing. A condition of this is that, "whatever our representation of the moral ideal", it excludes degraded labour.

Durkheim, like Kant, is wary of a morality that "paralyses" economic progress ([1893b] 1902b: 218; t.239), but also shares Kant's sense of the "glistering misery" of our society and of the problem it poses. It is that the conflict is at last overcome between man's development as a species and everyone's developing and flourishing as a person. This is above all in the ethical life, but must include self-realization in the *techne* of industry and the arts. It is significant that at the crucial point in Book II of *The division of labour*, when Durkheim turns from mechanical world evolution to begin to bring in ideals, his talk is of how "civilization" can become an ideal (*ibid.*: 330; t.339). It is significant because "civilization" is precisely a term that emphasizes *techne* and requires its inclusion in a vision of the ethical life. It is in an uncramped, neo-Aristotelian vision of this that the spontaneous division of labour's "free unfolding" of everyone's social powers is an ideal of an ethical republic that at last overcomes the conflict between man's development as a species and everyone's developing and flourishing as a person.

Part II

The kingdom and the republic

Chapter Six

Virtue ethics: duty and the good

A problem that underlies Durkheimian ethics is getting from a kingdom to a republic. The "kingdom" has two senses. In one, it is morality in its essentials, as it has always been, and the problem is how it can survive the spirit of modern rationalism. In the other, it is the Kantian ideal of a kingdom of ends, a society of free, autonomous persons, but one that also postulates God and an immortal soul and that realizes man's *telos* in a universal philosophical history. So the problem in republicanizing this kingdom is not just to rework Kantian autonomy. It is to dispense with God and the immortal soul, as well as with man as a universal moral subject.

Might ethics destroy morals?

Durkheim develops his ethical theory in various places. The most important is the first part of his course on moral education. Let us concentrate on this, and draw on other sources as and when appropriate.

The lectures begin, in effect, with the need to republicanize the kingdom. It is increasingly impossible to rely on traditional, religious morality. The modern world demands rational ethics. Yet there must remain a sense of morality's "majesty". This sets up the worry that Durkheim wants to tackle and resolve. It is a worry that ethics might destroy morals.

Enlightenment is often seen as "a purely negative operation", stripping morality of "all the adventitious, parasitical elements which have overlain it" (1925a: 9; t.8). The trouble arises if this also eliminates elements that are essential: "In the name of rational ethics there would only be impoverished morals" (*ibid.*: 10; t.9). Yet Durkheim himself goes in for stripping, laying bare and transparence. We must "seek, at the heart of religious conceptions, the moral realities that are as if lost and hidden in them" (*ibid.*). We must understand moral forces "in their rational nakedness" (*ibid.*: 13; t.11) – that is, "in their true nature, stripped of all symbols" (*ibid.*: 23; t.20).

In going into this, let us ask about God and His correct replacement. Is it society or man?

Durkheim looks to a "purely empirical reality", of which "the idea of God is perhaps only the symbolic expression" (*ibid.*: 12; t.11). He says more famously, in the paper on moral facts, that God is "society transfigured and thought of symbolically" ([1906b] 1924a: 74; t.52). This is nonsense if taken to mean that God is not integrally part of traditional life, but just a symbolic varnish that could be stripped away to reveal the same society.

God, as the centre of a system in which religious and moral ideas fuse, must be a constitutive idea of a way of life, entering into its very description. Traditional religion cannot decline without far-reaching changes in society itself, in the nature of core beliefs, and in our very ways of thinking. This is emphasized in *The division of labour*, and again in the moral education lectures. Rationalism, with its demand for free thought, "is only one of the aspects of individualism"; in turn, "rationalist faith reacts on and stimulates individualist sentiment"; and both concern the developing sense of "the dignity of man" (*ibid.*: 13–14; t.11–12).

Man's dignity suggests man as God's replacement. It is the same with *Suicide*, which is where man first becomes "a god for men" (1897a: 379; t.334). It is not much different in the paper on moral facts. Society displaces God – but it is to "consecrate" man ([1906b] 1924a: 77; t.54). God's Durkheimian successor must in some way be both society and man, but in what way?

God, in traditional worlds, is both the sacred source of things and the sacred centre of them. He is replaced in the modern world by society as the sacred source, man as the sacred centre. Just as God is a central, constitutive idea of traditional societies, man is a central, constitutive idea of modern society, the "god" and "sacred thing *par excellence*" that it consecrates.

We can now go to two basic ways in which ethics might destroy morals. One occurs if there is a failure, in demystifying the old world, to resacralize the new. The other arises if there is a failure, as part of this, to understand the essential nature and character of morality itself. The domain of morality is like that of religion:

> It is a sacred domain. All the things comprising it are invested with a particular dignity, that raises them above our empirical individuality and confers on them a sort of transcendent reality. Do we not readily say that the human person is sacred, and should be made into a cult? As long as religion and morality are closely bound up, this sacred character is not difficult to explain, since morality, as much as religion, is thought to depend on and emanate from the divinity, the source of all that is sacred. Everything coming from it participates in its transcendence and becomes by this very fact beyond comparison with everything else. But if appeal to the notion is systematically ruled out, with no replacement by another, the danger is that the quasi-religious character of morality may not appear to have any basis, since the idea that was its traditional foundation has been given up without its expression in another. The inclination to deny it is then almost inevitable; even feeling its reality is impossible. (1925a: 11; t.10)

This important passage brings out how the concern with sacredness, though more explicit in the paper on moral facts, already underlies the moral education lectures. It also brings out Durkheim's insistence that morality must involve a "transcendence", a power over and beyond us as empirical individuals, even though, with secular enlightenment, it itself must be an "empirical reality". Ethics might destroy morals from blindness to the need for something sacred and for something transcendent.

The topic, that ethics might destroy morals, was common in Durkheim's time. It is also discussed by Lévy-Bruhl, in a similar concern with morality as a human social institution and as an "objective reality" (Lévy-Bruhl [1903] 1910: 135–45; t.108–16). But it is just because Lévy-Bruhl so much emphasizes this reality as relative to changing social circumstances that there is an interesting, indeed fundamental, difference with Durkheim. Durkheim's republican hope is that we can understand morality's "majesty", "without destroying or even diminishing it" (1925a: 139; t.122). His route to this, far from just going on about the relativity of the moral, tries to get at its universal elements.

Enlightenment demands understanding both of the moral reality and rationale of our time and of morality's essential, universal nature. This leads Durkheim to a concern with sacredness, but also to other things – indeed, to an ethical theory tackling a whole range of questions. What is a moral character? What are the moral motivations? What is the nature of the right and the good? What is the relationship between reason, sentiment and belief? Who is the moral judge? This is the range of questions tackled by virtue ethics. Although Durkheim discusses them in terms of a dualism of "duty" and "the good", it is precisely not – as so often in contemporary ethics – to try to reduce everything to the single issue of the nature of the right and the good.

Duty and the "spirit of discipline"

Durkheim is explicit that his search for morality's essential elements is an enquiry into virtue and moral character. He says this does not mean trying "to draw up an exhaustive list of all the virtues, or even of the most important". It does mean looking for "the fundamental dispositions, the mental states, at the root of moral life" (1925a: 23; t.20–21).

He starts with a set of three, closely interconnected virtues. He does not himself name the first two. But we can discuss them as the virtues of dutifulness, justice and self-discipline. Dutifulness prepares the way for justice and self-discipline, which are the greater virtues.

Dutifulness concerns morality as a system of established rules. Durkheim is clear that they cannot do away with a need for judgement, to decide which rule applies in a particular case or how, exactly, to interpret it. This does not have to let in appeal to an abstract principle, from which to deduce everything every time we act. The need for judgement can still arise in the context of definite, pre-established rules, governing action in its essentials. As a system of such rules, morality's role "is, in the first place, to determine conduct, to fix it, to remove it from individual discretion" (*ibid.*: 26–30; t.23–7).

Durkheim's next point is that it is not simply the content of this or that particular rule that is of moral value. He emphasizes the importance of "regularity", of the development of engrained, "powerfully formed habits". They are "internal forces within the individual", and in this sense a "spontaneous" basis of action (*ibid.*: 30–32; t.27–8).

But he also emphasizes that a rule cannot be all spontaneity. It must involve something that is independent of personal wishes and can resist them. A line of action that, even as a habit, we ourselves construct and can change "is a project, not a rule" (*ibid.*: 33: t.29). So a next question is: what is this "something"?

Durkheim sees it as the impersonal, imperative power of the rule, and identifies it with the idea of authority. He sees it as involved to some extent in all rules. But he sees it, in the case of moral rules, as "absolutely preponderant". Other rules let in considerations of their usefulness to us in following our particular personal projects, interests and concerns. The moral rule does not. It claims obedience "out of respect for it and for this reason alone". It owes all its hold over our wills "to the authority with which it is invested". It consists "entirely in a command and in nothing else" (*ibid.*: 34–5; t.29–31).

Durkheim's concern, at this point, is just to drive home the moral rule's authority. It is through respect – even reverence – for the rule that it is felt as necessitating, forcible, obligatory. Later on in the lectures, and again in the paper on moral facts, he associates emphasis on this authority with Kant. Later on, too, he traces the source of the moral law's authority to society. It also becomes clear that his main worry about modern demands for rational ethics and autonomy is a loss of the sense of authority. But let us worry, for the moment, about virtue ethics.

Does Durkheim really work with virtue ethics? Dutifulness is certainly about moral motivation and character. But its virtue might seem completely derivative, since it is so tied up with respect for pre-established rules. Value attaches to these first. Virtue is then just read off as the dispositions and qualities needed to do what has already been identified, in its essentials, as the right.

In fact, Durkheim himself goes to the heart of the issue:

> Ordinarily, discipline appears useful only because it compels certain actions considered useful. It is only a means, in prescribing these, of bringing them about. It draws its *raison d'être* from them. But if the analysis just given is correct, it follows that discipline has its own *raison d'être*, that it is good that man is disciplined, independently of the actions to which he thereby feels bound. (*ibid.*: 36; t.32)

How can this be? He states, briefly, an argument that might be expected from him. It concerns the needs of society. He then concentrates on an argument that might come as a surprise. It concerns the needs, welfare and flourishing of the individual.

The argument about society is still of interest. It disconnects discipline from conformity to the particular norms of a particular society to insist on its indispensability in any society – including an ideal of the good society – as a basis of a shared moral code and organization of relationships. This is to disconnect discipline from dutifulness and to insist on its place in a virtue of justice, concerned with moral rules as they ought to be, and as the moral law. It might still seem that virtue is derivative. Value attaches to the moral law first, and justice is read off as the set of dispositions needed to do something a set of principles has already established as the right. Let us return to the point, after going into the argument about the virtue, for the individual, of self-discipline.

Durkheim emphasizes that an account of discipline in terms only of social needs is "insufficient". It must be anchored in individual needs. Social institutions cannot survive if they undermine "individual life at its source", and hence "the source from which they draw their own life" (*ibid.*: 42; t.38). There is then a long discussion about "balance", "limits" and "definite goals", the "disease of the infinite", and discipline as an essential basis of character. We "confront the multiple requirements of life with a limited amount of vital energies", and must control our activities according to "the strength at our disposal" and the "relative importance" of all the different things of concern to us (*ibid.*: 44; t.39). It is "the power to master oneself, the capacity for restraint or, as it is said, inhibition, that allows us to contain our passions, our desires, our habits, and subject them to law" (*ibid.*: 52; t.46).

Self-discipline is a fundamental virtue, as a fundamental part of individual flourishing. Durkheim does not talk of an Aristotelian *eudaimonia*. But his overwhelming emphasis is on a life of happiness. It is not, of course, a happiness just of satisfaction of desires. It depends on learning "the control of desire", and on a capacity "to resist ourselves" (*ibid.*: 55; t.48). Negatively, it is a middle way between two self-destructive extremes – an asceticism that crushes desire in a loathing of our embodiedness and sensibility, versus a hedonism that unfetters desire and sees any restraint as a violation of our nature (*ibid.*: 57–8; t.50). Positively, it is about self-development and realiza-tion (*ibid.*: 58; t.50–51). It involves the integrity of "the whole man", of working for some sort of balance and coherence in our lives.

It also involves integrity in the moral sense of standing by values that are rooted in the conscience and that, if we betray them, can en-gulf us in the unhappiness of guilt, shame and loss of self-respect. Lives of virtue and happiness are linked in this intrinsic way, whatever other ways.

Thus it is not Durkheim's argument to see self-discipline as just a socially "useful" virtue. But it is not his argument, either, to see self-discipline as just personally useful, for carrying out projects we choose and controlling desires in conflict with them. It is not the mere strength of will to do as we would wish – as in a lightweight liberal-ism's "second order preference" and desire to have this or that desire. The virtue of self-discipline is involved in the choice of projects itself, not just to constrain but to assess and direct desires, to fix on limited goals, to balance them and to achieve coherence. It is active, critical, emancipatory. "Self-mastery is the first condition of all true power, of all freedom worthy of the name" (*ibid.*: 50–51; t.45).

So self-discipline is fundamental to individual flourishing, because fundamental to lives of happiness, virtue *and* freedom. How, we might now be anxious to ask, does it come about? "Because of their authority, moral rules are real forces which our desires, wants and appetites of all kinds run up against when they tend to become immoderate" (*ibid.*: 46; t.41). "Together, moral rules really form around each person a sort of ideal barrier, at the foot of which the wave of human passions dies away, unable to go further" (*ibid.*: 47; t.42). In sum, and in another epigram: "will is formed in the school of duty" (*ibid.*: 53; t.46).

This is to say, in effect, that it is dutifulness – the internalization of existing norms – that prepares the way for self-discipline, freedom and all, and that is "the indispensable condition of the emergence of the personal, reflective will" (*ibid.*: 56; t.49). Similarly, it prepares the way for justice, as a reflection on existing norms themselves that rejects their "blind and slavish" acceptance (*ibid.*: 60; t.52), and shakes off "the yoke of traditional discipline" (*ibid.*: 61; t.53). How is dutifulness the school of the will in the all-important sense of the reflective will – the route to the spirit of discipline's other, greater virtues?

It has to involve judgement, and Durkheim repeats the point that, since circumstances are never the same, there is always a need to interpret and apply moral rules "with intelligence". But it is not, as earlier on in the argument, to emphasize how a moral code governs conduct in its essentials. It is to emphasize a different, if also favourite, theme – that social life always evolves, and moral rules and codes must evolve with it. Just as he argues in *The rules* that it is pathological if the *conscience collective* is too strong, he again insists that a morality must not be so internalized that it "is above criticism and reflection, the agents *par excellence* of all change" (*ibid.*: 60; t.52).

Thus Socrates stars in *The rules* as a man of justice and as a "criminal", championing a new ethic to replace the traditional one, at odds with the "conditions of existence" ([1895a] 1901c: 71; t.102). He reappears in the lectures as an exemplar of those who, considered "deviant" in their time, are at the forefront of the "moral revolutions through which humanity has passed" (1925a: 60–61; t.53). He again features in the paper on moral facts, as someone who "expressed more clearly than his judges the morality suited to the society of his time" ([1906b] 1924a; 93; t.64–5). But the lectures focus on a particular problem in all this. It is the risk of confusing "two very different feelings: the need to replace an old with a new order, and impatience with all rules, abhorrence of all discipline" (1925a: 61; t.53). The moment of challenge to traditional authority is a time when we most need to keep in mind the indispensability of discipline and rules. Yet it is precisely the time when we are most likely to reject this, as in the contemporary world's "anarchic aspirations" (*ibid.*: 61–2; t.54).

Let us pause here, to sum up the situation. Durkheim obviously works with virtue ethics in his account of self-discipline, does so again in his account of justice, and also, it turns out, in his account of dutifulness itself. Dutifulness is not just a dull old disposition needed to act in terms of ideas that already define the right. Audaciously, it is seen as the route to other, greater virtues. It becomes this partly through a respect that, instead of being chained to particular, preestablished conceptions of the right, is for the idea of the rule itself and so is generalizable via the virtue of justice to other, different beliefs about the right. But the main route is via the reflective will. Far from reducing, in the case of the virtue of justice, to a disposition needed to act in terms of some abstract principle that already defines the right, it is the complex of qualities needed to seek out, and to persevere in seeking out, what, as an ideal of the right, justice is.

A virtue ethics issue tied up with this is the identity of the ethical judge. Clearly, as far as Durkheim is concerned, it cannot simply be the individual: Socrates, otherwise, could in no way be a "criminal". Nor, however, can it simply be the the collectivity: Socrates knew better "than his judges the morality suited to the society of his time".

With his commitment to justice, Socrates is also taken as a paradigmatic case of respect for the moral rule, even in challenging the moral norm in the name of the moral law, of not confusing "two very different feelings" – opposition to particular rules and opposition to all rules. Are there difficulties, however, special to our own society? Durkheim talks of two "apparently contradictory" movements: the need for authority and insistence on scrutinizing it (*ibid.*: 60; t.52–3). This is an expression not just of "anarchic aspirations" but of the ideal of autonomy, so that a problem built into the modern world is how authority and autonomy might combine.

But it is necessary, before going into the problem, to continue with the account of morality's universal elements.

The good and "attachment to social groups"

Durkheim sees an irreducible dualism between duty and the good, though these two aspects of moral experience have the same underlying source in society (1925a 111–14; t.97–9).

It is partly a distinction between moral rules and moral ends and ideals. It is also very much about moral motivation. In essence, with the rule, there is a negative constraint of desires through respect for an imperative authority and exercise of the reflective will. In essence, with the ideal, there is a positive attraction, enthusiasm, spontaneity.

It is obviously a complex dualism, rolling all kinds of things together. Let us concentrate on three issues. They concern motivation, identity and the interrelationship of ends. And let us start with motivation.

The dualism between negative constraint and positive attraction comes down to some sort of dualism between reason and sentiment. Despite Durkheim's talk of a "feeling" of respect, even reverence, for the moral law, this is inseparable from reason in the form of the reflective will that orders and controls the crowd of desires. It is in effect a Kantian constraint of reason on the desires. The force of Durkheim's Humean appeal to sentiment lies elsewhere, in his insistence on positive social sentiments that attach us to one another and to a group as ends. But the motivational dualism of reason and sentiment is threatened in two very different ways.

Durkheim remarks, in his discussion of autonomy, that "thought is the liberator of the will" (*ibid*.: 136; t.119). He emphasizes, in preparing the ground for his discussion, the importance of the emotions, "since they are the moving forces of conduct". But he at once adds that they need to be aroused and guided by "the justiciable procedures of reason" (*ibid*.: 107; t.94). The coming of autonomy might therefore dissolve his dualism, in favour of reason. An escape clause is that autonomy, though something to work towards, is never fully realizable. There is always a need for belief, faith and intensely felt convictions – although convictions remain justiciable by reason, in that we still have to argue as powerfully as possible for them. This must also be the basic response to the other threat, which would dissolve the dualism in favour of sentiment, in seeing "the good", with its feelings of attachment, as fundamental to morality.

Durkheim looks for something that transcends the individual in the authority of the moral law, and again in seeing the good in terms of "impersonal ends". Moral ends are "those which have as their object *a society*" (*ibid*.: 68; t.59). A fundamental axiom of general opinion is "that man acts morally only when pursuing ends superior to individual ends" (*ibid*.: 69; t.60). The good lies in "attachment to a group of which the individual is part" (*ibid*.: 73; t.64). So, with its positive, solidary social sentiments, is not the good fundamental and prior to duty?

Durkheim himself remarks, in *The division of labour*'s original introduction, that solidarity is not only an obligation like others but the very source of morality. One of the book's central arguments, that justice is full of charity, is that a duty to respect negative rights depends on a positive fellow-feeling and attachment to one another and to the society of which we are part. One of its central themes, running through arguments about exchange, the contract, the market and the division of labour itself, is that the play of interest must take place within a pre-existing social and moral relationship. The good is the source of morality in that attachment to one another and a society as ends rooted as such in our character is the core constitutive element of morality itself. It is prior to duty in the same way that it is prior to interest. It is the basis of acknowledgement of one another's moral status, coming under the moral law and with claims to respect and regard as members of the moral community of persons.

It is thus about identity, and Durkheim again works with virtue ethics in that his account of the good, along with his whole approach, is so much concerned with issues of social and moral identity. A central theme running through all his work is how our basic identities in the modern world become "the individual" and "man", but also how they require anchorage in intermediate identities of particular, definite connexions.

The good is thus prior to duty, in that its feelings of attachment and identity are constitutive of a moral community and the basis of duty's respect for one another as bearers of a moral status. Yet the dualism survives, in that it is because sentiments of identity are so important that they ought to come within the influence and justiciability of reason.

Durkheim's account of the good very much implies this. It involves a distinction paralleling the one between dutifulness and justice. It is a distinction between virtues we might discuss as loyalty and humanity. Thus he emphasizes that, in getting his account going, he has "so far talked of society only in a general way, as if it were only one", when, "in fact, man nowadays lives in the midst of many groups" (*ibid.*: 83; t.73). What, "nowadays", are these groups?

He concentrates, in the lectures, on three kinds – the family, the political group or nation (*patrie*), and humanity – and says that they can coexist together as a "hierarchy" (*ibid.*: 83–4; t.73–4). This is to see how there can be an interdependence, through hierarchy, of essentially segmentary groups. It contrasts with the interdependence, through a network, of essentially interlocking groups – the pattern emphasized in *The division of labour*. But both patterns of interdependence feature in the lectures on occupational and civic ethics, which are more or less of the same period as the lectures on moral education. And the search, throughout, is for a combination of attachment to particular identities with the extensive sympathy, demanded in the modern, enlarged world, of attachment to "man".

The virtue of loyalty is tribal, the narrow, confined generosity of the Humean *homme de clan*, and an obstacle to an extensive humanitarian sympathy. But it is also a necessary path to this greater virtue, in the way that dutifulness is both an obstacle and a necessary path to justice. It is only through particular connexions that we become moral and acquire and develop attachments to one another and a community as ends. Far from being an ideal of the good, the notion of a society without particular connexions is an abstract, anti-moral "monstrosity". Just as justice has to develop out of dutifulness, and the growth within it of the free kernel of reason and the reflective will, humanity has to develop out of definite loyalties and attachments, and the growth within them of the ethical kernel of the good will. It is because there is this kernel that reason can come in, to reflect on, guide and extend sentiments of identity themselves.

This must be so, given Durkheim's account of the good as attachment to social groups, his general evolutionary approach to ethics, and his vision of the city of modern citizenship as a republic and human *patrie*. There can be no doubt about his commitment, as a man of his place and time, to France. But there can also be no doubt that, as we have seen, he looks beyond the existing nation-state to the emergence of new groupings and identities. Loyalty is attachment to an actual, existing social group. France, despite far-reaching conflict and change, goes on being France, and he insists in the lectures, as elsewhere, that "a society remains, in some measure, the same throughout all the course of its existence" (*ibid.*: 121; t.106).[1] Yet France is not just France, but part of the modern social world and its dynamic, so that, just as he envisages, in *The division of labour*, the emergence of Europe, and sees, in *Suicide*, even more extensive societies than at present, so, in the lectures, he talks of a future in which existing national characteristics will "die away" (*ibid.*: 86, 89; t.76, 78). In any case, and in the here and now, it is out of attachment to France that he looks to it as a human *patrie*. There is no place in the modern world for the blind, uncritical nationalism that, as in the Dreyfus Affair, he always opposed, or for the unquestioning loyalties of the *homme de clan* and "the hatreds, so frequent wherever the family vendetta still prevails" (*ibid.*: 240; t.210).

Thus Durkheim continues to urge the development of intermediate groups, linking us with one another, within the republic itself. For once, it is not to go on about the need for them as occupational groups. It is a general argument about the "spirit of association" (*ibid.*: 266–73; t.232–9).

This corresponds with the more famous "spirit of discipline". It is perhaps overlooked because it is discussed not in the account of the good that follows the account of duty but much later on in the lectures. It also returns to a concern with a network rather than a hierarchy of groups, involving us, outside of the family, in general social life. Durkheim worries about the relative lack of such a network in France compared with other modern societies.

The Revolution, in its drive for unity and animus against particular groups, encouraged a cult of the state but also a "ferocious individualism". This combination, with its exclusion of intermediate groups, is attacked in the lectures on Rousseau. It is based on "a contradiction" ([1918b] 1953a: 187; t.128). It attempts a cohesion that "attaches individuals to the society but not individuals to one another; their only linkage with each other is that they are all linked to the community, that is, alienated within it" (*ibid.*: 170; t.112). The lectures on moral education thus see French society and culture as caught in "a vicious circle" (1925a: 273; t.238–9). There is a need for cohesion through a whole network of intermediate groups. But they have to develop spontaneously and through the very thing that is lacking, a "spirit of association".

It is the same vicious circle that dogs Durkheim's general proposals, as in *The division of labour*'s new preface, for social and moral reform, and his search for a route into a virtuous circle. His solution, both in the new preface and in the moral education lectures, in effect lies in a deliberate effort, through a reasoned understanding of our situation, to find ways existing in it to develop and renew the "spirit of association" itself.

Reason comes into the good in other ways, if only because the human ideal is itself an ideal of reason, autonomy, enlightenment. To look to a human *patrie* is to look to a society committed to such things. But this also takes us to other problems, involving both identity and the nature and interrelationship of moral ends.

Durkheim insists that the good must concern impersonal ends. He then argues as if these must directly refer to social groups such as France. Yet are there not many ideals – such as freedom – that are impersonal but do not refer to a social group in this way? Indeed, his own standard view in the case of the ideal of humanity is that it can never refer to a social group in the form of a worldwide human *patrie*.

This ideal can of course enter into a description of a particular society as humane. Then in the same way other ideals can enter into a description of it as a society of freedom, equality, justice, developing and flourishing, enlightenment. In fact, however, this is a list of the constitutive ideals of the republic itself. They do not just come into its description. They are at the core of its description, forming its very identity as a society.

They thus raise a problem, of a society's identity as a society, that Durkheim's discussion glosses over. What, after all, is "France"? Does it have a meaningful social and moral identity separate from ideals that do not refer only to it? The Revolution got rid of Louis XVI, the three-in-one symbol of monarchy, the true faith and France, and brought in Marianne, the three-in-one symbol of liberty, the republic and France. Are Louis XVI and Marianne, as representations of France, representations of the same thing or of different things?

It is only if Durkheim sees them as completely different things that he can keep to his apparent equation of impersonal ideals with the group. Ideals of monarchy and the faith and of liberty and the republic are constitutive of France, so that its identity is transformed by them. If, without going so far as to see its identity as the same unchanging thing, he sees continuities, he must give up equation of impersonal ideals with the group. Particular impersonal ideals are to an extent separable from France, so that its identity survives changes in them. Since he sees such continuities, he must give up the equation.

What, at bottom, is at stake? In the article on the Dreyfus Affair, he insists that the ethic-cum-cult of the human ideal is "the only system of beliefs which can ensure the country's moral unity" ([1898c] 1970a: 270; t.66). In the article on the definition of religious phenomena, he observes that "our country, the French Revolution, Joan of Arc, etc. are sacred things for us" ([1899a(ii)] 1969c: 157; t.91). Perhaps it is because Joan of Arc is more like Marianne than Louis XVI that she can be run together with the Revolution. It is still to run together symbols of conflict, yet also of a common identity, needed to attach us to one another and take the strain of our disputes. Yes, society needs some sort of cohesion around beliefs, and in modern society it has to be around the human ideal. But this is precisely why there must also be a solidarity with one another, as citizens of the same city, that transcends and copes with the multitude of disagreements around the human ideal itself. It is vital that, instead of any close equation between impersonal ideals and the group, there is a looser inter-relationship between them. "A city is not made up of people who are the same: it is different from an alliance."

Integrity and duties to oneself

This leaves in place Durkheim's insistence on impersonal ends, transcending the individual, but complicates his insistence on them as social ends, attaching us to a group.

Let us just assume, from now on, a complex mix of supra-individual concerns in concerns for "society". Let us next tackle the interrelationship of ends, conceived very generally as concerns for oneself, for others and for society.

This means tackling their interrelationship in a hierarchy versus a network of ends. Another problem is their interrelationship in a fusion versus a balance of ends, and again brings in the links between virtue and happiness. Another involves "individual morality", in the Durkheimian sense of the branch of morality concerned with one's own good and such things as duties to oneself, ideals of personal flourishing, and pride and self-respect.

Durkheim's search for moral transcendence leads him into an argument that interrelates moral ends in a hierarchy. Concerns for society are primary, and concerns for one another are secondary and subordinate (1925a: 64–8; t.56–60). The argument is repeated in the paper on moral facts ([1906b] 1924a: 71–7; t.49–53). It has three steps. The first denies moral value to concerns wholly for oneself. The second questions the moral value of concerns for other individuals. The third eliminates anything that, though supra-individual, is supra-empirical, and so finds only society.

Action in one's own interest can be moral, if it is motivated by a collective good such as of one's family (1925a: 64–5; t.56–7). The same applies to action of benefit to others. In that they are moral, concerns for one another as individuals derive from attachment to a group. They are "secondary and subordinate" (*ibid.*: 94–5; t.83) and serve "a higher end" ([1906b] 1924a: 73; t.51).

The argument, from the point of view of secular ethics, is open to two possible criticisms. Let us shelve the first, which is that concerns for oneself or others can be moral but have nothing to do with an impersonal, collective good. Let us concentrate on the second, which is that concerns for one another and for society can be just as important, interrelated in a network rather than a hierarchy of ends.

Let us start with the case of friendship. It plays a crucial role, both in Durkheim's account of the organic self and in his whole theory of the organic society of a division of labour. It no doubt involves an impersonal ideal of friendship, which obviously varies from culture to culture. But there are clearly ideals of friendship that involve, at their heart, attachment to one another as flesh and blood individuals. That is, it is the content of the impersonal ideal itself that centres friendship around friends. It is not just focused on the group they might constitute. There are also ideals of the family that, instead of just placing it above individual members, centre it around them too.

Perhaps these are modern rather than traditional views of the family. But this takes us to modern society itself, and Durkheim's own view of its central, constitutive belief as belief in the individual as man. So, as with friendship, it is the content of the impersonal ideal that centres society around persons.

Indeed, it is just after concluding the case for the primacy of the group as an end that Durkheim argues that the social ideal becomes "only a particular form of the human ideal". It attaches us "to man as man", a process that "explains the moral character attributed to sentiments of inter-individual sympathy and to the actions they inspire" (1925a: 94; t.82–3).

We have been here, of course, before. The lectures on Rousseau insist on the attachment of individuals to one another, since if there is attachment only to the community they are "alienated within it". The article on the Dreyfus Affair emphasizes how it is the cult of the person that protects us as individuals. The paper on moral facts replaces God with society but also with man, whom it "consecrates". So society is primary and fundamental as the source of ideals – as the source of the sacred. But is it the centre of the sacred? It is hard to see how, given the human ideal it itself generates, persons can be secondary and subordinate as ends. They must be just as central as the society of persons that sacralizes, via the idea of the person, persons themselves.

This is a network, not a hierarchy, of ends. As such it still leaves society as an end, and not simply as a means to the other interrelated, personal ends – just as it still leaves these as ends, and not simply as a means to society as an end. Hence it meets Durkheim's anxiety on two very important points.

One is that a society forms a reality of its own and is not just an association of individuals, so that it must be an end "in and for itself, and not just to the extent that it serves the individual" (*ibid.*: 76; t.67). The other is that it cannot be an end of our conduct if it "soars above us with no flesh-and-blood bond uniting it with us" (*ibid.*: 75–6; t.66). In effect, it is the same argument as in the account of discipline, something Durkheim himself draws to our attention (*ibid.*: 82–3; t.73). The spirit of discipline is fundamental to personal development and flourishing, and so is society, including, he could have added, the spirit of association. He again attacks "egoism", to emphasize our incompleteness as individuals. Egoism is an impossible attempt to live as if an independent whole, a "cult of the self" based on misunderstanding of the self, an ignorance of the "art of happiness" (*ibid.*: 78, 81–2; t.69, 71–2). But the art of happiness does not lie, either, in a cult of society soaring above us, in a mysticism, as he says elsewhere, seeing in it "an end superior to individual ends and unrelated to them" ([1950a] 1969g: 90; t.54).

Does he nonetheless proceed to dissolve a distinctness of interrelated ends, in a familiar emphasis, going back to his earliest writings, on how we are "the product of society" (1925a: 78; t.69)? As in the situatedness argument, society is at the core of our being and forms "the most important part of ourselves". As in the identity argument, we therefore "cannot alienate ourselves from it without alienating ourselves from ourselves" (*ibid.*: 80–81; t.71). As in a characteristic metaphor, it "puts down deep strong roots within us – it is not enough to say that the best part of ourselves just comes from the collectivity" (*ibid.*: 83; t.73).[2]

But this does not commit him to a fusion of moral ends, in which concerns for oneself, others and society are always and in principle the same. It can still leave us with different concerns, even if the claim is that they all come from society, even our ideas of self-interest itself. The same is true, even though it is an account of how social concerns become our own concerns, in the sense that they become part of our own motivational structure. Concerns that are our own in this sense can still be distinct if interrelated concerns for oneself, others and society. Nor does it follow that they are always the same, even though, as in Durkheim's example of a concern for oneself and for one's family, they are sometimes the same. In sum, it is completely consistent with his emphasis on our sociality that we have different ends that we need to relate, organize and balance, in order to deal with conflicts between them and find the integrity of some sort of overall coherence in our lives.

Indeed, he seems committed to a balance rather than a fusion of moral ends in his whole emphasis on the reflective will and the virtue of self-discipline, which is all about the need to deal with different, potentially conflicting kinds of concerns. The only hint that he is after fusion, even so, is in an argument in which he sums up his overall account, and which involves the intrinsic links between virtue and happiness.

The individual gets something out of the sacrifice and idealism that morality demands, since it is through duty that we learn self-discipline, "the necessary condition of happiness", and since we cannot flourish without social and moral attachments, but "can have only a precarious existence" (*ibid.*: 141; t.124). This can seem like fusion because it is to question if, without virtue, there can be anything that really counts as wellbeing. But it is not to claim that virtue ensures happiness, and it rules out fusion in that it still sees something that really counts as sacrifice of wellbeing.

The article on the Dreyfus Affair quotes the line, "and, for the sake of life, to lose the point of living".[3] It is particularly appropriate, since the article is about the demands of justice and the line is from the passage:

> Or if, in a case where justice hangs in the balance,
> you appear as witness, then, though Phalaris bids you deny
> the truth, brings in his bull, and dictates the lies to be told
> count it the worst disgrace to prefer survival to honour,
> and, for the sake of life, to lose the point of living.[4]

Such situations force a choice, between life and virtue. But if virtue is a necessary condition of happiness, so is one's life. Giving it up is still a sacrifice in the sense Durkheim must have in mind in talking of the "demands" of morality and in his opposition to ascetic contempt for our embodied existence. This is so, even though to give up integrity is also a sacrifice, indeed both an easier and a greater sacrifice. Durkheim says, elsewhere, that we sometimes "excuse the man who sacrifices duty to save his life" ([1906b] 1924a: 83; t.58). This cannot be because of a fusion of things of value. It has to be because of a conflict between them, but in which one ought to override the other and it is sometimes excusable that it does not.

It is not just a conflict between concerns for oneself and concerns for others and society. It is partly a conflict between different kinds of concerns for oneself: a duty to oneself, of integrity, versus attachment to embodied existence and life. It is further complicated by Durkheim's views on suicide. He seems to condemn suicide without exception, even in cases motivated by honour and integrity. This is not because he rules out duties to oneself. On the contrary, it is because he insists on them.

Duties to oneself make a brief appearance in the moral education lectures: "It is society that prescribes even our duties to ourselves" and "requires that we realize in ourselves an ideal type" (1925a: 99; t.87). They also make a brief appearance in the lectures on professional and civic ethics. But it is brief because it is where Durkheim explains how he had discussed duties to oneself in the first part of the course – which is unpublished and seems to have been lost. He distinguishes a universal morality concerned with everyone "as man", rather than as members of a particular social group, and the plan of the course as a whole involved starting with duties to oneself as man, then going on to the morality of particular social milieux, and then finishing with duties to one another as man ([1950a] 1969g: 43; t.3).

A similar division is reported in notes on a course of 1909, and in which the general moral rules governing oneself, rather than relations with others, make up "individual morality" (1975b, vol. 2: 310).[5] There is also an outline, in notes on another course, of a lecture on "Duties of man towards himself" (Lukes 1968, vol. 2: 237–41).[6] It includes the case of suicide, where the argument is essentially the same as in *Suicide* (1897a: 378–84; t.333–8). It is thus possible to reconstruct a Durkheimian account of duties to oneself, and it is important to do so.

He approaches them from two directions. One is to argue that there cannot be duties to oneself unless something superior to the individual is involved, and there is, in individual morality's impersonal ideals and in society as their source. The other is to argue that the ethic-cum-cult of the person sacralizes the humanity in everyone, oneself as well as others. So, along with duties to respect others there must be duties of self-respect. The 1909 lectures categorize respect for others as a negative duty, in contrast with positive duties to them of charity (1975b, vol. 2: 310). This fits in with Durkheim's whole approach. But nothing is said about the application, to duties to oneself, of the dualism of negative respect and positive regard, attachment, love.

A trap is if the other, positive side of self-respect comes out as self-love – not an obviously Durkheimian virtue. Hence it is of interest that the lecture on man's duties to himself not only asks about the more positive side but names and identifies it as "pride" – pride in oneself as a man, "the motivation *par excellence* of this part of morality" (Lukes 1968, vol. 2: 238–9).

Various problems arise. One of them again concerns Durkheim's persistent Kantian dualism between our sensibility as desire-governed individuals and our humanity as reason-governed persons. It often seems, in his use of it, that he treats the first as profane and sacralizes only the second. But he needs to sacralize both if his general appeal to the moral emotions and his particular arguments about suicide and so on are to go through. This is precisely what happens in the debate on sex, with his insistence on the body as a central sacred symbol of the person. It is a reassertion, in effect, of the integrity of the body, individual and person.

Durkheim argues in *Suicide* that, just because in modern society we cannot belong to anyone else, we do not therefore become our own property, with rights to do as we wish with ourselves (1897a: 383; t.337). But it is anyway clear from his whole approach that he rejects self-ownership and instead emphasizes self-mastery, self-government and autonomy. This is fair enough. Talk of self-ownership is sordid, a category mistake that reduces persons to the level of things, and that is usually made without discussion of the ideas, proper to the domain of persons, of self-government and autonomy. But we must still acquire, with such ideas, modern liberty's rights to some sort of charge over our lives and a freedom both as individuals and as citizens. The dignity of the person, in the modern human ideal, is meaningless if it does not include these. Durkheim is completely correct, however, to worry about a libertarian abuse of rights that systematically undermines the dignity of the person and destroys the sacred centre of the modern moral world on which our claims to freedom, self-government and autonomy depend. His fundamental argument against the suicide's self-injury and violation is that society itself is injured by the violation of "the sentiment on which its most respected moral maxims nowadays rest, and which is almost the only bond between its members" (*ibid.*: 383; t.337).

Libertarians, despite their enthusiasm for freedom as a general, overriding principle, explain only some of the things it lets in, such as suicide and prostitution. They fail to explore others, such as the sale of one's body for canning, on death, as supermarket cat and dog food, or, for that matter, human food (cannibalism between consenting adults cannot be wrong). The libertarian might reply that these are outrageous, indeed unthinkable things, or that they are anyway not at issue since there is not so far any demand for them. But why, if it is not because the modern moral world has its own taboos that limit freedom and simply rule some things out as outrageous and incompatible with notions of the status and dignity of the human person? Libertarianism is a paradigmatic case of how ethics might destroy morals in its lack of any sense of the sacred. The central, paramount value of the human person, to which it appeals, cannot in fact be a central, paramount value unless there is a zone of the sacred that constitutes it through collective taboos that mark it off from the zone of the profane. The market is a zone *par excellence* of the profane, of a cash nexus and trade in things. The body is an integral symbol of the person and there is no way in which the person can be sacred without taboos that block an extensive, let alone complete commodification – that is, profanation – of the body and bodily parts.

Just as he is against suicide, Durkheim, with his views on sex, is clearly against prostitution, and with his views on pride and self-respect he is also against reduction of the division of human labour into a market in labour as merely another, thing-like commodity. He may or may not be right in particular cases, such as suicide. He is right in the general point that in our decisions over the range of cases that centrally involve the human body and bodily parts we must end up with an important, extensive zone of sacredness around the human person. This both constrains and protects freedom, in upholding the collective "sentiment" of the status of the person on which it rests.

In sum, the "individual morality" of integrity, pride and self-respect turns out to be crucial in all this. As he says in the lectures on civic ethics, it fixes "in the individual conscience the basic, general foundations of all morality, the foundations on which all the rest depends" ([1950a] 1969g: 43; t.3). In the modern human ideal it also keeps, as he is so anxious to keep, a sense of something transcendent. Yet it can do so in a network rather than a hierarchy of interrelated ends, with the person, a society of persons and the impersonal ideal of the person at its centre. Nor can the sense of this sacred centre just be a "sentiment". It must bring in both the authority and autonomy of reason: "the application of reason to morality tends more and more to become a condition of virtue" (1925a: 140; t.122).

Chapter Seven

Rational ethics: autonomy

The division of labour tackles the "apparent contradiction" of how the modern world can bring both autonomy and cohesion. It is in a way a sociological version of Kant's hopes for a kingdom of ends. But Kant's approach to autonomy very much involves philosophical issues of freewill. *The division of labour* skirts these, to concentrate on a sociopolitical freedom in which individuals, released from the collective yoke, become increasingly distinct, self-governing centres of thought and action. As a conception of freedom and autonomy, it is not at all strange. Things are different with the conception developed in the lectures on moral education. This very much involves philosophical issues, and might well seem strange. Autonomy lies in enlightened acceptance of the social and moral realities of our time.

A modern "fact"

How does Durkheim work towards this view? His first main move sees modern attachment to the ideal of autonomy as a "fact", to be understood and accepted as such. He begins with various standard expressions of the ideal, and connects it with modern morality's "fundamental axiom", that "the human person is the sacred thing *par excellence*". Thus any "kind of restriction on our conscience seems immoral, since it does violence to our personal autonomy". A "particular way of thinking should never be forced on us, even in the name of a moral authority". Our "reason should accept as true only that which it has spontaneously recognized as such". There must also be liberty to act on our beliefs: "what does it matter that thought is free, if action is constrained?" (1925a: 123; t.107–8).

It can sound, so far, just like *The division of labour*'s autonomy. But Durkheim switches interest from an "apparent contradiction" between freedom and cohesion to one between freedom and determinism. He reports various standard claims that our "personality can be nothing but the product of the milieu", whether social, physical or biological (*ibid.*: 123–4; t.108). He is then ready with his own argument that, even so, aspirations to autonomy constitute a modern "fact":

> Given the generality and persistence of this demand and the ever-increasing clarity with which it is affirmed, it is impossible to view it as the product of who knows what delusion of the public conscience. It must correspond with something. It is itself a fact, as much as the facts going against and opposing it, and instead of denying it, of disputing its right to exist, it is necessary, because it exists, to give an account of it. (*ibid.*: 124; t.108)

The argument is vintage Durkheim. Appeal to general persistent belief in autonomy recalls the appeal, in early work, to general persistent belief in the principles of 1789 and invokes, like it, an idea of the normal. Insistence that such belief "must correspond with something" recalls the insistence that the principles of 1789 must be rooted in changing social realities and invokes, like it, an idea of a dynamic. Autonomy is thus approached from a long-held basic position. Every type of society has a normal morality rooted in the conditions of the time, in our society it is the human ideal, and demands for autonomy are part and parcel of this. Or, taking solidariness as the very source of moral life, it must attach us, in the case of our own society and its ideals, to autonomy. So we again have a "paradoxical" combination of autonomy and solidarity. Now, however, it is to ground autonomy of the will on attachment to the hegemonic, socially generated ethic of our time. Is this possible?

The lectures, in discussing autonomy, raise the general question of paradoxes, seeming contradictions and, in Kantian terms, antinomies. Durkheim complains about being trapped in these by "abstract" philosophical thinking, when the need is to understand them as part of the single but complex "reality" of social and moral life (*ibid.*: 127; t.111).[1] Even so, his problem is that his whole approach to ethics rules out a root and branch rejection of our ideals of autonomy, yet itself might be ruled out by these as they stand, and must find a way of inter-preting and reworking them that does not so transform their meaning that it amounts, in fact, to their rejection. Indeed, it is part of his gen-eral programme, as set out in *The division of labour*, that the task of understanding, instead of rejecting hegemonic ideals, may involve a need to rework them.

Autonomy and the natural world

It is to go on to rework the ideal of autonomy that the lectures pro-ceed to discuss its original articulation by Kant. But Durkheim so criticizes this that he comes close to its radical rejection. Then perhaps he falls into a trap. Given Kantianism's authority as a basis in our cul-ture of thinking about autonomy and what it means and represents, perhaps his need is to convert it into line with his own views. This is not just an interesting challenge or a way of meeting one of the main sources of opposition to his approach to ethics. It may be required by the approach itself. So an attempt will be made to rework, step by step, Kantian into Durkheimian autonomy.

However, we first have to understand Durkheim's own ideas. He ends his critique of Kant by insisting that what is wanted is a "progres-sive autonomy" – something that is not simply a "logical possibility, always equally true in the sense of an altogether abstract truth", but that "grows, develops and evolves through history" (1925a: 130; t.114). In fact, Kant also wants this. Durkheim is misleading if he implies otherwise. But let us consider how, to introduce "progressive autonomy", he takes the example of our relationship with nature. It is not necessarily a persuasive example. Durkheim's discussion is brief and soon becomes problematic.

It begins straightforwardly enough. Man does not make the laws of the physical world, but discovers them through science. Yet we look for a greater independence in relation to this world, rather than only in the realm of moral ideas. So we have to look for it through science, the source of our "relative liberation" (*ibid.*: 130–31; t.114).

We might now sit back and expect a standard instrumentalist account of how science delivers power over nature in the service of human ends. We would be mistaken. Durkheim instead asks us to imagine that science is complete. We can then know not just the laws but the reasons of things, and see a rational order in the world. We can also identify and correct deviations from it. Above all, we can submit to this order and accept the world as "good".

Is Durkheim serious? What can be scientific, rational and enlightened about valuing mere things, not in terms of human interests but as in themselves "good"? It is true that the physical world, as he defines it, encompasses the organic world and, in the relevant aspects, ourselves. Yet his concern is with extending respect for intelligent beings not just to sentient beings or even to all life but to all "creation". It covers, as he clearly intends, inanimate things, and has roots, as he is clear too, in religion:

> What brings the believer to see that the world is good, because the work of a good being, we can arrive at *a posteriori* and to the extent that science lets us establish rationally something faith postulates *a priori*. (*ibid.*: 132; t.115)

This might confirm the view that it is all metaphysics, briefer, but like Kant's efforts in the third *Critique* to see a *telos* in nature and through it God.

On the other hand, perhaps Durkheim raises crucial issues for modern secular enlightenment. Must it lead, in the search for autonomy, to a deep refusal of a givenness of things? Does it have to involve an instrumentalism that so little "respects nature" that it ravages it? If there is a solution here, it is not necessarily a reform of society without any reform of our worldview itself. But it would still have to do more than Durkheim attempts, in sketching out his ideas, to integrate in the same worldview our relationships to "nature" and in social and moral life. In the meantime, let us turn to these ideas.

With science complete, the milieu of physical things becomes "part of ourselves, since there is within us a system of representations which exactly expresses it". Science even becomes like geometry or mathematics. We no longer have to go beyond ourselves in order, at a given moment, to understand and adapt to the world. It is enough to analyze, interrelate and work through our notions of it, that is, to take careful thought and achieve self-awareness. This is to achieve a "first degree of autonomy" (*ibid.*: 131; t.114–15). But what is the claim's point? With or without going beyond ourselves, it still seems to rest on a correspondence between our ideas and the world, and a requirement that they express it.

Perhaps the answer lies in the next claim, about discovering a rationale. Durkheim talks of going beyond knowledge of the "laws" to the "reasons" of things, and says that "if, to resurrect an old expression, it is not we who made the plan of nature, we rediscover it through science, we rethink it and understand why it is as it is" (*ibid.*: 131; t.115). So this can be taken as a difference between knowing "that" and knowing "why", since laws can be taken as descriptions of observed regularities rather than as explanations of them. There is of course the view that bans science, as an empirical knowledge, from going beyond such description or that equates it with explanation and the only idea of causality science may have. But, as has been argued, it is not Durkheim's view, any more than, according to Boutroux, it is Hume's or Kant's. In *The rules* and elsewhere Durkheim works with an idea of causality in terms of necessary and intelligible connexions. He seems to do so again in the lectures, both in emphasizing how science is made up of our "representations" – through which it might become like geometry or mathematics – and in wanting to go from laws to a rationale that understands and explains things through "rethinking" them. To bring out his anti-empiricism, we could talk of "re-thinking" and "re-presentations". Science constructs in the mind a knowledge of things, in constructing intelligible stories of them. Not least, in Durkheim's case, they are stories of systems and dynamics with an internal ideal rationale, and of deviations from this, whether or not because of external contingencies. Yet science, as far as he is concerned, is still about truth. It loses its point if it does not seek a knowledge that captures the world, even in rethinking it. So perhaps we need to understand and accept science's commitment to both an empirically based knowledge of things and, as part and parcel of it, an empirically underdetermined ordering of them.

This is all very general and can be articulated in very different ways. It still matters for understanding Durkheim, who is not an archsceptic or a simple celebrant of positive science, but, as he himself insists, a "rationalist". Thus, if science can ever be complete, it is not just as an empirical study of things. We also need to rethink these, in search of a clear, coherent, intelligible order in our ideas and in the world. Can we ever achieve the aim – and for Durkheim it is an aim – of science's completion? Although believing we can come closer and closer to this, he goes on to emphasize that it is an unrealizable ideal (*ibid.*: 132; t.116).

So, in effect, we should look for a rationale at work in the world, and can imagine yet can never have certainty that such is the case. It might still be that, when we argue as far as we are able that it is the case, we should not just stop there but go on to endorse the world and its rationale. In Durkheim's words:

> to the extent that we are sure that it is all as it should be – that is, as the nature of things implies – we can submit to it, . . . because we judge that it is good and that we cannot achieve a better. (*ibid.*: 131–2; t.115)

Yet are these evaluative judgements necessary if, through understanding, there is to be "submission" to the world?

Durkheim insists that it "is not passive obedience but enlightened adherence", and that:

> to will freely is not to will the absurd; on the contrary, it is to will the rational, that is, to will to act in conformity with the nature of things. (*ibid.*: 132; t.115) [2]

Then surely we can have the autonomy that this describes if, having sought and argued our way towards a reasonably based understanding of "the nature of things", we accept it as a given. It is neither good nor bad. It is just a fundamental "fact", constitutive of our situation, even our existence and the kinds of beings we are.

But perhaps Durkheim's worry is that to accept the world as a given we need more than its valuelessness. Indeed, it is as a "fact" constitutive of our existence that it might seem inevitably drawn into the human evaluative realm, and not simply as an instrument of human ends and interests but again as something that, very generally, helps to constitute them. Durkheim's argument about autonomy, through science, in our relationship to physical things stresses their internalization in our representation and rethinking of them, so that the world becomes "part of ourselves". This is not to deny that it is already in a very basic way part of ourselves, in our physical and, in Kantian terms, "sensible" being. On the contrary, it is very much to do with Durkheim's belief that through knowledge's opening up of the world, not least in ourselves, we can become "our own masters" and that, as he goes on to remark, "thought is liberator of the will" (*ibid.*: 136;

t.119). It also returns us to his attempts, in seeing self-discipline as a fundamental virtue, to work out a position that neither rejects nor embraces but somehow accepts our embodiedness. The issue is as perplexing as it is central, running, for example, through the whole of Kant's ethics and worldview, including the teleology of nature. In Durkheim's case, acceptance of our embodiedness and acceptance of the world seem to be tied up with one another as acceptance of essential givens of human existence as, at bottom, a human good.

Even so, he invites easy defeat in linking the good of the given with not being able to achieve a better world and rationale. This still lets in imagining one, and if we can imagine a better one, why endorse our own?

It is necessary to bring out his assumption that the good, in such matters, is not just something we can desire as a conceivable, "abstract" possibility. It is something we can will. It has to be a reality inherent in our situation and an ideal that we can struggle to achieve.

The distinction is important, and not to be easily given up, though again inviting easy defeat. When Durkheim imagines and subscribes to the aim of science's completion, he himself emphasizes that we can never achieve this. So even in wanting, through science, a progressive rather than merely abstract autonomy, he seems, like Kant, to want human pursuit of a humanly unattainable ideal.

It will not do just to say that the real ideal, here, is always to work towards the unattainable. The real ideal *is* the unattainable. Nor will it do just to lower our sights. The ideal of knowledge and truth is a necessary, guiding myth, embedded in science, even, more generally, in philosophy, as human activities, and giving meaning and direction to them. The same is the case with autonomy, as a social and moral ideal of our time, and so even with the ideal of a republic of persons itself. An ideal is not ruled out just because, in its full, complete realization, it may seem unattainable, and when, on the contrary, it will not go away but is rooted in our society and its collective imagination and aspirations.

In *The division of labour*, as we have seen, Durkheim himself tries appeal to unattainability in order to rework modern egalitarianism as an ideal of equal opportunity, only to land up with something that itself seems completely unattainable. Some ideal or other of equal opportunity is indeed rooted in our society. But the real objection to its expression in the liberalism of equal life chances is not that this is impossible, but that it is undesirable, as a vision of an abstract society of abstract individuals that can have nothing to do with a republic of everyone's developing and flourishing. Let us now turn to autonomy in regard to the social and moral world, which has everything to do with the ideal of a republic.

Autonomy and the social world

Durkheim warms up with a preliminary on moral life and how we can develop a science of it. There is also, after the main section, a discussion of various problems and a general summary. In the main section itself, however, he reruns things as before.

He imagines moral science's completion, and goes over how we can then internalize the moral world, see a rationale and correct deviations from this, but, above all, accept it. Thus we become masters of the moral world: "Our heteronomy is at an end" (1925a: 133; t.116).[3]

Durkheim goes on to say that autonomy is morality's third element. It lies in understanding morality and in its "free acceptance", which is nothing other than "enlightened acceptance" (ibid.: 137; t.120). A question is whether he simply means understanding and acceptance of the elements basic to all morality – as suggested at one point by Gurvitch (1963, vol. 2: 175). He is certainly concerned with the recognition rather than the undermining of these by the secular rational ethics our world demands. But it follows that we need to situate them in our own world and in a grasp of its nature and its demands, including for autonomy itself.

Indeed, it can seem that Durkheim wants a life wholly transparent to us. Autonomy develops "to the extent that we achieve a more complete knowledge of things" (1925a: 135; t.119), and requires that, "whether in deference to a rule or devotion to a collective ideal, we have the clearest, fullest consciousness possible of the reasons of our conduct" (ibid.: 137; t.120). But what matters, above all, is understanding an essential dynamic to see if our social and moral world is everything "implied by the natural make-up of the reality it expresses", and to be able, to the extent that it is not, to restore it to its "normal state" (ibid.: 133; t.117). So Durkheim continues to appeal, at a crucial point, to an idea of the normal. This is to try to articulate how autonomy means both a power to act on and change our world and a submission to a givenness in it. It does this as an idea emphasizing not what is general but what is "implied" by an underlying reality and its rationale. As such, it is part and parcel of Durkheim's fundamental ethical position – that the real and its rationale are the good – and of his view of autonomy as enlightened acceptance of the social and moral realities of our time.

A next question is whether this view of autonomy is essentially procedural or is also substantive. It seems essentially procedural. It does not spell out the nature of the social and moral worlds it might endorse. Thus Durkheim is a liberal, committed to a republic of persons and the human ideal. But is he a liberal by chance? Even if, nowadays, his view of autonomy happens to back a republic of persons, can it not subscribe to any ruling regime and ideology, however nightmarish? It is therefore important to try to show that his view of autonomy means that there is only one social ideal able to pass the test – the human ideal of a republic of persons.

A preliminary task is to do more to explore the procedural and substantive sides to autonomy. Let us take the example of Kant's idea of it. A canonical expression is: "man makes the moral law." An unusual expression is: "So I will, so I decree." But in both cases the first part sounds procedural and the second substantive, since, regardless of the substantive nature of the law, procedurally it is what "man makes" or "I will". It is true that Kant's idea of the basic moral law is standardly seen as formal and procedural, and in a way it is, relative to the substantive maxims that it tests to see if they might or might not pass as laws. But the basic moral law is also itself substantive in its inclusion of a universalist requirement to respect everyone as a person. This content limits the proceduralism in which the law is what "man makes" or "I will".

As a proceduralism, Durkheimian autonomy is a collective autonomy since, with its source in science, it lies in the social practice of collective, free, public enquiry. But a process of collective argument does not in itself entail a collective verdict. On the contrary, a possible norm is that the participants must each draw their own individual conclusions and make and indeed act on their own individual judgements. Hence an absolutely crucial issue in ethics is the identity, in enquiry about the right and the good, of the final, authoritative, moral judge. A general, generally unexamined assumption is that it is and must be the individual. It is mistaken to go on as if it is obviously

Kant's assumption ("man makes the law" is not the same as "I will"), while, of course, it is an assumption Durkheim spends much of his time attacking. But does he always just substitute society? His modern moral judge might instead be the person, that is, the individual as man.

To go into the proceduralism of Durkheimian autonomy we thus need to investigate both the collectiveness of ethical enquiry and the identity of the ethical judge. We can then tackle how its necessary substantive entailment is the ideal of a republic of persons. We shall still have to tackle, with necessary connexions themselves in mind, Durkheim's equation of enlightened autonomous acceptance with freedom of the will. This done, the way is ready to argue that Durkheimian and Kantian autonomy are, near enough, two versions of the same thing.

Procedural autonomy

It is easy enough to see that Durkheimian autonomy, with its source in science, must lie in collective processes in which, for example, we look to one another to test an argument for mistakes, gaps, etc. The problem is to clarify this basic view.

In imagining that natural science is complete, Durkheim also imagines that we each have knowledge of it (1925a: 131; t.114). In going on to moral science he seems to hold up the same ideal, of a world at last transparent to us all. He seems hopeful, too, about the basis already laid for such an understanding, whereas in the paper on moral facts he stresses our remoteness from the full moral self-knowledge demanded by the modern conscience. This is still to accept the ideal and to see moral science as the route to it ([1906b] 1924a: 109–10; t.74–5).

A world transparent to all implies a same full, clear consciousness in everyone. So let us talk of it as an ideal of mechanical enlightenment. This points up the difference from *The division of labour*'s autonomy and general picture of things. Modern society opens the way to a "growing multitude of individual disagreements" ([1893b] 1902b: 147; t.172). We each have and hang on to "our own opinions, beliefs, aspirations" and "cast of mind" (*ibid.*: 175–6; t.198). Everyone's development as an "autonomous source of action" means everyone's development as a distinct autonomous centre of thought: "the very materials of consciousness must have a personal character" (*ibid*.: 399; t.403–4).

Can we look to science to sort things out and establish an enlightened consensus? Durkheim certainly insists that "understanding guided by science must take a larger part in the course of collective life", but also insists that "the science everyone is thus required to know hardly merits the name". Science, properly so-called, goes far beyond this and is "accessible only to an elite" (*ibid*.: 15; t.52).

In fact, of course, science is no longer accessible to anybody. Its development and expansion through the division of labour mean that an individual can cope with only highly specialized bits of it. In discussing how science might cohere, Durkheim rejects appeals to encyclopaedism, general philosophy and even rules of method. Instead, the solution lies in "the living unity of an organic whole". To bring science together "it is not necessary that all of it is grasped by one and the same mind – which is anyway impossible – but it is enough that all those cultivating it feel they are collaborating in the same work" (*ibid*.: 363: t.371).

So let us talk, here, of an ideal of organic enlightenment, since there could still be an increasingly complete science of both the natural and the moral world. It is just that none of us can have knowledge of it. It is this that is the important if paradoxical point, rather than the more pedestrian one about elitism, and that really contrasts with mechanical enlightenment's ideal of a world known and transparent to us all.

It is true that it can let in hope that science can reach out to us to disseminate a basic social and moral understanding. It remains in tension with the mechanical enlightenment of the moral education lectures, and again surfacing in the paper on moral facts. But it itself also very much comes into this, so that the tension between organic and mechanical enlightenment runs through Durkheim's work and exists, as here, in the same discussion.

So let us turn to the discussion, and especially to replies to comments about the importance of the individual. One is to Frédéric Rauh, whose book on moral experience had appeared a few years earlier and made something of an impact. Durkheim accepts that of course individuals each have their own inner moral life. It is just that its investigation is inadequate for understanding society's moral life. There is "no individual conscience that exactly translates the communal moral conscience" ([1906b] 1924a: 115; t.78). This in a way sums up an earlier reply to Alphonse Darlu (who had tutored Proust):

> Each of us manages to assimilate only bits and pieces of the sciences and is open only to certain aesthetic impressions. It is in society and through society that science and art live in their wholeness. There is talk of the moral richness of the individual! But of the many moral currents at work in our era, each of us is aware only of the one passing through our individual milieu, and then has only a fragmentary, superficial feeling of it. How much richer and more complex is the moral life of society with all its different complementary or conflicting aspirations! But we know almost nothing of this intense activity fermenting around us. (*ibid.*: 98; t.67–8)

The basic point – that individuals draw on, without ever capturing, collective thought and experience – thus has a number of very important implications.

It carries all the way through from the lay world to science itself, including any science of morals (no individual sociologist can capture its collective thought about collective life). It carries all the way through to even the most central collective notions. It is a matter not just of differences but of disagreements between individuals in their understanding of these. It is a matter of differences and disagreements not just between individuals but between movements, tendencies and factions. It can still mean unity around a collective ideal.

Let us shelve science for the moment, to concentrate on the point's implications in lay life. The reply to Darlu is explicit that it carries all the way through to even the most central collective notions. In giving examples, Durkheim cannot resist highlighting as just such a collective notion the "individual ideal" itself (defining personal developing and flourishing, ends, duties to self):

> each of us colours this communal ideal in our own way, marking it with our own individuality, just as each of us practises charity, justice, patriotism etc. in our own way (*ibid.*: 99; t.68).

He then concludes where he wants to conclude, with an emphasis on the moral unity round these ideals. But throughout the reply and in the discussion as a whole, he is very much concerned with disagreements, above all between different social movements and tendencies. He criticizes the romance of the individual pitted against "society". It is in reality an expression of conflicts within collective life itself.

It is of interest to ask which of the moral factions making up the modern world has Durkheim's own support. But the fundamental question raised by all this takes us back to moral science. How can it decide between these tendencies to say to any of us which to support, and, if it cannot, what use is it as a key to ethics?

Durkheim is naturally optimistic about finding a solution, and his approach goes back to *The division of labour* and even further. It depends on an appeal both to an underlying dynamic and to understanding of it. But it also depends on a basic contrast between traditional beliefs and new ideals. Thus he argues that, in showing their rootedness in a vanishing versus an emergent order, as well as in helping us to clarify and direct the new, science "lets us take up a position between these divergent moralities" (*ibid.*: 87–8; t.61). So, if his sympathies are not with tradition, they are not just with actual, existing manifestations of the new. He goes on to talk of confused aspirations and movements that each express, if not very well, "part of the underlying social reality". Science's task is understanding this reality – a task that is also, in practice, reflective and that helps the age achieve "self-consciousness" (*ibid.*: 92–3; t.63–4). Or again, in replying to Darlu, he emphasizes an opposition between the collective and the collective itself, only "better understood" and "more self-aware" (*ibid.*: 96; t.65–6). The reply, however, is where he gets into difficulty:

> It is the *true* nature of society that is conformed to when obeying traditional morality; it is the *true* nature of society that is conformed to when in revolt against this same morality. (*ibid.*: 95; t.65).

So how is he able to take sides?

It is no doubt possible to rule out some positions as hopelessly reactionary, some as hopelessly utopian. This still lets in a whole range of tendencies, whether the more conservative and cautious about change, or the more radical and enthusiastic for it, or the more moderate wanting a middle way. What help is it, in order to decide between them, to appeal to a better understanding and fit with an underlying reality? On such appeal, the Durkheimian answer may be the need to understand that they are all part of the same dynamic – even to look for a division of labour in which the conflicts of moral factions contribute to the stability and movement of the social whole.

So the answer is not vacuous. It instead suggests that the Durkheimian approach to ethics must, in a sense, be neutral. Its business is not to try to decide between any of these "divergent moralities". To do so is to try to decide the *individual*'s question of which to support, as if there is only one choice, in reason, one can make (and when it would be disastrous if, say, we all became moderates). Its proper concern is with the *social* question of acceptance of some range or other of different, even conflicting, tendencies as both necessary and legitimate.

There is something in this. But it gives up too easily on Durkheim's urge to point the way. The question at stake is not just a diversity of opinion. It is its centre of gravity. For Durkheim, it is about changing this and moving social debate on to a new, more progressive agenda. Thus, as in the intervention on the Dreyfus Affair, it is about moving individualism on, from a campaign for basic, negative rights to a campaign for a more positive, far-reaching justice.

It is above all a question, again as in the intervention on the Dreyfus Affair, of battling against traditional and other forces to defend the human ideal itself, with its very belief in free, enlightened enquiry and in everyone's status as a person and centre of autonomous thought and action. It is an ideal he himself sees at the core of the modern world's dynamic and rationale. But the need is for its establishment as an ideal around which there may be continuing dispute over how to interpret and justify it yet there is also a fundamental unity of commitment.

The discussion on moral facts is of interest as an occasion when Durkheim argues as powerfully as he can for his way of interpreting and justifying the ideal while arguing with others sharing this commitment – for example, there is the important pro-Dreyfusard article, in the same year as Durkheim's, by Darlu (1898). Durkheim does not comment, in the business of arguing his case, on the norms governing the discussion and scientific and other enquiry in general. But the issue comes up in the lectures, some years later, on pragmatism and sociology.

He is still concerned with science as a search for impersonal truth. He is still concerned with its collective, collaborative division of labour. However, he also emphasizes that science is pluralistic, tied up with the diversity of individual temperaments, minds and opinions, and, in a word, highly personal. This is not a licence to believe what one likes. Instead, it is partly that "there are separate tasks in a common work and in this work each can carve out a task according to temperament, attracting them in a particular direction". It is mainly that reality is so complex that "for every object of knowledge there are differing but equally justified ways of examining it", while individual minds are so finite that "none can work from all points of view at once". Like modern society itself, science requires norms of free thought, mutual respect in criticism, and tolerance:

> Each must be able to admit that another has seen an aspect of reality they had let escape them, but which is as real and as true as those to which they had gone from preference. (1955a: 186–7; t.91–2)

So let us draw some conclusions.

The lectures clearly work with and develop the organic view of enlightenment. This is also clearly a way in which Durkheim's individualism becomes part of his holism, as well as of his ideal of science's completion and insistence on science's necessary, guiding myth as the search for truth. Collective development of understanding of the moral and natural world – and so the development of autonomy – has to be through the diversity of minds, perspectives, temperaments and opinions. But the other side of the process – and the lectures refer back to the paper on moral facts in emphasizing it – is that "collective thought is only feebly and incompletely represented in each individual consciousness" (1955a: 204; t.104).

So we might now wonder, in all this, about the identity of the ethical judge. It cannot just be the individual. We are feeble and incomplete. Yet how can it be society? Its knowledge is not known to us.

Perhaps the best and indeed only candidate left is the individual as man. We in fact judge personally and partially as individuals. Yet we seek to be able to judge impersonally and universally, and, in a word, as man. We can then reintroduce, instead of forgetting all about, mechanical enlightenment. Its imagination may sustain the will to try to judge universally, and indeed imagining something of the sort seems a necessary expression of this will itself.

What about the individual as man and judging between particular tendencies and their visions of the good? Contemporary liberal neutrality on the issue leaves us to our own devices, to the extent that it withdraws ethics from relevance to most of our moral concerns and reduces judgement on them to preference and mere choice. Preference also comes into the individualistic side of Durkheim's views, even of science. Yet so do the demands of public enquiry, argument and exchange, whatever the interest and perspective we are drawn to by temperament. This lets in hope of particular moral choices as reasoned, particular judgements – but precisely not just on the assumption there is only one, in reason, for anyone to make. The assumption cannot be part of organic enlightenment. Or rather it can come into it, with the individual as man as the ethical judge, only through some sort of continuing role for the ideal of mechanical enlightenment.

There is a more concrete and immediate way of trying to express things. A remark in the discussion on moral facts concerns points of conscience that are "always delicate" ([1906b] 1924a: 88; t.61). Then it may well require "delicacy" to keep within civilized norms and still argue with power for a particular position, but at the same time to accept that it is not the only position to adopt, while arguing as if it is. Yet this is a requirement of the human ideal, in the republic of science and in the republic of a wider, liberal society.

Autonomy and the republic

Everything is now more or less in place to examine how Durkheimian procedural autonomy relates to substantive social ideals. Can it endorse only the human ideal of a republic of persons? Or does it just endorse this contingently, if it happens to be the hegemonic ethic of our time?

Thus under mechanical enlightenment autonomy lies in a world transparent to everyone. Then an objection is that a world could be more or less transparent to its inhabitants, accepted by them and yet, say, a dictatorship. Can wholly illiberal worlds run only on delusion? The only thing that seems certain – and the point of the objection – is that they do not run on respect for *la personne humaine*. Transparency need not be a sufficient condition of this ideal.

Is it even a necessary condition? It is possible to extricate Durkheim from the whole problem by emphasizing how he works with organic rather than mechanically transparent enlightenment, and how we can rethink the lectures on moral education in line with it. This still has to involve some sort of understanding of the social and moral realities of our time. Otherwise we also leave behind the whole approach of the lectures to autonomy. But it may be a way of trying, autonomously, to understand things that is bound up with republicanism as a social and moral ideal, and cannot commit us to any other.

The concern in all this is rooted in Kantianism. It is about hope of a society that can have everybody's ethical, since autonomous, acceptance. It is not about hope of one still dependent on force and other heteronomous compliance. There is therefore the question of how such an ideal might make its way in the heteronomous world. For Durkheim, as for Kant, it is not at all just a problem of how to convert a particular individual to the universalist ethic of everyone's autonomy. It is about the conversion of particular groups, societies and indeed humanity as a species – so that, as for Kant, the ethic at last emerges as the conscious aspiration of an "age of enlightenment", and is at last realized in practice in the society of an "enlightened age". But this problem of conversion is separable from the one at stake here, which is how the procedural ideal of a society that can have everybody's autonomous acceptance has to be the substantive social ideal of a republic.

The division of labour emphasizes our development as autonomous centres of thought and action, with our own distinct views. So only a society in which everybody can develop in this way can have everybody's autonomous acceptance. Like any other society, it requires some sort of unity of commitment to a collective ideal. But it is to the human ideal, with diversity and disagreement, as well as active citizenship, built into it. So all this, it might seem clear, rules out illiberal regimes. Yet how can it be clear that it leads to a republic? Enlightenment is not transparent, because of its society's built-in differences of view, even in interpretation of its human ideal. It is still possible to search for a rationale, at work in the very processes of conflict and argument and developing through them. It is to be sought, in Durkheim's argument, in the rationale of a fully free division of labour, pointing to the more complete justice, personal flourishing and cohesion of an ethical commonwealth.

But it is also a consistent part of the argument that every social and moral order, even at its most ideal, secretes its own pathologies. In our own world they include, as well as "anomic", aggressive self-interest and "egoistic", intellectual self-absorption, the drive to authoritarianism. Thus Durkheim sees the modern state as one of the most powerful sources of this, yet also of the individual's emancipation, and looks for a solution in the intermediate groups of corporatist reform. But is it not in science, the Durkheimian hope for autonomy, that authoritarianism has its deepest modern roots of all?

It might well be that science itself, with its need of diversity, freedom, tolerance, etc., must be a republic. It might also be that the same spirit must permeate the wider society and because of the same rationale. There is still the problem that it is just because of organic enlightenment's rationale of a division of labour that we must trust in the experts to guide us and defer to their republic's authority. It is even all the more of a problem because they can and should reach out to our lay republic to disseminate some semblance of understanding amongst us. This is an open invitation to dogmatize and to abuse science's authority – which is why it also risks undermining it and generating, in the lay, free-thinking republic, scepticism about any claim to knowledgeability.

Durkheim does not come to grips with such issues in his enthusiasm for specialization in *The division of labour*'s original edition. But he engages with them – long before the lectures on pragmatism – in his various courses on education, in insistence that only a "broad, human culture" and "truly human culture" can give modern societies the citizens they need ([1903b] 1922a: 116; t.121; 1904a(40): 684).

A basic problem, as we might now put it, is that all of us must be able, as individuals, both to draw on and to contribute to a collectively created "culture" and "knowledge" that none of us, as individuals, can master. In looking for a solution Durkheim rules out a narrow, premature specialization, as well as a would-be generalism that can be only a bricolage of this and that, but also a generalism philosophizing in thin air. Intead it is necessary to develop a transferable power to think and enquire critically, but which has to be anchored in experience of reflection on *something*, and across a span of things. Durkheim distinguishes and interrelates the concerns and approaches of three cultures – the modern humanities – forming this span: the study of science, of history, and of language and the arts.

There is an interesting shift in his view of the arts. The lectures on moral education exclude them from the core of the *vie sérieuse*, yet see them as its extension in the *vie légère*, giving this greater value (1925a:

313–14; t.273–4). The lectures on the evolution of educational thought reintegrate the arts into the *vie sérieuse*, in seeing literature as essential for an imaginative yet disciplined understanding of other peoples and of our own society; it is not just to cultivate "taste", but always, at bottom, "to arouse and exercise this sense of humanity" (1938a, vol. 2: 205; t.332). And although separable from history and the social and natural sciences it must interrelate with them, both in what they study and, not least, in the critical, collaborative ways they study them.

In discussing the natural sciences, Durkheim emphasizes the need to get away from dogma and to do so through a sense of how they work, how their knowledge is constructed through "experiments, gropings and failures of all sorts", how this knowledge remains open to revision and is "provisional" (1925a: 300–301; t.262); but also how logic and critique develop through science itself, which is a "product of cooperation" (1938a, vol. 2: 215; t.340). In sum, he envisages a new humanism spanning the sciences and the arts and opening them, through experience of their cultures, to a lifelong access everyone can develop in their own particular ways – and it is lifelong and for everyone, as in the hopes of *The division of labour*'s second preface (1902b: xxxi; t.26–7). At the same time he sees it as a new rationalism, acknowledging the irreducible complexity of things but knowing "how, without loss of nerve, to look this complexity in the face" (1938a, vol. 2: 225; t.348).

So Durkheim, it is clear, looks for a republican culture that opens the way to a republican society. But in doing so, it also seems clear, he is not just anxious to see off authoritarianism. The very arguments against this – stressing complexity, critique, difference and disagreement, the provisional status of science's knowledge, truth as its guiding myth – can let in something else. There is a need, "without loss of nerve", to face up to a thoroughgoing scepticism. This can assume all kinds of forms, such as the pragmatist doctrine Durkheim opposed in his own day. Far from being "postmodern" it is a recurrent feature of modernity, and can be added to Durkheim's list of built-in modern pathologies. His view of these means that, although autonomy is necessarily connected with a republic, there is no straight, sunlit deductive path from one to the other. It is risk filled. By the nature of its own rationale the republic will remain this, should we ever get to it.

Freedom and necessity

Everything is now almost in place to ask how Kantian autonomy and the kingdom might come out, more or less, as Durkheimian autonomy and the republic. The lectures on moral education, let us recall, set out in search of a secular rationalism in ethics that does not undermine morality itself. But Durkheim seems either unaware or unconcerned, in reviewing the project, that autonomy might collapse his dualism of duty and the good in making sentiment completely justiciable by reason. Instead his worry is that reason might collapse duty itself – since moral rules, as soon as we understand their why and wherefore and freely accept them, might "lose their imperative character" (1925a: 134; t.117). It is all the more of a worry because a main (textually well-founded) complaint he makes against Kantianism is that it does away with the moral law's necessary imperativeness. Anxious in case he does the same, he insists that to obey freely is still to obey, and adds:

> When . . . we blindly carry out an order not knowing its meaning and implications, yet knowing why we should take on this role of a blind instrument, we are as free as when we alone have all the initiative in our action. (*ibid.*: 135; t.118)

This backs away from the ideal of our increasingly complete understanding, and might help with rethinking the lectures in terms of organic enlightenment. It does not help with explaining how the moral law remains imperative when, in some sort of understanding, we accept it freely.

We must return to Durkheim's concern with the necessary connexions of a social and moral rationale. Autonomy lies in discovering this rationale. He is adamant that, just as we do not make physical laws, we do not, as individuals, make the moral law (*ibid.*: 133; t.116). It does not even seem his view that the individual as man makes the moral law. Yet this need not oppose him to Kant. On the one hand, the Kantian sense in which man makes and declares the moral law – far from just being that man makes it up – is much more that man acknowledges, sees, indeed discovers the moral law. On the other hand, Durkheimian autonomy does not just find out a rationale but is itself a reflexive, constitutive and creative part of this. It is a working out in the mind of a set of necessary connexions seen as at work in the world, of a logic of the real. Not least, it again involves the tie with a republic. The autonomy we require for discovery of our world's social and moral rationale can develop only in an "age of enlightenment", so that the only rationale it is in a reflexive position to discover contains the ideal of some sort of republic. It is still to try to understand as well as we can, and in such reflexiveness, a set of necessary social and moral connexions, an objective logic we cannot simply make up, a "thing" resistant to change at will, even our collective will. So it still has a constraining, imperative force, and, as autonomy, freedom of the will is enlightened acceptance of necessary connexions.

Is there therefore a fundamental conflict between Durkheim and Kant? But both insist on the need to combine freedom and necessity. Both insist, in doing so, on a freedom that goes beyond mere arbitrary choice and on a causality in the human as in the natural world that goes beyond mere regular concurrence. The lectures on the evolution of educational thought again make clear Durkheim's commitment to the causality of necessary connexion (1938a, vol. 2: 212–13; t.338), just as the lectures on pragmatism make clear his continuing concern with contingency versus necessity as an issue (1955a: 186; t.91). Yet does he not himself see "contingent", "accidental" causes, and does he never use them as a soft route to freewill's compatibility with social science?

A note in *Suicide* warns that freewill is a "metaphysical question outside our province". Durkheim still wants to say something about it, not least to trap supporters of methodological individualism. Their view means that social patterns must be explained by the characteristics of individuals; so they must characterize individuals themselves as all predictability and pattern; so they in effect deny freewill. In contrast, his own holistic approach explains social patterns such as the suicide rate in terms of the social milieu itself, without looking inside individuals to determine who in particular commits suicide. So it can leave us with freewill (1897a: 368, n.1; t.325, n.20). The trouble is not just that this ignores his interest in looking inside the individual at "deep, strong roots" put down by society. It seems to equate freewill with arbitrariness, leaving us with only an accidental, contingent causal power over our individual lives, and only residual, if any, power over our collective life. It is certainly not autonomy's freedom.

Autonomy, although a collective self-determination, still cannot deliver a power to transform our social and moral world completely, but is on the contrary to accept its necessary rationale. The Durkheimian hope is that it is this understanding itself that delivers a real power of transforming our world in line with its own human republican ideal. It is through it that we can see and tackle externalities working against the ideal-rationale, but also, and not least, see and contain internal pathologies coming from the rationale itself. So, whether or not limited to externalities, contingency remains part of an account that nonetheless combines and centres on freedom and necessary connexion.

Like Kant's, it is not at all a soft route to the compatibility of man's freedom with man's causation. But is it a development of Kantianism or something in complete conflict with it? Has Durkheimian autonomy and freedom of the will anything to do with Kantian autonomy and freedom?

Chapter Eight

From the kingdom of ends
to the republic of persons

Kant first made an impact in France during the Revolution.[1] By Durkheim's time he had long occupied a central place in French philosophical teaching and debate.[2] The leading academic authority was Durkheim's "dear master", Boutroux, who was invited to write the article on Kant for the *Grande Encyclopédie* (1895c). He is also acknowledged as his "dear master" by Victor Delbos, in *Kant's practical philosophy* (1905). Even if this does not go much beyond Boutroux in its essential interpretation, it is the outstanding work of French Kantian scholarship of the period.

There were many attempts to build on Kant, without accepting every aspect of his doctrine. Renouvier's "neo-critical" philosophy – developed in *The science of morals* (1869) and elsewhere – became one of the most influential. Renouvier's death coincided with the centenary of Kant's, and the whole of the 1904 issue of the *Revue de métaphysique et de morale* is devoted to discussion of their work.

There were also extensive commentaries on Kant of a highly hostile kind, and one of the clearest and most effective is to be found in Fouillée's *Critique of contemporary ethical systems* (1883). This includes an attack on Renouvier's neo-critical philosophy, both in itself and as having little or nothing to do with Kant, despite its Kantian pretensions. Criticism of Kant and Kantianism became, moreover, a standard and almost obligatory feature of expositions of other approaches – as in Léon Ollé-Laprune's Catholic, neo-Thomist *On moral certainty* (1880), Guyau's free-thinking *Sketch of a morality without obligation* (1885), Lévy-Bruhl's naturalist *Ethics and moral science* (1903), and, of course, Durkheim's own work.

Durkheim still stands out. He is not just a commentator or a disciple. He is an original driving force in the development of a distinctive vision of things – as in his emphasis on "the person", not just in reference to persons but as an abstract collective representation necessary to sacralize everyone as a person, and as in his radical reconceptualization of autonomy itself. What, however, has it to do with Kantian autonomy? In tackling this question, it is not simply that it helps to see Durkheim, and what he has to say about Kant, in the context of his time. It is also that it helps if, in reworking Kantian as Durkheimian autonomy, appeal can be made to the authoritative interpretation, by Boutroux and Delbos, of *Kant à Paris*.

Durkheim's critique of Kant

As in *The division of labour* and elsewhere, there are all kinds of points of entry into the Kantian system. As we are concerned with autonomy, let us concentrate on the point of entry in the lectures on moral education. It is about the authority that must be part and parcel of autonomy, the "majesty" that must remain part and parcel of the republic, and recalls the problem introducing the lectures as a whole. How might ethics, instead of destroying morality, preserve its imperativeness?

In wanting autonomy, Kant wants obedience to the moral law – only as self-legislated law. But if it is self-legislated, how can it be binding and imperative; indeed, how can it be law at all?

The second *Critique* takes up the motto, "so I will, so I decree" – *sic volo, sic jubeo* (Kant [1788] 1913: 31; t.32). This comes from Juvenal's *Satires*, with which Kant was completely familiar, and from the passage:

> [wife] "Put that slave on a cross!"
> [husband] "What crime has he done to deserve it?"
> . . .
> [wife] "You fool! Is a slave human? What if he hasn't
> done wrong?
> That is my wish, my order; my will is reason enough."
> Thus she rules her man.[3]

The passage is about arbitrariness, in fact, woman's arbitrariness and man's subjection to it. It might demonstrate Kant's sense of humour. It certainly underlines the question: if, with autonomy, the law is what

I will, how does it command and constrain me, where is its obligatory force, and, indeed, how is it law at all?

Let us now go to Durkheim's own discussion. On the one hand, he says, there is Kant's great sense of "the imperative character of the moral law", demanding complete obedience. On the other hand, it is obedience to something of our own making, and Kant is adamant that will cannot be moral "when it submits passively to a law of which it is not itself the legislator". Are the two views not contradictory?[4] To bring out the problem, Durkheim goes to the point in the second *Critique* just after the motto about willing and decreeing the moral law. He quotes from a French translation as follows:

> The relationship of human will to this law is a relationship of dependence (*Abhängigheit*); it is termed obligation (*Verbindlichkeit*), which designates a constraint (*Nöthigung*).

Even so:

> The autonomy of the will is the sole principle of all moral laws and of all duties corresponding to them; all heteronomy of the will . . . is opposed . . . to the morality of the will. (1925a: 124; t.108–9).[5]

Let us note that (a) Kant's distinction between will as *Wille* and *Willkür* disappears from the translation, (b) the text between the two passages is one of many places where Kant himself argues for a developmental, progressive autonomy, and (c) his distinction, here as elsewhere, between a human and a "holy" will underlies but is not explicit in Durkheim's comments. What are these comments?

A purely rational will (that is, a holy will), free of human desires, inclinations and sensibility, would "move spontaneously towards duty by the impetus of its nature alone". So, when autonomy is complete, the moral law "loses its obligatory character, its coercive aspect". It is not something binding at all. It is binding only in relation to human sensibility, and it is our reason that "makes the law that imposes itself on the inferior parts of our being" (*ibid.*: 125; t.109).

Hence a first criticism. In Kantian ethics "the law is not necessarily imperative". Its character as this is contingent and "accidental", dependent on a conflict with human passions. On the contrary, Durkheim argues, "the moral law is invested with an authority that imposes respect even on reason"; it governs not only our sensibility "but our whole nature, even our rational nature". Indeed, he then seeks support from Kant himself for this view:

> Kant has shown better than anyone that there is something religious in the sentiment that the moral law inspires even in the loftiest reason. *But we can only have a religious sentiment towards a being, real or ideal, that seems to us superior to the faculty conceiving it.* (*ibid.*: 126; t.110; italics added)

This completes the first main criticism, and opens the way to others that are even more fundamental:

> Our reason is not a transcendent faculty: *it is part of the world and so is subject to the world's law.* (*ibid.*; italics added)

Looking for autonomy in "a reality set apart from the world" leads straight into a metaphysical mire and does not get us anywhere. How "can a reason, which by hypothesis lies outside of things, outside of the real, lay down the laws of the moral order if, as we have established, this expresses the nature of the real and concrete thing that is Society?" (*ibid.*: 130; t.113). We need a developmental, progressive autonomy, which is not simply a "logical possibility, always equally true in the sense of an altogether abstract truth", but "grows . . . and evolves through history" (*ibid.*: 130; t.114).

In sum, the first stage of Durkheim's Kantian critique insists on an autonomy in which the moral law remains imperative, with authority over even our rational selves. The second stage insists that it is no solution to look for something inscribed, eternally, in a mysterious transcendental realm. The third stage insists on both an unmysterious developmental autonomy and an unmysterious transcendent authority. This then leads to autonomy as understanding the social and moral realities of our time, and as enlightened acceptance of them.

Reworking Kantian as Durkheimian autonomy

Autonomy makes its first clear appearance in Kant's *Groundwork*, as Delbos points out ([1905] 1969: 305, n.1). As he sums up:

Kant's practical philosophy was definitively constituted from the time that the notion of the categorical imperative was linked with the idea of transcendental freedom through the concept of autonomy of the will. The principle of its systematic organization and development lies in this link and the concept effecting it. (*ibid.*:593)

So Durkheim goes straight to the heart of Kantian ethics in asking how, with autonomy, the moral law is imperative, and in questioning appeal to reason's transcendental freedom.

But it is less that he rejects any supersensible freedom as such, more that he rejects it as the key to morals and ethics. The way therefore remains open for a reworking of Kantian autonomy, rather than a mere theft of the name. We must leave a notion of supersensible freedom in place as something central to Kant's articulation of autonomy, even in looking with Durkheim for an articulation of autonomy as rooted in the world, not set apart from it.

Delbos helps with another essential condition of reworking the one into the other. He argues that Kantianism not only does not oppose but sanctions a positive social and moral science (*ibid.*: 601). So the way is open to Durkheimian autonomy, at least in its aspect as an enlightened understanding of our social and moral world.

Delbos is in fact interested in a possible *rapprochement* between Kantian and Durkheimian approaches to ethics. But he also makes clear the sticking point. Kantianism does not oppose moral science as such, only if it goes beyond the limits of theoretical, scientific reason with "claims to furnish the supreme law of the determination of the will" (*ibid.*: 602), with "a definite rule that prescribes to the will the ends to choose" (*ibid.*: 603). This, on the contrary, is the task of practical reason.

On the general issue, about the necessity of "art", there is no dispute. The science of morals is not a science of ethics, which is a contradiction in terms. It is the key to ethics. It is the basis of understanding a reality resistant to change at will, and is the basis of acceptance, on practical rational grounds, of the real's rationale. If there is a dispute, it must concern the nature of practical reason itself and, in relation to Kantianism, the Durkheimian sticking point.

Delbos insists that it is impossible to "reduce the will to an object of scientific knowledge" (*ibid.*: 604). This cannot be to insist on a freedom of the will that is completely set apart from the world, in that it is completely unformed and unconditioned by it. He argues that moral science, in describing customs, institutions, etc., can get at the given of an already accomplished "*volonté voulue*" but never at the active direction of effort, in face of the given, of a "*volonté voulante*" (*ibid.*: 603). Yet how, in our situation and character, can the will as *volonté voulante* escape the influence of the "practico-inert" and the will as *volonté voulue*? Delbos is anxious to keep Kant's ethical insights fresh and alive, which cannot be done by freezing them in Kant's thought in its entirety. In particular, he argues, it is necessary to do something about the chasm separating the "sensible" from the "intelligible" aspects of our being, when, on the contrary, man "acts on his reason in the middle of a nature and of a society with which he is in direct relation" (*ibid.*: 604). But, again, in that case, the freedom and practical reason even of a supersensible will cannot be completely set apart from the world and completely unconditioned by it – that is precisely the general Durkheimian sticking point.

This has an especial bearing on the nature, status and origin of "the moral law" as the universalizing ethic, demanding everyone's recognition as a person, proclaimed in *The groundwork* in 1785, then a few years later, in 1789, in the *Declaration of the rights of man and the citizen*. It is not much in evidence amidst the "oppression" and "glistering misery", as Kant puts it, of ancient empires, and of course for Durkheim it is not man's but modern man's moral ideal. So it is important, in the conversion to Durkheimian autonomy, to press Kant for an account of how and why it is only the practical reason of a modern "age of enlightenment" that discovers the moral law.

Or does he believe that it has always been the moral law, in fact and not only in right, and if so is it an integral part of his approach? *The groundwork* involves a journey from the *bonne volonté* to the *volonté bonne*, as explained by Boutroux (1926: 298–302). Kant starts by going to the ordinary moral world, which is where he identifies the good with a good will (*bonne volonté*). He then arrives, through its analysis, various formulations of the moral law and the statement of the principle of autonomy, at, let us say, the ethical will (*volonté bonne*), so that Boutroux sees the one as the source of the other. This need not mean there has always been recognition of the moral law, and indeed Boutroux seems to imply some sort of evolutionary movement in commenting that "the good will is the beginning of the realization of the ethical will" (*ibid.*: 302).[6]

Kant himself seems to imply otherwise. His first formulation of the moral law comes early on, in discussing ordinary morality, when he suddenly just asserts that it is a morality of "universal law". He also just asserts that the ordinary reason of mankind "agrees completely" with his principle, and always has it "before its eyes" (Kant [1785] 1911: 402; t.67). This looks as if it involves an empirical claim, and as such, in a Durkheimian view, is mistaken. In a Durkheimian *Groundwork*, the good will is first and foremost attachment to one another and a group as ends, and its unconditioned, disinterested obedience to duty arises in this context, which need not at all mean a universalist duty recognizing everyone as a person. It is a different matter if "the will is essentially for Kant the power to act through the representation of rules [in which] the tendency to universalize the maxim is immanent", as suggested by Delbos ([1905] 1969: 298). This again implies a need for a sociohistorical, evolutionary account of the tendency's realization, and also fits in with Durkheim's emphasis on the rule as an essential element of morality both as law and as the virtue of self-discipline.

A simple solution to the problem is just to say that the issue of the recognition of the moral law as an anthropological fact has nothing to do with the issue of its justification by pure practical reason and an ethical principle of the right, which is what the Kantian project is "really" all about. At one point, in discussing Kantian versus evolutionary ethics, even Boutroux seems tempted by this line (1926: 316). The trouble with it is that it ignores Kant's interest in finding in the ordinary moral world the "source", as Boutroux himself says, or the "roots", as Durkheim would say, of the ethical will, the moral law and the coming of the kingdom of ends. The demand for a sociohistorical account of how we move towards recognition and realization of the law arises from within the Kantian project itself, and is not just imposed from outside by a Durkheimian approach.

If we now begin to rework Kantian as Durkheimian autonomy, let us return to the passage quoted by Durkheim from the second *Critique*, and to the distinction in the original text between will as *Wille* and *Willkür*.

Discovering the moral law as an objective necessary rationale

The ordinary sense of *Willkür* is arbitrariness, and is the background sense, as we have seen, of *sic volo, sic jubeo*. Kant does not make the distinction between the two aspects of the will fully explicit until *The metaphysics of morals* (1797), and even then makes it in more than one way. The complex, changing usage of the two terms in his work as a whole is explained by Delbos ([1905] 1969: 351, n.2).[7] But let us concentrate on it as a distinction between the legislative will (*Wille*) and the executive will (*Willkür*), such that, as in *The metaphysics of morals*: "Laws come from the legislative will, maxims from the executive will" (Kant [1797] 1914: 226; t.52).[8] The legislative will states the moral law's basic form and tests substantive maxims to see if they can pass as law. The executive will, the source of the maxims, is free to choose to act in light of the law.

Then the law can have authority over our rational rather than just sensible nature, in that the executive will seems in some sense part of our rational being rather than just all sensibility. This complicates Durkheim's criticisms. Yet does it meet them? It is one kind of reason binding another. It is also still the case, as he complains, that the law is not necessarily imperative.

Kant repeatedly talks of "obligation", as Durkheim indicates, as forcible, coercive, constraining. This is how the law is imperative for humans. It does not have such imperativeness for holy beings. He says in *The groundwork* that obligation has no reference to a "will whose maxims necessarily accord with the laws of autonomy", that is, "a *holy*, or absolutely good, will" (Kant [1785] 1911: 439; t.101). He says in the second *Critique* – in the section from which Durkheim quotes – that a holy will is "incapable of any maxims which conflict with the moral law", and that the reason that commands human will is "an inner but intellectual compulsion" (Kant [1788] 1913: 32; t.32–3). He says in *The metaphysics of morals* that an imperative "*makes* necessary" action conforming with the law, but that there is no imperative when the action "already inheres by an *inner* necessity in the acting subject (as in a holy being)" (Kant [1797] 1914: 222; t.48–9).

So it seems that a holy will can do no other than act on the necessity inherent in the law's very rationale. It is bound by such necessity, although free from any determination by the sensible world. The legislative will commanding humans is bound by the same necessity, and Kant says at one point that it "cannot be called either free or unfree". It is our executive will, in which we have to choose how to act in light of the law's necessitating constraints, that is "free" (*ibid.*: 226; t.52).

Durkheim does not quite capture all this in saying that the pure will would "move spontaneously towards duty by the impetus of its nature alone". The holy will represents an ideal, a morality without obligation. So it is like the ideal of spontaneity sought by Guyau. But it also represents the law as a necessary objective rationale. This is the law's authority, binding the autonomous ethical will, even as the legislative and not simply the executive will. The law is not something we are free to make up. Autonomy does not lie in the individual's arbitrary, anything goes, put-the-slave-on-a-cross *sic volo*. It lies in something transcending the individual. It lies in the individual as man, in the person's acceptance of a moral rationale that is necessary, objective, in its ideal way real, and an expression, as Boutroux says, of a collective, "common will" (1926: 304).

Kant often says that autonomy means that man makes the moral law and is its author. Again, this cannot mean that, as individuals, we merely make it up. Perhaps holy beings *express* a necessity and rationale inherent in their very nature. What about humans? Just as in *The groundwork* the moral law is somehow lodged in everyone and "before our eyes", the second *Critique* appeals to it "as if a fact" of which we are all *a priori* conscious (Kant [1788] 1913: 47; t.48), and as "a principle recognized by every natural human reason" (*ibid.*: 91; t.95). Perhaps, even so, this is not the universalism of 1789, but the kernel of it in the rule and sense of duty constituting an elemental, Durkheimian "fact" about all moralities. The essay on universal history insists that reason "requires trial, practice, and instruction in order gradually to progress from one stage of insight to another" (Kant [1784a] 1923: 19; t.30). So, in that the human legislative will reasons, "from one stage of insight to another", to the principle "before its eyes", autonomy is to *discover* the moral law.

Delbos again and again talks of "discovering" the law, if without making a special point of this. Durkheim does make a point of it, emphasizing, in the lectures on pragmatism, that given Kant's view of the fixity and impersonality of the law then "in a way we find it in ourselves, but we do not invent it; we make it only in that we discover it" (1955a: 48; t.13).[9]

Humanizing the moral law

Kant is obviously concerned, as is Durkheim, with working things out by ourselves as distinct centres of thought and action. *The groundwork* is perhaps the text that most emphasizes this aspect of things. But the essay on enlightenment also stresses the importance of public reason, and an enlightened milieu and collective mentality and "way of thinking" – *Denkungsart* (Kant [1784b] 1923: 35–42; 41–6). In the essay on universal history, the remark about reason's need of "practice and instruction" comes from a passage that explicitly sets aside the individual to focus on the development of our reason in society, over generations, and as a species. Kant is not an out-and-out individualist. He does not treat a life in common as automatically autonomy-threatening and "alien". On the contrary, through its development of our reason and the culture of an enlightened *Denkungsart*, a life in common is a condition of our autonomy.

Autonomy is also both individual and social in its character as an ideal. The Kantian good will, in the first part of *The groundwork*, lacks the Durkheimian good will's sense of attachment to one another and to a society as ends. However, this seems to come to the fore later on, when Kant discusses the formulation of the moral law that concerns "the end in itself", and that is the famous imperative: *"always treat humanity, whether in your own person or in the person of any other, never simply as a means, but always at the same time as an end"* (Kant [1785] 1911; 427–9; t.90–91). This still does not bring in, or does not obviously bring in, attachment to a society as an end. But it leads on to the statement of the central principle of his ethical system. He immediately writes, after baptizing it as "the principle of the *Autonomy* of the will":

> The concept of every rational being as one who must regard himself as making universal law by all the maxims of his will, and must seek to judge himself and his actions from this point of view, leads to a closely connected and very fruitful concept – namely, that of *a kingdom of ends*. (*ibid.*: 433; t.95).

He at once adds that by a kingdom he means "a systematic union [*Verbindung*] of different rational beings under common laws", so that a kingdom of ends is "a whole of all ends in systematic conjunction".[10] He also makes it clear that it is everyone's autonomous moral capacity, as a rational being, that qualifies everyone as a "law-making member in a kingdom of ends", and that is "the ground of the dignity of human nature" (*ibid*.: 435–6; t.96–7). So autonomy lies in membership of such a society – a "society of persons", as it is called by Renouvier (1869, vol. 1: 168), a "republic of persons" by Boutroux (1926: 373), a "republic of wills" by Delbos ([1905] 1969: 308). But have we got a Durkheimian attachment, not only to one another as ends but to society itself as an end and so as something more than an association of individuals?

It looks as if we have. *Verbindung* can just mean association. But it reads like union, in the emphasis, in the context, on "a whole of all ends in systematic conjunction", and in the concern, elsewhere, with an enlightened culture and with man's development in society, over the generations and as a species. It nonetheless has to be in a network of interrelated ends in which, as in our earlier discussion of Durkheim, society is an end that at the same time serves persons as ends, far from just "soaring above us" or treating its members "simply as means", and in which the idea of the person is a central, constitutive idea of the society itself.

In working his way through various formulations of the moral law, then coming to the principle of autonomy and the ideal of a kingdom of ends, Kant, surely, is working his way up to them. The principle of autonomy, as Delbos brings out, links the concepts of the categorical imperative and of transcendental freedom. But it also contains within it the idea of the person and the "closely connected, very fruitful" idea of a union of persons – the ideas, it can be argued, that drive the universalism of the moral law. And it is the dignity of the person – demanding reverence, but also a republic – that underlies the universalizing moral law as an objective necessary moral rationale and its authority as such. Thus the key to the Durkheimian–Kantian problem, of how with autonomy there is also authority, lies in the transcendence, neither of "Society" nor of "Reason", but of the person in a union of persons.

Yet even if it is the same solution to the problem, and so a help with conversion, is it not reached by completely different routes, ruling out conversion? Thus it still leaves us with Durkheim's criticism, that the Kantian moral law is not necessarily imperative, and this is because Kantian ethics, even if a cult of the person, is a cult not necessarily of the human person, but of the person as any "rational being", human, holy or whatever.

For Durkheim, as for Hume, ethics must be based on a secular scientific study of the human world, since morality is part and parcel of the human world, and it is mere metaphysics and fancy to approach it in any other way. But for Kant, with all his talk of rational and holy beings, is morality anchored in the human world at all? *The groundwork* might start in this world. But its account of the ordinary human good will is also predetermined, from the start, by its preoccupation with other-worldly rational and holy beings. This is why the Kantian "human" good will cannot be identified in terms of Durkheimian feelings of attachment to one another and to society as ends. It is also why caution is required in interpreting the formulation of the end in itself as in fact bringing in attachment to one another as ends, even attachment to society as an end. In discussing the formulation, Kant argues that ends need not be merely "subjective", that is, based on desires and impulsions. They can be "objective", in that they "depend on motives valid for every rational being". There is indeed such an objective end, in that "man, and in general every rational being, *exists* as an end in himself". There is then talk of the attitude towards persons – that is, rational beings – as being to "view" and to "treat" them as ends (Kant [1785] 1911: 427–9; t.90–91). There is no Durkheimian talk of positive social and moral feelings of attachment to one another as ends. Can Kant let in these feelings without "tainting" objectivity? Can he exclude them and still have an account that has anything to do with morality and its human motivations and concerns?

For Durkheim, as for Hume, reason cannot stir us up on its own, and moral motivation must be found in feeling. Kant is often accused of reliance on an emotionless, "apathetic" reason, and Boutroux insists that Kant in fact brings in sentiment as a moral motive, in the form of the sentiment of respect for the human person (Boutroux 1926: 338–41). Indeed, Delbos points out Kant's long, anxious search for a moral motive, which he finds not in reason on its own, but in sentiment (Delbos [1905] 1969: 274). It is again the sentiment of respect, indeed reverence, which is different from merely "subjective" inclinations, since it is a sentiment of respect that is both for the objective rationale of the law and generated by it. So if this is Kant's own way of humanizing, without subjectivizing, the ethic of the moral law, we can do the same with positive Durkheimian feelings of attachment to one another and to society as ends. They are attachments to objective ends, in that they are to persons and a union of persons, and can be injected into Kantian ethics without radical upset.

We can similarly go on to eliminate holy and other-worldly rational beings, or, rather, just to take them as our own, human representations of ideal and other-worldly possibilities. As Delbos sees it, Kant's use of them is as an analytical fiction and "in no way implies the existence of a hierarchy of rational beings outside of man" (*ibid*.: 252, n.4).

Then the moral law is man's law, nobody else's, and the person is the human person, nobody else. In Kantian as in Durkheimian ethics, morality is a human institution.

But if Kant is for anthropology, he is still insistent on "anthroponomy" (Kant [1797] 1914: 406; t.206). It is one thing to explain the conditions of man's progress to the good. It is quite another to determine, through principles of right, the good itself. Anthroponomy – a humanized metaphysics of morals – identifies the good through *sui generis* ethical critique. Anthropology deals only with "the subjective conditions in human nature that hinder men or help them in *fulfilling* the laws of a metaphysics of morals" (*ibid*.: 217; t.45).

Then how can we get any further? The Kantian kingdom declares, via anthroponomy, an ethical commonwealth of man. The Durkheimian republic declares, via anthropology, an ethical commonwealth of modern man. The autonomy of the one can be reworked, even so, as the autonomy of the other.

Man's philosophical history

"The philosophy of history was of far-reaching importance in the constitution of Kant's practical philosophy", according to Delbos ([1905] 1969: 239). So let us turn to the various essays dealing with this history.

The essay on universal history begins:

Whatever concept one may form of *freedom of the will* in a metaphysical context, its *appearances*, human actions, like all other natural events, are certainly determined in conformity with universal natural laws. (Kant [1784a] 1923: 17; t.29)

An example worthy of Durkheim points out how social statistics occur in conformity with such laws, regardless of anyone's freewill. The argument is then that, regardless of our particular intentions and decisions, there is a patterned, developmental history of man, in which we "unconsciously proceed toward an unknown natural end, as if following a guiding thread" (*ibid*.). The essay on speculative history draws on the evolutionism of the Scottish and French Enlightenment to peer into the dawn of human society; man is first a hunter–gatherer, then there is pastoralism and agriculture, and then the rise of luxury, oppression and "the glistering misery of the cities" (Kant [1786] 1923: 118–20; t.55–7).[11] The other essay continues at this point with recorded history, to see societies "in turn overthrown by their inherent deficiencies, always leaving behind a seed of enlightenment that developed more with each revolution" (Kant [1784a] 1923: 29–30; t.38–9). Kant's "philosophical history" does not seek to replace *detailed* empirical research. It constructs a larger, speculative, yet still empirically based account of human social evolution. Why, otherwise, not go to the Brothers Grimm, to peer into the mysteries of fairyland? But it constructs, as he adds, "a world history that is to a certain extent led by an *a priori* guiding thread" (*ibid*.: 30–31; t.39).

What is this guiding thread? How can Kant provide a sociohistorical explanation of progress towards the good, without threatening transcendental, supersensible freedom and the independence of ethics?

A solution is to see a spontaneous growth in freedom itself, a movement that, once started, gathers its own, ever-increasing momentum. Some such view is involved in the essay on enlightenment. There exists in us *an ability to think freely*, and "once nature has removed the hard shell from this kernel . . ., the kernel gradually reacts on a people's mentality (whereby they become increasingly able to *act freely*)" (Kant [1784b] 1923: 41–2; t.45–6).

It is also a vital part of Kant's general philosophical history that there arises an "age of enlightenment", increasingly conscious of the good, and opening the way to its realization in practice in an "enlightened age" (*ibid*.: 40; t.44–5). At the same time, of course, the new era's increasing consciousness of the good leaves behind the dark ages in which man stumbles, blindly, towards it. Yet how is this a spontaneous, self-generated change? It is "nature", after all, that removes the hard shell of traditional subjection from the kernel of a supersensible free ability.

It is nature, however, in the form of social processes. So a solution might be to treat the whole of culture and society as a *sui generis* intelligible reality. The movement from traditional to enlightened ways of thinking remains causal. But it is a causality within culture, and is intelligible in that it is essentially a movement of ideas, rather than of more "sensible", material conditions.

The solution, if applied to Durkheim, has to dematerialize the division of labour, population size and density, the struggle for existence, etc. It even runs into trouble with beliefs. They are forever run together as beliefs *and sentiments*, while a logic of such social "things" is not so much of clear ideas as of obscure needs, stirrings, aspirations. So the solution seems, in the case of Durkheim, a non-starter. What about the case of Kant?

The transition from hunter–gatherers to pastoralism–agriculture to despotic wealth is almost as if everything happens mechanically and is due to the forces and relations of production. It is certainly emphasized, in the essay on universal history, that a general motor of evolution lies in competitive struggle:

> *the means that nature uses to bring about the development of all man's capacities is the* **antagonism** *among them in society, as far as in the end this antagonism is the cause of law-governed order in society.* (Kant [1784a] 1923: 20; t.31–2)

This is what he famously calls our *"unsocial sociability"*. Perhaps it can let in the communitarian yet murderous tribal altruism of the Humean *homme de clan*. As Kant's key to ethical progress it comes across as self-love – and in the Rousseauan form not of *amour de soi* but of an ugly, egoistic *amour-propre*. But whatever its exact kind, unsocial sociability helps to power a general empirical history of man's development of man's law. Like Durkheim's, it is an account that very much involves a "sensible" and material social causation. It does not just involve ideas, or an effervescence of collective supersensible freedom.

Thus another essay, on theory and practice, says of long-term moral progress:

> [It] depends not so much on what *we* do . . .; instead, it depends on what human *nature does in and with us so as to compel us on*

to a path that we ourselves would not readily follow. (Kant [1793] 1923: 310; t.87)

Kant repeats, in the conclusion, his belief in "the nature of things" to compel man along such a path. Yet he also emphasizes his belief in a theory, saying where it ought to lead, that "derives from the principle of right" (*ibid.*: 313; t.89). So he still asserts the independence of ethics, even if, in his own social history, supersensible freedom can seem to disappear.

But if it is there, nonetheless, it is still possible to see and explain a development and emergence of the human ideal and of commitment to its moral law. This is to explain development of the will. It can therefore be to incorporate, as Durkheim demands, legislative ethical reason within the world and the world's law. If so, the way is clear to rework autonomy as enlightened acceptance of the moral dynamic of our time.

Man's *telos* and modern man's consciousness of it

The kingdom of ends is itself an end. Indeed, it is man's *telos*, or overarching, final end (*Endzweck*). Does an "end" have to be a self-aware, consciously intended aim, project and purpose? Kant does not think that animals go around with such purposes. Yet he argues in the essay on universal history that a science of living beings and creatures requires understanding of how their *"natural capacities are destined to develop completely and in conformity with their end"*, and adds that in a teleology of nature "an organization that does not achieve its end [*Zweck*] is a contradiction" (Kant [1784a] 1923: 18; t.30). Even so, does man's *telos* have to be a self-aware purpose? Yet the whole point of the essay is that, whatever our particular intentions, it can still be that we "unconsciously proceed toward an unknown natural end [*Naturabsicht*]" (*ibid.*:17; t.29), and this concerns the full development of our reason *"in the species, not in the individual"* (*ibid.* 18; t.30). So the human ideal, as man's *telos*, can still be unknown to individuals and indeed whole societies – until, as part of its own unfolding, man is at last conscious of it in an age of enlightenment. We read in *The groundwork*:

Teleology views nature as a kingdom of ends; ethics views a possible kingdom of ends as a kingdom of nature. In the first case the kingdom of ends is a theoretical Idea used to explain what exists. In the second case it is a practical Idea used to bring into existence what does not exist but can be made actual by our conduct. (Kant [1785] 1911: 436, n.1; t.98, n.1)

Man's overarching, final end is thus a natural end, in that it is a realization of a kingdom of ends as a kingdom of nature. But although the practical idea envisaging this possibility helps to bring it about, it does not follow that it always does so, since it does not follow that it is always man's conscious, self-aware *telos*. Again it can still be that most of the time and, as in the essay on theory and practice, we are compelled "on to a path that we ourselves would not readily follow". Kant's teleology precisely does not commit him to the view, which Durkheim so much criticizes, that history is driven by an always conscious end.

Let us now turn to this teleology in the third and final *Critique*, which can be seen as the completion of Kant's system. It can also be seen as motivated, in its urge to find a teleology of all of nature, animate or inanimate, by a religious horror of just viewing the universe as a blind, meaningless "mere mechanism".

In introducing the question of a teleology in all of nature, Kant sees two possibilities if we want more than the "mere mechanism" of efficient causation and want to bring in the causality of ends and purposes. Teleology could come in as a "regulative" principle, to view something through an "*analogy* with the causality in terms of purposes, without presuming to *explain* it in terms of that causality". Or teleology transforms into a real, "constitutive" principle of explanation if we really do attribute final causes to nature. But we then bring "a new causality into natural science, even though in fact we only borrow this causality from ourselves and attribute it to other beings without wishing to assume that they and we are of the same kind" (Kant [1790] 1913: 360–61; t.236–7).

The introduction is as if teleology – whether regulative or constitutive – concerns ends only as intentional, conscious purposes. The situation changes as the discussion develops. Kant contrasts mere mechanisms with "organized beings", in which "*everything is an end [Zweck] and reciprocally also a means*" (*ibid*.: 376: t.255). Each of its parts not only exists *"for the sake* of the others and a whole", but is "an organ that *produces* the other parts (so that each reciprocally produces the other)", and there is a *"formative* force" contained within the organized being, organizing it and propagating itself (*ibid.*: 373–4; t.253). So it is not only that ends are not necessarily conscious purposes, but that there is an obvious sense of a whole that is itself an end, and of an active dynamic within it. It is also in this context, with its emphasis on an organized–organizing whole, that there is a reference to the human social world and a transformation of a people into a *Verbindung* (*ibid.*: 375, n.1; t. 254, n.38) – confirming the idea of it as a union rather than just an association of persons.[12]

If we now concentrate on the case that interests us, the human social world, Kant continues to work with an account of man's unconscious progress, in and through his nature, towards man's end. Moreover, he identifies and endorses man's end, not through an independent principle of right, but through the anthropology-cum-anthroponomy of philosophical history. His discussion identifies it step by step. In the first it is not happiness but culture. It is then man as a social and moral being. It is, finally, morality plus happiness in conformity with it.

Like Durkheim, Kant attacks appeal to happiness *per se* as the end guiding man's development. Happiness is an idea that man formulates so diversely and changes so often that it is a completely "wavering concept" (*ibid.*: 430; t.317). At bottom and like Durkheim, Kant looks for something within nature and within man, yet that also *prepares man* to transcend and master his nature. Then where Durkheim always finds this in "society", Kant at first finds it in "culture". This is because he dissociates it from any particular purpose. Culture is the development of "man's aptitude in general for setting himself purposes" (*ibid.*: 431; t.319). Kant emphasizes, in a passage Durkheim might have noted, the necessity of a culture of discipline. This lets us order and select our purposes in its "liberation of the will from the despotism of desires" (*ibid.*: 432; t.319). But he also emphasizes a culture of skill.

We can see, underlying Kant's argument about the development of a culture of skill, the antagonism of unsocial sociability and the struggle for existence in a division of labour. His explicit argument is that it is difficult for such a culture to develop without inequality, oppression and the troubles and conflicts of a class-divided society. He again talks of a "glistering misery". But it is a misery that is part of our progress as a species; "nature still achieves its own purpose, even if that purpose is not ours" (*ibid.*: 432; t.320).

Kant sets out "the formal condition under which nature can alone achieve this final aim":

> [It] is that constitution of human relations where the impairment to freedom that results from the mutually conflicting freedom is countered by lawful authority within a whole called *civil society*. For only in this constitution of human relations can our natural predispositions develop maximally. But this constitution requires something further, . . . [a system of all states in] a *cosmopolitan* whole. (*ibid.*)

He is then ready to go on to identify man's end as man "as a moral being" (*ibid.*: 435; t.323) and as "*man under moral laws*" (*ibid.*: 445; t.334).

This is *not* to identify it as man in complete compliance with moral laws (*ibid.*: 448, n.1; t.338, n.39). It still means trying to comply with these as far as possible, and so takes us to the ideal of the kingdom of ends as a kingdom of virtue. It also takes Kant to man's end as virtue plus happiness. Durkheim, too, wants a way of bringing happiness back into the moral life, though not in this way. Their reunion, in Kant's case, leads to the claim that it is "necessary that we assume a moral cause of the world: in other words, that there is a God" (*ibid.*: 450; t.340).

Let us leave God for the moment, and concentrate on how we can let in a supersensible freedom while insisting that morals and ethics must be rooted in the world and the world's law, and not declared completely independent.

All the way through the arguments about happiness versus culture, skill, discipline, civil society and man under moral laws, man's end does not seem derived from independent ethical principles at all. Civil society, for example, is identified and endorsed as a condition of continuing cultural development, through sorting out conflicts and getting cohesion. Moreover, the freedom it delivers might be taken as sociopolitical, without anything obviously transcendental about it. In fact, the issue of supersensible freedom underlies even this part of the account and moves into full view when man's end is identified as man as a moral being. How is such freedom described?

The essay on enlightenment talks of a kernel within everyone, which is the *ability* to think freely. Similarly, the third *Critique*, when identifying man's end as man as a moral being, sees man as the only natural being in whom we can cognize, as part of his constitution, a freedom that is "a supersensible ability" (*ibid.*: 435; t.323).

Freedom as a supersensible ability is not a power that exists, fixed and fully formed forever. It is a potential to be developed, a power to be realized, so that for Kant "freedom increasingly ceases to be a thing, *res aeterna*", as Delbos emphasizes ([1905] 1969: 597). Moreover, both as potential and power, and as in the journey Boutroux describes from the good will to the ethical will, it is a collective supersensible freedom. It is not a merely individual affair. Nor does it just grow of its own, supersensible accord. It grows in interaction with the world, as part of the world and the world's law. It involves the nature pushing in and through us and unconsciously to *prepare man* for man's end, autonomy as a person in a union of persons and under the authority of the moral law. In sum, the development of reason and the legislative will to discover the universalist ethic of the person – like the development of the executive will to revere it in a universalist cult of the person – is sociohistorical and empirically conditioned.

This eliminates the independence of ethics, as an anthroponomy that does not need any basis in anthropology. It does not eliminate supersensible freedom, or a role for practical as against theoretical reason. On the contrary, it is here that, instead of trying to Durkheimianize Kant, it might be necessary to Kantianize Durkheim.

The kernel of a free ability in everyone's constitution can remain supersensible, empirically unconditioned, and cognizable, as if a fact, only by practical reason – even though the end that, as a formative force, it contains *in potentia* and its development towards this are empirically conditioned and determinable by theoretical reason. This end is a union of persons of which everyone, as a human person, can be a full *sui juris*, civic, law-making member, since the power to become so lies in the free ability in everyone's human constitution. A necessary part of the modern republican demand to extend the full status of a person and a citizen to all is that all have the potential to qualify for the status. An important, perhaps necessary appeal is the Kantian one, to the free ability inherent in us all, cognizable by practical reason whatever the arguments of reactionary versus republican anthropology.[13]

Why cannot practical reason go on to become a completely independent anthroponomy, claiming to deduce from the kernel of our free ability, and as an eternal ethical truth, its full social and moral implications in a kingdom of ends? Even if they do not stop this as a genuine Kantian route, the arguments here still succeed if they point to and keep open another Kantian route, convertible to Durkheimian autonomy, the route through anthropology and history.

Apart from anything else, everyone's free ability might be a necessary but not a sufficient condition of justifying a republic, and it is questionable if, in his own time, Kant in fact justifies this. His views on man as woman suggest otherwise. Indeed, most of his fellow men (labourers, servants, etc.) also seem excluded from citizenship (Kant [1793] 1923: 295, n.1; t.76, n.1).[14] Yet he again talks, in the same essay, of the insights of higher stages of morality, in which "one can see further still and can make more rigorous judgements regarding what man is in comparison with what he ought to be" (*ibid*.: 310; t.87). And what about the oppression, inequality and "glistering misery" that he sees not just in ancient empires but in his own age, and that he both condones *and* condemns?

Kant's ambivalent account of a "progress" in inequality owes much to Rousseau. In commenting on the ills of modern society he says that "Rousseau was not so far from right in preferring the state of savages" (Kant [1784a] 1923: 26; t.36). It is untrue that he just criticizes early man's stationariness and "bovine contentment" (Kant [1786] 1923: 120; t.57). The problem is "the inevitable conflict between culture and the human race as a *physical* species whose every individual member ought fully to fulfil its vocation". The question is: "how must culture progress so as to develop the capacities belonging to mankind's vocation as a *moral* species and thus end the conflict within himself as a moral and a natural species?" (*ibid*.: 116; t.54). The answer is: "finally, after many revolutions of reform, nature's supreme objective – a universal *cosmopolitan state*, the womb in which all of the human species' original capacities will be developed – will at last come to be realized" (Kant [1784a] 1923: 28; t.38).[15]

The vision of a time in which the conflict will at last be overcome between man's development as a species and everyone's developing and flourishing as a person is also the vision of *The division of labour*. It means that a human *patrie*, realizing the human ideal, is the only *society* that autonomy as enlightened acceptance can endorse without fundamental criticism. It involves an argument and a hope that our existing society contains within its rationale not only the human ideal itself but an impetus, despite everything, towards its realization. It also means that this is the only *rationale* that autonomy as enlightened acceptance can endorse, and indeed as a self-reflexive, constitutive part of the rationale, with everyone's social and moral status as a person at its centre. It is the way in which Kantian autonomy can convert, more or less, into Durkheimian autonomy.

Chapter Nine

A secular religion?

The transformation, by secular ethics, of the kingdom of ends into a republic of persons runs up against Kant's insistence that God and an immortal soul are necessary postulates of morality. Durkheim gives short shrift to the immortal soul – an "illusion" (1897a: 228; t.213).[1] He is more attentive to how to dispense with God, in that he is convinced that it cannot be to dispense with religion. Even in the modern secular world there is and will always be a need for some sort of "religion".

Let us try to concentrate on the meaning of this claim for ethics and morals, and steer clear, as far as possible, of controversies over Durkheim's account of religion itself. Then it can be seen to involve three main concerns, and let us examine them in turn. They are to do with core beliefs, faith and sacredness.

Core beliefs

The division of labour insists: "In the beginning . . . everything social is religious" ([1893b] 1902b: 143; t.169). But other functions gradually break away from it and religion encompasses an ever smaller part of social life. It does not cease to exist, since "to the extent that all the other beliefs and practices assume a less and less religious character, the individual becomes the object of a sort of religion" – "a cult which, like every strong cult, already has its superstitions", "if you like, a shared faith" (*ibid.* 147; t.172). Just before all this we read:

> It is indeed an established fact that when a conviction of some strength is shared by the same community of men it inevitably

takes on a religious character; it inspires in consciences the same reverential respect as properly religious beliefs. It is therefore highly likely . . . that religion corresponds to an equally, very central region of the *conscience commune*. (*ibid.* 143; t.169)

So religion is a matter of core collective beliefs. So it is also a matter, since the two go together, of strong, intense sentiments – of the belief-cum-sentiment of a "conviction". There will always be a need for some sort of religion, because there will always be a need for morality, which is nothing without such convictions. So the moral-religious core of things is also a matter of obligatoriness. Durkheim insists on this from the beginning, in his reviews of Spencer and Guyau, and again in the article on the definition of religious phenomena:

> *Phenomena called religious consist in obligatory beliefs, connected with well-defined practices which relate to given objects of the beliefs.* As for religion, it is a more or less organized and systematized whole made up of phenomena of this kind. ([1899a(ii)] 1969c: 159–60; t.93)

The obligatoriness of core collective beliefs remains part and parcel of the concern with the sacred in *The elementary forms* (1912a: 65, n.1; t.63, n.68). It is also part and parcel of the idea of "mythological truths", which is so crucial to the argument of the 1913–14 lectures on pragmatism (1955a: 184; t.91).

It is muddle-headed to see the modern liberal ethic as an exception to all this, because of its emphasis on freedom, diversity and tolerance, just as it is muddle-headed to criticize it as intolerant and so "self-contradictory". Liberalism would not be a morality without core convictions, and without intolerance in its insistence on these. Liberalism, as a great historical social and moral movement, has fought to outlaw and ban one thing after another, in a passion for justice and outrage at injustice, but above all in the demand to recognize everyone as a person. Durkheim himself drives the point home in the article on the Dreyfus Affair. The ethic of the human person is a religion, and a "religion which tolerates acts of sacrilege abdicates all sway over people's conscience" ([1898c] 1970a: 274; t.69).

Tolerance must still remain a liberal virtue. There are many things, on issues that matter to us, that we see as wrong, yet that we also see it as wrong to try to prohibit. We can then be quite precise about a point where, in the Durkheimian view, and even in the case of liberalism, morality and religion join up. It is where core convictions define something not just as wrong but as an intolerable wrong that it is right to try to prohibit.

It is impossible to be precise in drawing up a complete, definitive map of where liberalism hits moral bottom lines and arouses us, right-eously, against intolerable wrongs. This is not just because liberalism, like any great social movement, develops and evolves. It is also be-cause of the individualistic altruism that is built into it, and in which we can each become zealous, even fanatical, about a particular good cause. But there is at least this difference between a liberal and a hair-brained fanatic: the latter hits too many bottom lines on too many issues too soon. If liberalism is a religion fired by intolerant, core con-victions, it nonetheless also has to be one in which we are each ready, on an extensive range of issues, to settle for accommodation, compro-mise and the mediocrity of moral *politique*. Indeed, this might be one of the most important, intolerant core convictions of liberalism as a moral *mystique*.[2]

There is certainly much to explore in Durkheim's concern with convictions at the core of any morality, including secular liberal mo-rality, and his talk of "religion" emphasizes an essential feature of mo-rality that liberal ethical theory too often ignores or plays down. It need not seem talk of anything that seriously bars the way to a secular social and moral world. What about his concern with faith?

Let us first comment on his review of Wundt's *Ethics*. Let us then go into the challenge to his whole outlook represented by Guyau, in two books that went through innumerable editions, *A sketch of a morality without obligation or sanction* and *The non-religion of the future*.[3]

The non-religion of the future

Wundt is much duller than Guyau. His book has only a single chapter on religion, in fact, on religion and morality, and let us concentrate on his view of their future.

Durkheim duly reports Wundt's account of an evolution in which, as "morality separates itself from religion, religion seems to try to draw nearer to morality"; religion "moralizes its concepts so well that they stand as useful auxiliaries for ethics"; indeed, religion is modelled "in the end" on morality (1887c: 117–18; t.94–5).

Wundt himself writes:

> The religious thus increasingly joins with the moral in an inseparable unity, but one at the same time purified of all ethically worthless elements. Religion and morality are no longer different in their content, but only in the *point of view* which they adopt towards this content. Religion becomes, as Kant expresses it, the moral law seen as divine command. (Wundt 1886: 86; t. vol. 1, 123–4)[4]

But Durkheim ignores Wundt's view of where all this might lead: "nothing proves the impossibility of some later stage of moral life in which morality completely cuts free from its religious roots" (*ibid.*: 87; t.125–6).

It is true that in the first edition of his *Ethics* (1886), the edition that Durkheim read and reviewed, Wundt is circumspect about the matter. He comes out fully into the open in the third edition:

> Finally, in a last stage, which in general we may well see as already reached by civilized peoples, moral opinions separate from religion to form a completely autonomous domain. Moral precepts now appear as norms which have value independent of any religious conviction, and which in the process become so dominant that religious conviction by and large disappears. (Wundt [1886] 1903: 105)

So Wundt does not assist with Durkheim's campaign against a non-religion of the future, even if he does not do much to challenge it and is easily brushed aside. Let us now turn to the confrontation with Guyau.

Durkheim's review of *The non-religion* acknowledges Guyau's insight and originality, yet is also highly critical. There is a response from Guyau's stepfather, Fouillée (1889: 135–7), but not from Guyau himself, who was already very ill and died in 1888 at the age of 33. Durkheim complains that although Guyau treats religion as a social institution he does not see it as first and foremost this. He is too "intellectualist", preoccupied with religion as metaphysical speculation about the world. He fails to understand that its beliefs are obligatory, that they are above all practical, anchored in pre-existing social concerns, that they attach us to society rather than just to one another, and that they lie in the need for and power of faith (1887b: 307–11; t.34–8). Are the criticisms justified?

Guyau's introduction sets out a basic way in which he sees religion. This is: "every historical, positive religion has three distinctive, essential elements." These are: myths, dogmas, and cults and rites. Myths try to explain natural as well as historical facts. Dogmas are "symbolic ideas and imaginative beliefs, impressed on faith as absolute truths". Cults and rites are "more or less immutable practices, seen as having a miraculous power to affect the course of things". It is in terms of these three elements that religion is distinguishable from mere philosophy: "A religion without myths, without dogmas, without a cult and without rites" would just "dissolve into *metaphysical* hypotheses" (Guyau 1887: xiii; t.10).

Hence a central sense of Guyau's non-religion of the future is the withering away of traditional *positive* religion – myths, dogmas, cults and all. It is still the case that "something of religion" will remain – the most fundamental thing of all. This is its expression of sociability, its concern with the joining of lives in the assembly and community of "the church". The sociohistorical development of enlightenment can throw out myths, dogmas and cults of traditional religion, but keep, in secularized form, the community of the church.

There is another way in which Guyau sees religion as social, and which helps to explain the sub-title of his book, "*étude sociologique*". Religious ideas are "conceived *by analogy with human society*" (*ibid.*: ii; t.2). They are, he says, "sociomorphic". It is because they are sociomorphic that they constitute a sociology. But it is "a mythical or mystical sociology". It is also a "universal sociology" – a mode of thought about natural forces, animals, the dead, spirits, good and evil, the origins of things, etc., that can extend to all questions in all realms. He writes, in offering a formulation of this basic theme:

religion is a *physical, metaphysical* and *moral explanation* of all things by analogy with human society, in an imaginative and symbolic form. It is, in a word, a *universal sociological explanation, in mythical form.* (*ibid.*: iii; t.2)

The first part of his book, with its chapters on "religious physics",

211

"religious metaphysics" and "religious ethics", concentrates on the evolution of religion as a sociomorphic and so, in its mystical, meta-phorical way, a sociological mode of thought.

The idea of society as a model of beliefs, concepts and categories does not show up in Guyau's essays on time (1890). It is introduced and explored, rather than really developed in *The non-religion of the future*. It is reported without comment by Fouillée (1889: 131–2), who criticized the idea many years later (1911b: 81–93). But this criticism is directed at the idea as pushed and developed by none other than Durkheim himself, in the essay on primitive classification:

> It was because men were grouped, and thought of themselves in the form of groups, that in their ideas they grouped other things, and in the beginning the two modes of grouping were merged to the point of being indistinct . . . Things were thought to be inte-gral parts of society, and it was their place in society which deter-mined their place in nature. ([1903a(i)] 1969c: 456; t.82–3)

The early review is positively unreceptive to the idea, condemning it as part of Guyau's unsociological intellectualism (1887b: 307; t.34). Durkheim insists on religion as an expression of practical interests and sentiments.

Guyau introduces his book by emphasizing its concern with reli-gion as social sentiment. He writes, poetically, that this enlarges and "reaches to the stars" (Guyau 1887: i; t.1). Hence Durkheim's remark: "Religious society is not human society extended ideally to beyond the stars" (1887b: 310; t.36).

His point is that primitive gods form a society of their own, separate from human society, and are far from just and benevolent ideal beings. This is a strange criticism. Although Guyau says of religion, "in the beginning it was only an extension of society", it is to insist that its extension of human society "was not the perfection of this society" (Guyau 1887: 82–3; t.114–15). His argument, on the con-trary, is that primitive gods are far from ideal beings. They reflect the divisions and faults of humanity. But a moralization of religion takes place in which it more and more becomes the expression of a human ideal, and reaches for the stars in that God is identified with the good and "appears as a sort of mystic realization of the universal society *sub specie aeterni*" (*ibid.*: 102; t.135).

Hence religion's journey to beyond the stars is also to its own annihilation, via mythical physics and metaphysics to secular science and philosophy, and via mythical ethics to secular enlightened humanism. It is not so much the power of myth over reason that holds up the journey. It is the power of the dogmas and cults that entrench the myths in an obligatory faith.

The opening chapter of the second part of Guyau's book has as its title and topic, "Dogmatic faith". He emphasizes its intolerance and "obligatory credulity" (*ibid.*: 104; t.136). He discusses its insistence on texts that must be revered, doctrines that must not be questioned, practices that must not be deviated from:

> The sphere of dogmas and sacred rites can widen or narrow; discipline can be loose with some, with others a regulation even of the dietary regime; but there must always be a minimum of absolute dogmas and absolutely necessary practices without which there could no longer exist a truly religious church. (*ibid.*: 111–12; t.145)

It is little good just appealing to reason in all this. It is difficult to persuade the faithful to listen, or to sway with argument anyone who "believes he is in error the moment he calls certain dogmas or authorities in question" (*ibid.*: 108; t.141). The issue for Guyau is not, simplistically, the power of reason in itself and of free, critical enquiry. It is the development of a commitment to reason and to such enquiry, through complex, long-term sociohistorical processes.

These are both internal and external to religion. Durkheim has cause for complaint, in that Guyau's discussion of the external, wider social processes is weak and unsystematic. These processes include the rise of science, economic change and, not least, the French Revolution – something that, far from being "over", is still going on, and which, far from being a "new religion", is the "first liberal and egalitarian movement in the world outside of any religion" (*ibid.*: 206; t.251).

Guyau comes into his own in discussing internal processes, undermining religion from within, as, above all, with the emergence of Protestantism. This is still in part an instance of recurrent heretical challenges to orthodoxy, essential to sustain a traditional faith as a living faith, and it still involves "dogmas which it is impious to reject" (*ibid.*: 154; t.194). But in its at first hesitant commitment to the authority of individual conscience, Protestantism "contains in germ the negation of all positive religion" (*ibid.*: 154; t.194).

Hand in hand with this, the critical examination of sacred texts and doctrines entails a move away from naïve, literal belief in even the most fundamental of them. There is instead a search for a "symbolic faith", in which God Himself ends up as poetry – a beautiful, inspiring, even forceful way of expressing things, yet not the reason for accepting them. It is by our own judgement that we shall find and revere the justice in the word of Christ, "and this word is not true because it is divine, it is divine because it is true" (*ibid.*: 147; t.185).

Do we then need myth? We might as well concentrate on truth. "The real world, that is, the moral along with the physical world, should be fully sufficient for our thought" (*ibid.*: 152; t.191). Guyau is withering in his criticism of parodies of religion that appeal to its outwards forms when the core of faith has gone. Nor is a search for a new faith a brighter prospect than attempts to hang on to the old. The demands of freedom, conscience and the human ideal are not the inventions of philosophers, but moral realities, built into the nature and dynamic of the modern world.

The third part of Guyau's book tries to work out a picture of modern society developing and flourishing in accordance with its ideals. This part, like the book itself, announces "The non-religion of the future". Yet the opening chapter emphasizes religious individualism, while the next emphasizes the continuation of religious society.

The other chapters go on (and on) about the principal metaphysical hypotheses that replace dogma, and help to let in Durkheim's accusation of intellectualism. They nonetheless offer a clue to the religiousness of "non-religion". Whatever else it is, it is not the traditional trinity of dogma, cult and myth.

Guyau's "religious individualism" revolves round the ideal of *anomie*. He refers to the ideal, in his earlier book, of moral *anomie*, and defines it as "the absence of universal, fixed and apodictic rule". He continues: "the ideal of all religion must be to move towards *religious anomie*, towards the emancipation of the individual, towards the deliverance of his thought, more precious than life, towards the suppression of all dogmatic faith under whatever form it is concealed" (*ibid.*: 323; t.374–5).

Thus "religious individualism" in an enlightened anomic society has nothing to do with religious pluralism in the softheaded liberal sense of a coexistence of all manner of dogmatic faiths within any of which we are free to imprison our minds. It involves a society in which religions of this kind have withered away. Then what is religious about "religious individualism"? It cannot just be freedom to think and philosophize, since Guyau explicitly rejects a reduction of religion to philosophy. Rather, it lies in the sociability and community essential to religion, in its union of persons.

Just as Guyau emphasizes this in the introduction, he emphasizes it again. "The most enduring practical idea at the basis of the religious spirit . . . is the idea of association", so that "religions rightly describe themselves as *associations* and as *churches* (that is, assemblies)" (*ibid.*: 339–40; t.391–2). "Religious individualism" must have meaning in terms of the continuation but at the same time transformation of "religious society", and it has this meaning in Guyau's ideals of individual freedom and diversity in and through an enlightened community as a "true church". The error of traditional religions is their picture of society as homogeneous, as made up of individuals "forming a single intellectual and moral type" (*ibid.*: 341; t.393). But what, for Guyau, is the secret of freedom plus diversity plus union?

It is a secret that, if Durkheim noted it, his review does not give away, for it is, at least in part, the division of social labour. Guyau latches on to this as a solution to modern demands, but again without really pushing and developing the idea, and without Durkheim's deeper understanding of the division of labour as a dynamic that also helps to generate modernity's demands. It is nonetheless of interest that he focuses on the division of labour within and between groups. In discussing a range of these, he takes associations for scientific enquiry as exemplars and "the type to which every association will without doubt draw nearer in the future". They are free, voluntary associations, based on a division of labour that is also the basis of their co-operation and cohesion. "These societies are true churches", their "community of inquiry creates a fraternity like the community of faith, but often superior and more fertile", and "they reconcile the best elements of individualism and socialism" (*ibid.*: 341–2; t.393–5).

Guyau insists on talking of a "non-religion of the future" as an antidote to all the talk of a "religion of the future", which he sees as hypocritical in the way it appeals to myth and symbolism to seem to support traditional religion when in reality undermining it (*ibid.*: xii; t.9).[5] His own ideal is both religious and non-religious, since it aspires to the essentials of religion while unambiguously abandoning the characteristics that mark out and mar traditional faith – not just myth but, underlying and sustaining it, dogma and the cult.

So Guyau links enlightened "religious society" with the free and diverse society of a division of labour. Durkheim, in contrast, always locks religious society into a community of belief, into the core convictions of a *conscience collective*, including the core belief in the individual as man of the modern *conscience collective*. Does not Guyau also see the need for a community of belief, above all, in the modern world, in the individual as man? Perhaps – but not as a cult of man, and not as an obligatory, dogmatic faith.

Modernity transforms religion: "We are coming to love God in man ... The man of evolution is truly the Man–God of Christianity" (*ibid.*: 170; t.211). But God become man is not man become God. Guyau is all against mystification, not least this remystification. "Love of humanity is one thing, idolatry of man another ... A sincere, enlightened love of humanity is the very opposite of such idolatry and would be compromised and corrupted by it" (*ibid.*: 391; t.445).

Durkheim obviously misrepresents Guyau in accusing him of a failure to see the obligatoriness of religious beliefs. The obligatory and dogmatic character of traditional religious belief is precisely one of Guyau's main objections to it, at least as something that has any place in the modern world. If there is anything behind the accusation, it must concern the place of such belief in the modern world. In fact, Guyau, like Durkheim, looks to the development of a secular, scientifically and empirically based morality that "will more and more suffice in the ordinary course of life" (*ibid.*: 374; t.427). But it is also here that they part company.

Both emphasize, as part of enlightenment, recognition of the limits of knowledge, even in the effort to extend it. For both, therefore, a question that must always arise in enlightenment concerns the need to go beyond knowledge in order to act. Durkheim's answer is that we then need to act on the basis of faith. Guyau's answer is that the very meaning of enlightenment is that we must then act on the basis of uncertainty and accept "the admissibility of doubt where things are subject to doubt" (*ibid.*: 328; t.379).

Thus his *Sketch of a morality without obligation* is as much as anything a sketch of a morality without faith. In enlightenment all faith is bad faith:

In the domain of thought there is nothing more moral than truth; and when it cannot be secured by science, there is nothing more moral than doubt . . . But, it will be said, if it is irrational to affirm in thought as true that which is doubtful, it is still sometimes right and necessary to affirm it in *action*. Perhaps, yet it is always a provisional situation and a conditional affirmation: I do this only in *supposing* it my duty, even my absolute duty. (Guyau 1885: 127–8; t.63)[6]

"Happy are those today to whom a Christ could say, 'Oh, ye of little faith!'" (*ibid.*: 235; t.143).

Faith versus doubt

To see what is at stake, we need to try to sort out ideas of "belief", "certainty", "dogma" and "faith". Both Durkheim and Guyau often run them together, in the way, for example, they talk of "dogmatic faith". But it is not an accident that Durkheim so often runs "beliefs and sentiments" together. "Belief" includes an emotive dimension. It is not simply cognitive as in the idea of knowledge as true justified belief. It might be strange or redundant to say: "I know and very much believe that $E = mc^2$". It need not be strange or redundant to say: "I know and very much believe that there is a God". Unlike "I know", "I believe" expresses a strength of feeling that is appropriate in the case. Similarly, with the arrival of Durkheimian and Guyauan enlightenment, we could say we not only know but very much believe that the modern social ideal is the human ideal. Indeed, even when we have a more or less established knowledge of the human ideal as the ethic of our time – and Durkheim often argues as if we already have such a knowledge – there is still a need to believe in the ideal, given his view of the practical, motivational power of sentiment, rather than just reason on its own. So he does not necessarily imply that the human ideal is not grounded in a knowledge, even in continuing to discuss and emphasize it as a belief.

What about "certainty"? Again it need not simply describe a cognitive state in which we possess or claim to possess knowledge and truth, but can include a feeling of conviction, with practical, motivational implications. So it can again mean that, even with knowledge, we still need certainty. Indeed, this is the starting point of Ollé-Laprune's *On moral certainty* (1880). It also fits in with Durkheim's discussion of the subject in the lectures on pragmatism. He emphasizes "the necessitating character of the true idea", so that "we feel obliged [*contraints*] to adhere to the truth" (1955a: 201–2; t.101).

Guyau rules out obligatory faith and credulity. His ideal of a morality without obligation does not rule out the obligatoriness of truth. It instead involves two basic things. One is that he looks for a more positive sense of a spontaneous feeling, impulsion, power, and rejects the Kantian sense of obligatoriness as a negative, necessitating constraint – which is also criticized by Fouillée ([1883] 1921: 166). The other is that he limits the obligatoriness of a collective, social ethic to what can be established "with sufficient rigour" (Guyau 1885: 3, 33; t.3, 97); "belief beyond the range of our knowledge can never have anything obligatory about it" (*ibid*.: 122; t.58). Beyond it lies, or ought to lie, the ethical world of pluralism, doubt and *anomie*, where there is "the greatest possible diversity of action and the greatest variety of ideals pursued" (*ibid*.: 231; t.139).

The irony is not simply that Guyau's social and moral ideal of *anomie* is taken up by Durkheim and transformed into a social and moral malaise. It is also that Guyauan *anomie* is in a way itself a Durkheimian ideal. On the one hand, there is the collective ethic of the modern human ideal, linked up with a division of labour. On the other hand, it is an integral part of this that we each have our own views, that we are distinct, autonomous centres of thought and action, and that there is a "growing multitude of individual disagreements".

In any case, Guyauan enlightenment spreads everywhere, in that the pluralism of moral as of religious *anomie* is not a softheaded liberal licence for retreat into private worlds of dogma and faith. Enlightenment, with its commitment to free thought, and by its very nature as an ideal, opens up everything to discussion. Nothing should be protected as a "dogma", that is, as a taken for granted, not to be questioned, not to be criticized belief. This applies to "the presupposition", supposedly at the foundation of things, and hence often declared beyond examination – "The greatest enemy of human progress is the presupposition" (*ibid*.: 127–8; t.62–3). And it applies to all claims, hypotheses, inferences and deductions whether of theoretical or of practical reason. It is irrelevant to complain about a search through theoretical reason for moral "knowledge", in contrast with a search through practical reason for moral "certainty". Enlightenment means that even the claims to knowledge that seem most established must remain open to challenge. The same goes for the claims to apodictic certainty even – or especially – of Kantian pure practical reason.

Before arguing for a morality of doubt, Guyau goes over moralities of "practical certainty" and then of "faith" (*ibid.*: 107–28; t.45–63). He discusses, under both headings, the Scottish appeal to the presupposition. Either way it runs into the sands, and whether as appeal to a moral sense, or to intuition, or to a necessary trust in the opinion of the general run of mankind.[7] Kantianism also fails in its aspiration to deliver us, via the metaphysics of practical reason, moral certainty. The neo-Kantianism of Renouvier and others is a morality of faith. In settling for a "duty to believe in duty", it gives up on the apodictic truth of the moral law and just treats it, like God, as a postulate. There is "no essential difference between moral faith and religious faith", but moral faith has "a more universal character than the other". The increasing "non-religion" nowadays – the first time Guyau introduces the term – is a sort of provisional triumph of a "purer faith". "In becoming exclusively moral, faith does not alter; on the contrary, it casts off all foreign elements" (*ibid.*: 116–17; t.53). Like the neo-Kantian duty to believe in duty, modern moral faith is an insistence on a need to affirm something's certainty and truth, even when we have given up on mystical or other claims to certain possession of its truth. It is "to will an artificial truth" (*ibid.*: 127; t.62).

Guyau criticizes this refusal to face up to and accept doubt as in itself unenlightened. But he also criticizes moral faith because it remains dogmatic and, like traditional religious faith, declares itself "above all discussion" and rejects "the scientific spirit". "All *problem* disappears, for a problem would imply many different solutions calling for verification; so one does not verify duty; there are questions that we may not address even to ourselves; there are questions we must not raise" (*ibid.*: 118–19; t.54–5). Guyau does not consider the possibility of an undogmatic faith, which on his view might seem a contradiction in terms, and which he would in any case still criticize as unenlightened, in that, dogmatic or undogmatic, it is still faith.

Early on in Durkheim's Latin thesis, there is a statement of a theme running through all his work, that life cannot wait for science. In this particular version, in face of an urgent practical problem we come up with a variety of reasons to ground action, yet these can offer "only doubtful probabilities" and we act on them, "not because the arguments on which they seem based leave no room for uncertainty, but because they fall in with our personal feelings" (1892a: 14; tf.33; t.6). In the version in *The elementary forms*, "theories destined to make men live and act . . . push thought in advance, beyond that which science permits us to affirm". But the system of ideas that we may continue to call religion is different from traditional faith: to have the right to go beyond science, it must "begin by knowing and being inspired by it" and must "submit to its criticism and control" (1912a: 615–16; t.479). It is accepted, however, that most of our concepts still come from common experience, "without submission to any criticism" (*ibid.*: 624; t.486). This recalls the point, in the essay on the definition of religious phenomena, about "general beliefs of all kinds" in democracy, progress, equality, one's country, the Revolution, etc.; "the community will not tolerate open denial of them without resistance", and they are to some extent indistinguishable from "religious beliefs proper", since they are beliefs in things "sacred to us all", which are not to be challenged or interfered with ([1899a(ii)] 1969c: 157; t.91). All this prepares the ground for the argument, in the lectures on pragmatism, about "mythological truths".

Scientific truths are "always subjected to testing or demonstration" and constitute for us nowadays "the very type of truth" (1955a: 175, 178; t.86, 88). Mythological truths are accepted without such controls. They express a "unanimous conception, and it is this that gives them a force, an authority, through which they impose themselves and are protected from testing and from doubt". There are thus ideas in our society that we imagine are not religious but that nonetheless have "the character of dogmas, and are not to be questioned". "There is and there will always be a place in social life for a form of truth which will perhaps be expressed in a very secular way but, even so, will be at bottom mythological and religious" (*ibid.*: 184; t.91). Yet why do we still need, in the form of mythological truths, dogma and faith?

Life, we are reminded, runs ahead of science. Yet why can we not then be enlightened enough, both as individuals and as a society, to face up to and accept doubt? Durkheim criticizes the view – this time of Comte rather than of Guyau – that with the arrival of enlightenment it is possible to base our lives on "positive scientific truths, which can be considered as established ", and to give up on trying to decide questions beyond these, but just leave them "in intellectual doubt". This might be a possibility in the case of ideas relative to the physical world. It is not in the case of the social world. Here, society "cannot wait for its problems to be solved scientifically" and we need "something other than doubt" (*ibid*.: 183–4; t.90). Yet why?

Durkheim insists in a general way that, unless we are "certain", we must hesitate when the time comes to act (*ibid*.: 199; t.99). His specific answer, bringing in mythological truths, has to do with why society cannot wait for science: "it must decide what must be done, and to decide this must have an idea of itself", "a representation of itself, indispensable for its action and life" (*ibid*.: 184; t.90).

That is, a basic Durkheimian argument against doubt and for dogmatic faith concerns ideas that, in the form of mythological truths, are about our own and our society's very identity. They are core, constitutive beliefs, coming into a society's very description, and they also have a "creative power", bringing the society, historically, into being and developing it. In this case, indeed, "it is thought that creates the real, and the great role of collective representations is to 'make' the higher reality which is *society* itself" (*ibid*.: 173–4; t.83–4).

Perhaps, if we try to spell out the argument – which Durkheim himself does not do – it is this. Ideas of identity are so central to everything else that there has to be conviction about them. They have to be a faith because, in their very creation of an identity, they necessarily go beyond anything that theoretical or practical reason can establish as "true". Hence they also have to be a dogmatic faith, protected against an examination that can only unmake what they make, a *raison raisonnante* with a power to deconstruct social and moral community though not to recreate it.

But if mythological truths help to create, constitute and invent the social world, the other half of the story, Durkheim insists, is that they remain rooted in it. He asks if societies are "free to create whatever truths they please", and answers that "ideas cannot become collective if they do not correspond with anything real". Monotheism, for example, expresses "a tendency towards increasing concentration of the social group" (*ibid*.: 176–7; t.86–7).[8]

Then such ideas, if both socially creative and socially rooted, cannot be completely exempt from informed, enlightened examination, and we return to the position in *The elementary forms*, that modern faith must increasingly submit itself to such examination's control. Indeed, in the lectures on pragmatism, as in *The elementary forms* and elsewhere, there is a deep ambivalence in Durkheim's attitude to faith. There is and there will always be a place for mythological, not to be questioned truths, but they are "one of the great obstacles holding up the progress of sociology" (*ibid.*: 184; t.91). So, on the one hand, and as against Guyau, it seems to be part of enlightenment to recognize the need for faith. On the other hand, and as with Guyau, faith does not seem part of enlightenment at all.

The ambivalence is at its most deliberate and paradoxical in the article on the Dreyfus Affair. Enlightenment's cult of man has autonomy as its "first dogma", freedom of discussion and enquiry as its "first rite" ([1898c] 1970a: 268; t.67).

This identifies the problem with *modern* mythological truths. Our moral world's central, constitutive, mythological truth is the individual as man, and an integral, constitutive part of this is belief in autonomy and free thought themselves. A commitment to these rules out any legitimate place for dogma. So must it rule out faith? For both Durkheim and Guyau, faith more or less inevitably brings in dogma, to sustain and entrench it. But it is important to try to concentrate on the issue of faith itself, without prejudging whether or not it then brings in dogma. With enlightenment and its recognition of the limits to knowledge, is faith possible or even desirable, instead of "the admissibility of doubt where things are subject to doubt"? Or can we find, in something such as commitment, an alternative that somehow escapes this choice?

The risk society

For both Durkheim and Guyau it is a collective rather than just an individual issue, about a society constituted around the human ideal. It involves the ways in which, in its public culture, we understand a collective or an individual claim as knowledge, belief, article of faith, or more or less uncertain hypothesis. It is also, for Durkheim, very much about motivation. Where is the will to stand by our ideals, without feelings of conviction about them? But for Guyau, too, it is very much about motivation. The *Sketch of a morality without obligation* looks for motivational "equivalents" of the sense of duty of moralities of certainty and faith.

Guyau is perhaps the first to emphasize sociology as "the science of risks" (1885: 216; t.126). This concerns consequential risk, the uncertainty of outcomes of our action. But his deeper concern is with moral and metaphysical risk, uncertainty about the ideals themselves that govern action.

The difference can be brought out by a passage from Boutroux:

> the notion of duty . . . implies a risk, an adventure, a sort of logical absurdity. I do not know if what I hold by is possible, or if I and my fellows will find ourselves better for it; but I know that I should so act, whatever the consequences. To characterize such certainty, there is no other word than "faith". (Boutroux [1909] 1928: 172)

So here is a Kantian certainty of faith in the moral law, plus uncertainty about the consequences of acting on it.

It is of interest that Boutroux brings in the idea of an adventure, which suggests something positive, whereas duty in the face of risk suggests something negative, a need to control and overcome anxiety and fear. Guyau criticizes general views that just take such a negative attitude. They see only "the fear of risk". They fail to see and to understand "the love of risk" (1885: 212; t.123). Emphasis on this lets in an unKantian motivation of a positive desirability and attraction.[9] But, as an emphasis on consequential risk, it can still leave the urge to moral certainty untouched. Moreover, in criticizing the way attraction to risk is often ignored, Guyau is not asking us to simplify and suppress other aspects, or to rely on it as a motivation. His discussion instead leads on to another, more fundamental motivation.

He raises cases in which ideals – honour, justice, etc. – can demand action involving, not just a risk, but the virtual certainty of some sort of personal sacrifice, including of life itself. He then locates an unmystical, secular motivation in identity. It lies in attachment to others and to society as an integral, deeply rooted part of oneself. This contains in germ, whether or not it contributed to, Durkheim's account of the good. Indeed, to drive home his argument about the nature of the good, Guyau, too, appeals to the line from Juvenal – *"for the sake of life, to lose the point of living"* – and uses the same metaphor of the self's "rootedness" in society (*ibid.*: 223; t.133).

But how does he get from the social self, attached to a surrounding milieu, to individualism, *anomie* and metaphysical and moral risk? The answer is not that different from the way Durkheim gets from it to individualism, its anomic and other pathologies, and the human ideal. It is built into the modern world's developing rationale:

> Religious society (and every absolute moral philosophy seems to be the last form of religion) this society, united by a community of superstitions, is a social form of ancient times, which is in process of disappearing and which it would be strange to take as an ideal. (*ibid.*: 233; t.142)

The account of this process, which Guyau goes on to give in *The non-religion of the future*, has already been discussed. In criticizing it, and wanting to hang on to faith, Durkheim argues that to decide the matter we must look to changes "in the nature of societies" (1887b: 310; t.37). But this is precisely what Guyau, to decide the matter, tries to do. Modernity leaves less and less place for dogma and faith. The claim that all societies need belief ignores the specific nature of our own, and the way to discredit and undermine morality in our society is to go on insisting on unassailable, apodictic belief. The modern social self, attached to the society that puts down deep strong roots in it, is attached to free thought, argument and independent-mindedness.

In effect, Guyau's "love of risk" transforms into a need, in the modern world, to learn to live with and embrace moral, metaphysical risk. It involves the development of a public culture in a number of ways. One is a readiness to recognize "the hypothetical character" of our ideas (*ibid.*: 229: t.138). Another is a "division of thought and diversity of intellectual labour" in which disagreement, far from being feared, is encouraged (*ibid.*: 232; t.140–41). Moreover, acceptance of a diversity of views and of the hypothetical character of one's own views seems interconnected in his argument, each implying or tending to imply the other.

Then *anomie* might well entail a pluralism in which we are free to go off separately, in pursuit of our own ideals in our own ways. But it also involves something else. Guyau looks to a community of agreed norms, where we stay together, but understanding them in terms of all kinds of different philosophies, metaphysics and worldviews, rather than just a single system. This corresponds with the idea of "polytelism" later, and independently, discussed by Bouglé (1914). It is essentially as polytelism that Guyau contrasts *anomie* with autonomy, when embedded in the particular system of Kantianism. It is *anomie* that is "true 'autonomy'" (Guyau 1885: 231; t.139)

Guyau seems to reject not just a "community of superstitions" but any community of belief. He relies instead on a community of norms, the cohesion in diversity of a division of labour, and the sentiment – the essence of religion – of attachment to one another and society. It is more or less the package put together in *The division of labour*, except, of course, that Durkheim sees and insists on a continuing community of belief in a religion of man.

A basic criticism of Guyau is that in his complete commitment to the human ideal he explores and elaborates its implications but loses sight of the need, in the first place, for a community of belief in the ideal itself. A community of norms has to fit in with and develop in terms of this universalist, egalitarian ethic of the person. So must any of the diverse worldviews – whether in a pluralism or in a polytelism – of *anomie*. Indeed, we might almost stand Guyau on his head. It is autonomy that is true "*anomie*" – autonomy not as embedded in Kant's whole system of thought but in its essential emphasis on the person in a republic of persons.

Moreover, Guyau is committed to a community of belief in another way. He is committed to a common public culture, constituting modern society as a "risk society" – a culture in which there is a love of risk rather than just a fear of risk, and a culture, above all, in which we learn to accept free thought, disagreement and uncertainty more or less throughout morality itself. But the point, of course, of pressing him on a community of belief around the core idea and ideal of the human person is to ask if it is not here that his risk society has to stop, and it is Durkheim who is right in his sense of the need for conviction and faith.

Durkheimian modern society is also in many ways a risk society, and in many of the ways – free thought, disagreement, scientific truth as the "very type of truth" – that it is for Guyau. But the Durkheimian internalist programme brings out and emphasizes risks that Guyau does not. They are invisible risks. And they are systematic risks, built into the very nature of our social world.

225

They can threaten the individual, as with the suicidogenic currents that might sweep us off to our deaths, and, as generally, with the anomic and egoistic pathologies generated by the human ideal's individualism. It is of interest that Guyau in fact hints at these. He talks of a "pure meditation and solitary thought" that can numb us in a "sort of fever of infinite weariness", of a despair that lies in "infinite hope", and of a pessimism that lies in "infinite desire" (*ibid.*: 240–41; t.148–9). Infinite weariness, with its retreat into solitariness and thought, clearly has to do with Durkheim's diagnosis of "egoistic" individualism. The despair of infinite hope – Bouglé's feelings on reading Book III of *The division of labour*! – seems a mixture of this and "anomic" individualism's infinite desire. If we switch round Durkheim's labels, we can see a fundamental agreement between him and Guyau over *anomie*. It is both an ideal, of free thought, and a malaise contained within the ideal and generated by it.

But an essential feature of Durkheim's internalist programme is that, as in this case, the invisible, systematic risks built into our social world do not just threaten the individual. They can undermine from within, and collapse, liberal society itself.

This takes us to another way in which, taking Guyau and Durkheim together, we live in a risk society. They articulate a choice between a need in an enlightened liberal culture to acknowledge uncertainty and a need in a liberal ethic, as in any ethic, for conviction and some sort of faith in core ideals. Is there a way out of the dilemma in the idea of a commitment? Guyau, in effect, goes on to see some such solution:

> There is a middle course between doubt and faith, between incertitude and categorical affirmation – it is action. Only by it can the uncertain realize itself and become a reality. I do not ask you to believe blindly in an ideal; I ask you to work to realize it. Without belief? So as to believe. You will believe in it when you have worked to produce it. (*ibid.*: 239; t.147)

Commitment to an ideal is at the same time, and interactingly, working to bring it about, a feeling motivating working to bring it about, and a source of belief in it. Durkheim's account of mythological truths and of periods of ferment implies something similar – a process of creative collective action that in articulating and striving to realize an ideal is a source of a socially constitutive belief in it – rather than just that the belief comes first, motivating the action and constituting the society.

Indeed, the hope-cum-despair of his call for reform in *The division of labour*'s new preface has to do with modern society's lack of commitment to its own human ideal and a need for milieux that can stir this up and produce through action the belief constitutive of a human *patrie*.

A commitment to the human ideal can combine conviction with an uncertain and undogmatic free thought, precisely because a conviction in working to realize this ideal can also be in continuing to argue, through free thought, not only over detailed interpretations but over how – and as part of these efforts of interpretation – to justify and establish it.

The difficulties are not only in achieving but in sustaining such a culture, as Durkheim and Guyau, together, bring out. There is the risk of a slide, via belief and faith, into authoritarianism. There is the risk of a slide, via doubt, into scepticism. Each undermines a republic of persons, if in opposite ways.

Chapter Ten

The cult of man

The issues of faith versus doubt and of risk tie up with the dispensabil-ity, in a secular society, of God. Durkheim argues in the lectures on moral education: "Because God is beyond the world, he is above and beyond science; if, then, morality comes from and expresses God, it is placed beyond the grasp of our reason" (1925a: 138; t.121). But this deals just with the route to God via knowledge and theoretical reason. What about the Kantian route via practical reason? Durkheim turns to it in the paper on moral facts. "Kant postulates God, since without this hypothesis morality is unintelligible. We postulate a society spe-cifically distinct from individuals, since otherwise morality has no object and duty no roots." God is then seen as "society transfigured and thought of symbolically" ([1906b] 1924a: 74–5; t.51–2). What sort of society? And what else might the postulate of God, taken as a metaphor, be about?

The ethical importance of hope

Boutroux attacks "sociologists" who reduce morality just to attach-ment to actual society. It involves attachment to an ideal society (Boutroux 1908: 205–7). The criticism is off target if directed at Durkheim. Morality is rooted in the real rather than the actual, and attaches us to the ideal society it implies – in the modern world it is to the ideal of the person in a union of persons.

Though duty, for Boutroux, is a faith – implying "a risk, an adven-ture, a sort of logical absurdity" – it cannot remain a blind faith. It must try to understand its object. In doing so, it becomes a search for a supreme ideal. This has to be an ideal of community. "None of us, just by our own powers, could become all that we could be and do all that we could do"; a fully human life is characterized by "common love of the ideal and of one another" (Boutroux [1909] 1928: 173).

But in looking beyond duty and finding the kingdom, Kant also finds God. As Boutroux explains, it is not because we need God as a motivation to duty; it is because we need hope. "Religion, for Kant, is the hope that our efforts towards the establishment of a reign of justice and happiness will not be in vain" (Boutroux 1926: 367). So, if Durkheim is to secularize the kingdom, and see God as society thought of symbolically, it has to be as a symbol and metaphor of hope.

According to the second *Critique*, the necessary postulates of morality are "immortality, freedom . . ., and the existence of God" (Kant [1788] 1913: 132; t.139). The argument for an immortal soul runs into various problems.[1] It seems driven by a need to sustain belief in the moral law, through hope that we can progress towards a time when we live up to it – something impossible for the limited, mortal individual. Or is it impossible only for the limited, mortal individual as an atomistic self? The picture changes with the organic self, attached to a society that is not just made up of whichever individuals happen, for the moment, to be living but that continues through the generations, with debts to the dead, responsibilities to the unborn, and hopes for the future. Organic selves, with their interest in the future, can dispense with the immortal soul by collectivizing the hope it represents – that evil will not inherit the earth and that society will one day be just.

There remain the postulates of God and freedom. God, in the Kantian scheme of things, arranges the realizability of a union of virtue plus happiness. He does not arrange the realizability of virtue *per se*. This is the task of the immortal soul – and of freedom. Where would freedom be if human virtue became God's work? So without the immortal soul and as far as virtue is concerned we seem alone – collectively – with our freedom. But the kingdom, transformed into a republic, is still an ideal of a society in which everyone can flourish as a person. Is this not near enough to a Kantian union of virtue and happiness to have to postulate a providential God to see to it?

Happiness can be related to a life of virtue and flourishing in ways that are, let us say, intrinsic, compatible, inconsistent or contingent. God does not come in if happiness is related to virtue in any of the first three ways, that is if it is intrinsic, compatible or inconsistent. He is optional if it is contingent.

Durkheim emphasizes a happiness that is intrinsic to moral flour-ishing – in the virtue of self-discipline and in self-constitutive attach-ment to ideals. This is not to claim that the relationship is always intrinsic. It still lets in relationships in which happiness and virtue are separately defined, including a compatibility in which they are none-theless joined in the same lives. A Kantian route to this is if maxims involving the pursuit of happiness pass the test of the moral law. There may be other routes. But the general point about compatible happi-ness is that it is an interlinked part of the efforts, activities and rela-tionships making up a moral life. Although defined separately from these, it does not arise separately from them. Like intrinsic happiness it arises from within moral lives of developing and flourishing them-selves. It is therefore for man rather than God to arrange it, just as it is for man rather than God to resist happiness inconsistent with the law. It is not an external, contingent event, with an external, independent causation, which might require God's hand in it. So, to the extent that contingent happiness is kept out of the ideal of a republic of develop-ing and flourishing, God can and indeed ought to be kept out of it too.

But can the ideal exclude contingent happiness? A passage in the third *Critique* is addressed to the "righteous man" who is nonetheless an atheist. Kant descends from abstraction to give some idea of the happiness and unhappiness he has in mind in postulating God. Let us just say that one group of examples concerns the socially caused, the other the naturally caused. In one, people may be righteous yet expe-rience "deceit, violence and envy" all around them. In the other, how-ever worthy they are of happiness, "nature, which pays no attention to that, will still subject them to all the evils of deprivation, disease, and untimely death" (Kant [1790] 1913: 452; t.342).

It may be coherent to *hope* to avoid contingent, naturally caused unhappiness, lying completely outside of our control. Is it coherent to adopt this as an *end*? Of course we can adopt the end of trying, as far as possible, to bring "deprivation, disease, and untimely death" (and death itself?) within our control. But to the extent that things remain outside our control, and even if avoidance of the unhappiness caused by them is coherent as a hope, is it coherent as an end, in the sense, anyway, of a purpose and objective?

It is clearly included in the Kantian "highest good", defined as all the happiness consistent with virtue, which in turn seems clearly defined as an end in the sense of an agential objective. As in the second *Critique*, "we *ought to* seek to further the highest good (which must therefore be at least possible)" (Kant [1788] 1913: 125: t.131).

Yet although all the highest good *is* possible, thanks to God, the same passage makes clear how furthering it is not possible for *us*, where it is concerned – the passage's main concern – with happiness that is consistent with virtue but outside our power, and so, as discussed here, contingent.

We can both hope for a republic and seek to further it as an end, insofar as the obstacles to it – including "deprivation, disease, and untimely death" – lie within human power in that they lie within our society itself. The ideal then involves work enough. Indeed, it is all the *work* for us there can be, since anything more than it can only be a hope, and only in regard to a nature that, however great its impact on the social and moral world, lies outside it. God, as a hope, also lies outside of this world and its human ideal, and so is not society transfigured and symbolically thought of at all. He can still come in, and indeed cannot be kept out, but as an optional rather than a necessary postulate of an idea of human life within the totality of things. He is everywhere in Kant's metaphysics of nature, and nowhere in Durkheim's, who leaves us alone, collectively, with our freedom.

But freedom – whether interpreted as a thing *res aeterna* or as a sociohistorical development of man's *telos* and of the kernel, in everyone, of a supersensible ability – is the foundation of Kantian ethics. As such it leads to religion, and to God and the immortal soul as postulates. So a puzzle is what it is doing as itself a postulate.

The solution, for Delbos, is that freedom as a postulate has more to do with "belief in virtue", with a "human power confident of being able to do all it should if it so wills" (Delbos [1905] 1969: 400–401). That is, it has less to do with autonomy, more to do with what Kant calls "autocracy" (*ibid.*: 401, n.1). As in *The metaphysics of morals*, autonomy is enough for holy beings. Human beings also need autocracy, a "consciousness – though not directly perceived yet rightly inferred from the moral categorical imperative – of the *capacity* to master one's inclinations when they rebel against the law" (Kant [1797] 1914: 383; t.188). Philonenko draws on Delbos to argue that freedom as a postulate concerns the need to overcome doubt. "What is the belief in virtue if not the pure, simple annulment of all the doubts that man can experience in regard to his freedom?" In fact, each of the postulates is "a belief in the foundation" (Philonenko 1993, vol. 2: 172–3).

So is the sense of confidence, of belief-cum-hope, not also a *motive* to morality?

Delbos, like Boutroux, is anxious to make clear that Kant denies that hope is a moral motive. Indeed, he does deny this. But it is within the problematic of God, of hope of all the contingent happiness consistent with virtue, and of worry in case happiness then becomes a motive to virtue itself – which "would destroy the entire moral worth of the actions" (Kant [1788] 1913: 129; t.136). If we clear the problematic away, we can see the belief-cum-hope represented in the other postulates for what it is – an essential moral motivation.

"Autocracy"'s hope for autonomy and a republic of developing and flourishing based on it is for a society that is man's work, not God's, just as it is for a society in which "deceit, violence and envy" will not be all around us. But it is not, in a Durkheimian version, an ideal of perfection. A republic may always face contingent risks, coming from outside its rationale, just as there may always be in it contingent unhappiness. It necessarily faces risks inherent in its rationale and the specific, characteristic pathologies inherent in it too. What we may hope for is a republic that manages to contain and survive these. What we may also hope for is the coming, despite everything, of the republic itself.

There is good reason for optimism. This is all the more so in light of Guyau's expression of modern uncertainty – an expression that is part of his commitment to the human ideal and hope of a republic: "Religions say: I hope because I believe . . . It is necessary to say: I believe because I hope" (Guyau 1885: 240; t.148). Or rather it is *also* necessary to say this.

We can hope for a republic because of a belief that, despite all the uncertainties, obstacles and risks, its realization of the human ideal is written into modernity's dynamic. But commitment to the ideal is itself a core active element of the dynamic, pushing for a republic. So why, in face of the uncertainties, choose pessimism? It adds to the obstacles. A good reason for optimism is that it sustains and motivates the belief in the ideal that is essential if a republic is ever to come about. We can hope because we believe, and we can believe because we hope.

In Kantian terms, the person in a union of persons is both a postulate of the human ideal and its fundamental principle. As a postulate it concerns a hope that is inferred from the principle, yet that is also nec-essary for commitment to it. In that it concerns the executive will it might be called executive hope.

But moral and metaphysical doubt go beyond this, to strike at the legislative will. Boutroux accepts that Kantianism rests on faith, only a pure, practical, rational faith. It is not just a religion "without revela-tion" (Boutroux 1904: 525), "a sort of translation into rationalist lan-guage of a doctrine at bottom wholly mystical" (Boutroux 1926: 275). He fails to explain how, even so, it can have the adamantine cer-tainty it claims.

What might be called legislative hope is an alternative to faith as a basis of practical commitment to the republic. It is the other, positive side of moral and metaphysical doubt. It is hope in the truth of our ideals. It is hope in a power to develop our ways of understanding and grounding them. It is hope in doing so through a culture of free, pub-lic, critical enquiry.

The trouble with scepticism is the same as the trouble with faith. Both are blind to the other side of legislative, moral and metaphysical doubt – legislative, moral and metaphysical hope.

Sacrality

Durkheim turns to faith in a preoccupation with the need to develop commitment in our world to its own human ideal, to entrench it as a real, living, social ideal. The issue does not go away if we replace faith with hope. It becomes a question, instead, of how to entrench hope. Guyau denounces idolatry of man as a corruption of the modern ideal, whereas Durkheim sees a cult of man as essential to it. A "cult" that "sacralizes" man seems clearly linked with the issue of motivation and commitment. It is less clear what is meant by such a "cult" or by man's "sacralization".

In worrying, in the lectures on moral education, that ethics might destroy morals, Durkheim talks of a cult of the human person as sacred. He emphasizes, in the same passage, that we must keep a sense of the traditional divinity's sacredness: "Everything coming from it participates in its transcendence and becomes by this very fact beyond comparison with everything else" (1925a: 11; t.10). Similarly, in *The elementary forms*, he sees a "logical chasm" between the sacred and the profane: the "sacred thing *par excellence* is that which the profane must not touch, and cannot touch with impunity" (1912a: 55; t.55). He then defines religion as "*a unified system of beliefs and practices relative to sacred things, that is to say, things set apart and forbidden – beliefs and practices which unite into a single moral community called a Church all those who adhere to them*" (*ibid*.: 65; t.62).

A deflationary view of "the sacred" is that it comes down to his concern with core beliefs, plus an emphasis on how they are set above and apart from other things. Hence it does not follow that a Durkheimian "cult" of man means graven images and idolatry. It is just high-flown talk. Man as god = man as sacred = everyone's status as a person = everyone's importance.

But why does Durkheim talk up the important into the sacred? This takes us to a constative–constitutive view. It need not be enough to say something is "very important" or "all important" in order to state, communicate and constitute it as a Durkheimian "sacred" belief. It has to be in the right register, in a style of language that involves appropriate emotive force, that may therefore draw heavily on repetition, emphasis, metaphor and other devices of rhetoric, and that is in any case distinguished and defined through contrasts with other registers, not least of the ordinary, "profane" world.

The idea of a register of the sacred covers whichever ways discourses state and constitute something as a core, all-important, sacred belief, whatever the occurrence in them of the actual term "sacred". It does not imply that modern society must adopt Durkheim's own talk of man as "sacred" and "a god", but implies that it must find and adopt forms of talk that are appropriate in our culture yet up to the task. The task, to repeat, concerns a register that is constitutive of core beliefs and part and parcel of their statement. It does not just express them, in a language that might add an aesthetic or other quality, yet that could be replaced without loss of meaning by "plain", "naked", "literal" speech. The "logical chasm" that Durkheim mentions is as much as anything linguistic. The mistake of the deflationary view is to assume that the register of the sacred can be translated without loss of meaning into a register of the prosaic – that is, the profane.

A reason for insisting on the point is just because it is so important, not only to state and constitute beliefs, but to get across, communicate, *express* them, in the ways and with the force this requires. Stating, constituting and communicating core beliefs might well have to be done in the same ways. As Durkheim puts it: "Collective ideals can constitute themselves and become self-conscious only by becoming fixed in things that can be seen by all, understood by all, and represented to all minds – figurative drawings, emblems of all sorts, written or spoken formulas, animate beings, or the inanimate" ([1911b] 1924a: 137–8; t.94). This raises the stakes, taking the issue of a cult of man well beyond language, and closer to an idolatry involving symbols "of all sorts".

The article on the Dreyfus Affair is very much about the person's sacredness, very much insists on a cult of man, and very much draws on rhetoric. Yet it draws away from symbolism: "a religion does not necessarily imply symbols and rites in the full sense, or temples and priests; all this external apparatus is merely its superficial aspect" ([1898c] 1970a: 270; t.66).This is different from the impression given in *The elementary forms*:

> There is therefore something eternal in religion, destined to survive all the particular symbols in which religious thought has successively enveloped itself. There can be no society which does not feel the need to maintain and strengthen, at regular intervals, the collective sentiments and ideas constituting its unity and personality. This moral remaking cannot come about except through gatherings, assemblies and congregations where individuals, brought close to one another, reaffirm in common their common sentiments; hence the ceremonies that, in their object, in the results they produce, in the processes they employ, do not differ in nature from properly religious ceremonies. What essential difference is there between an assembly of Christians celebrating the principal dates in Christ's life . . . and a gathering of citizens commemorating the institution of a new moral charter or some great event in national life? (1912a: 609–10; t.474–5)

Far from being a superficial and by implication a dispensable aspect of religion, the rite, in some sense or another, has become part of Durkheim's long-sought answer to the question of what is "eternal" in religion and might survive the development of secular science, ethics and society.

Another important passage in the book concerns the emblem. Durkheim emphasizes that it does not just express an already existing social group and identity. Nor does it just sustain this. The emblem is "a constitutive element" of the society itself – both in helping to create it historically, and as an integral part of its self-consciousness and description (*ibid.*: 329–31; t.262–3). Durkheim goes on to argue: "Thus social life, in all its aspects and in all periods of its history, is made possible only by a vast symbolism" (*ibid.*: 331; t.264).

The rite and the emblem play a crucial role for him in this. Another type of symbol might be called "the image", which represents an abstract ideal such as liberty. Not least, there is the type of symbol that might be called "the icon". It might also be an emblem or an image or both. But the point is that it has a special value transferred on to it from whatever it represents. Durkheim writes, in the article on judgements of value and of reality:

> An idol is a very sacred thing and sacredness is the highest value that men have ever recognized. Yet an idol is very often only a block of stone or a piece of wood that, in itself, is without any kind of value . . . There is no faith with any life in it, and however secular, that has not its fetishes where the same disproportion is evident. A flag is only a bit of cloth; the soldier will die, even so, for his flag. ([1911b] 1924a: 126–7; t.86–7)

That is, the sacrifice is not for a bit of cloth. But it is not simply for what it represents. This is made clear in a lecture course on religion. The soldier "almost forgets that the flag is only a symbol; it is the image of the flag and not the idea of his country that grips his mind most at the moment of sacrifice". Similarly, "the totem is the flag of the clan, and it is on to it, rather than the clan itself, that the sentiments brought about by the clan are transferred" (1907f: 109).

So the icon is at the sacred symbolic heart of things in any faith, however secular. As if to drive this home Durkheim deliberately alludes to it as idolatry and fetishism. Is it possible, all the same, to recapture something of the more "iconosceptic" attitude of the Dreyfusard article, in which a religion of man might dispense with temples, priests, graven images, etc.?

A cult of man, symbol laden or not, is only one of the Durkheimian ways of looking for commitment to the human ideal as a real, living, social ideal. It is important not to lose sight of the organic self, intermediate groups, a human culture and, for that matter, actual social reform. The passage in *The elementary forms* about the need in a secular republic of the future for civic rites and ceremonies is followed by an interesting comment. It is that, if it is difficult for us to understand what these would be like, "it is because we are going through a stage of transition and moral mediocrity". Durkheim continues: "the idea which has been formed of human freedom and fraternity seems to us today to leave too large a place for unjust inequalities" (1912a: 610; t.475). This recalls the concern for reform in *The division of labour*'s new preface – but including the point that the traditional occupational group, as a moral milieu, was very much a milieu of symbols, ceremonies and rites (1902b: xii–xiv; t.11–12). So it seems as if such concern goes hand in hand with the argument for a symbol-laden, rather than symbol-free, cult of man. Yet what are the central symbols in this cult?

They can only be ourselves, the flesh and blood "icons" that personify it. We are our own temples and priests, with a sacrality that lies, or ought to lie, in our regard for one another in the actual relationships that constitute social and moral life. But we again have to remember the complexities of Durkheim's approach. The source of sacredness becomes society instead of God. Sacredness itself must then be transferred on to "man" as an abstract idea. It is only in this way that it can be transferred on to "men", on to all of us as empirical personalities, sharing, in our diverseness, a common moral status.

It does not follow, however, that it is possible to make do with a single symbol, the individual as man. There is still the need for a register of the sacred, stating, constituting, communicating and entrenching the core ideal of the person, not only through language and "written or spoken formulas" but through symbols of all sorts. These include the emblem, the image, the rite . . . But they also include the temple itself, in the sense of a special zone of sacredness, set apart from the business of ordinary life.

There are two different ways of understanding Durkheimian appeal to the individual as icon of man, on issues of suicide, the sexual relationship, the marketability versus non-marketability of bodily parts and services, etc. One is to carry it right through as a principle governing all issues. This is to apply it like the Kantian imperative to treat humanity, whether in one's own or anybody else's person, never simply as a means but always at the same time as an end. But it is to emphasize, in doing so, that symbolic considerations must always come into "reverence" for the dignity and sacredness of the person. The other way is to insist that such considerations must be overriding in a significant range of cases, if "reverence" for the person is to be constituted and sustained as a core collective value at all. These cases mark off a special collective zone of the sacred, a symbol of it, a temple where the market does not reach and where human dignity overrides individual libertarian rights. A complaint might be at imposing a collective line on "dignity" when individuals disagree over the idea. Why not complain at imposing a collective libertarian line on "freedom" when individuals disagree over this idea too? A republic entails continuing differences around these and other key ideas, a need to work out collective lines on them, and also a need to sustain respect for persons – including their freedom itself – through sentiments and symbols of dignity.

In sum, the central sacred symbol – the icon – in a cult of man must be ourselves, but within a network of symbols of all sorts. This brings its own risks, such as a ritualism in which moral concern is lost in preoccupation with a symbolic "external apparatus". Yet it is not just a superficial, external "apparatus", which the modern invention of man as a basic social and moral identity can do without. It is integral to the identity's development, in the republic's future and from its beginnings.

1789

The early review article on the Revolution sees it as a religion, which had its martyrs and apostles, and as a creative epoch of a new, audacious faith. It is this again in *The elementary forms*. Durkheim talks of the Revolution's new religion, with "its own dogma, symbols, altars and feasts" (1912a: 306; t.245), and about "those hours of creative effervescence, in the course of which new ideas arise and new formulas are found that serve for a while as a guide for humanity" (*ibid.*: 611; t.475).

He seems very enthusiastic, and in discussing the revolutionary religion, complete with symbols and rites, he draws on a work by Albert Mathiez (*ibid.*: 306, n.1–5; t.245, n.15–19). Mathiez was a young, radical historian, who went on to found the Society for Robespierrist Studies. In arguing in his book *The origins of the revolutionary cults* that the Revolution had a religion, he in turn draws on Durkheim himself and the article on the definition of religious phenomena.[2] His argument, however, includes an emphasis on a particular religious characteristic of the revolutionary movement – its intolerance, not just in regard to different beliefs but in a "destructive rage against the symbols of other cults" (Mathiez 1904: 12). He gives case after case of such iconoclastic "fanaticism", and cuts his discussion short by remarking that the examples are so numerous they could fill a vast volume (*ibid.*: 38).

Durkheim tends to turn a blind eye to all this. He stresses, as has been seen, revolutionary creativity. But there is the occasional, brief reference to a more violent and destructive side, as, for example, in the early review article itself ([1890a] 1970a: 216; t.35). Even in *The elementary forms* there is talk of the many scenes, "sublime or savage", of the Revolution: "Under the influence of the general exultation, the most mediocre or the most inoffensive citizen can be seen transformed, whether into hero or butcher" (1912a: 301; t.241–2). Or there is the remark, perhaps of more interest, elsewhere: "the French Revolution felt the need to substitute a new cult for the old one that it wanted to destroy" (1907f: 637). This is of interest because it suggests that the need to develop a new cult was not simply to express new ideas. It was to struggle against the vast symbolism entrenching the old.

The attack on the old regime did not just sweep away titles, coats of arms and "feudal" rights, rename the *Place Louis XV* the *Place de la Révolution*, or pull down the Bastille. It involved the destruction of symbols of all sorts – statues, tapestries, paintings, altars, churches, tombs, even the corpses of long dead kings and queens, and there were proposals to pull down Versailles. Yet the revolutionaries themselves invented the term "vandalism". They did so out of concern for something else they invented, the idea of a "national heritage". And they looked to "the museum" as an answer to the problem. The problem was how to destroy objects as political and religious symbols but without an unenlightened, vandalistic destruction of them as part of a national, indeed human, heritage, and the museum was seen as a way of stripping them of their old symbolic power while conserving and re-presenting them as works of art.[3]

It could be, at most, only a partial solution. It did not address the influence and importance of literature, music, opera and the theatre, or the "vandalism" of representing works of art piecemeal, torn from their original setting and destroyed as an ensemble. This was a persistent criticism, at the time and subsequently, of the museum. It is doubtful if it was a purely aesthetic criticism, since to preserve "works of art" in context and as an ensemble, in a palace or a church, is to help to preserve their power as ideological symbols. It is in any case difficult, even in a museum, to destroy their old magic completely. Yet a new era of enlightenment cannot contemplate the vandalism of their wholesale physical destruction. So by its very own principles it cannot have a clear, clean break with the past. Part of a cult of man is a culture of man, involving some sort of respect for a "heritage". Hence a cult of man that, even in respecting a heritage, can escape from the ideological grip of the past through the development of a whole new symbolic milieu seems all the more important.

Durkheim's list of symbols of all sorts includes animate beings. The most dramatic case of iconoclasm is "iconocide", the killing of human beings because they are symbols. The term is introduced elsewhere to discuss the killing of the king, as the sacred symbolic centre of the monarchy (Watts Miller 1993a).[4] But the issue has general, far-reaching significance. This is not because people can be important symbols in this or that political and cultural system. It is because in a Durkheimian view it is each of us as a person that must become, in the modern world, a sacred symbolic centre of things, a view that condemns anyone's iconocide, whether criminal or king.

Louis XVI was transformed by 1789 from king of France into king of the French and first official of the new constitutional state. It was as king of the French that he was later accused and convicted of the crime of treason against the nation. The trial itself was intended *as* a symbol, a showpiece of new era justice. But it violated liberal justice in all kinds of ways – not least because it was also the trial *of* a symbol, an attempt to destroy monarchy by destroying the man who, as sacred absolute king of France, had personified it.

Michael Walzer defends the episode as part of the long march, in the modern world, towards democracy. The revolutionaries had to settle with the old monarchy, to find "some ritual process through which the ideology it embodies (and the man who embodies it) can be publicly repudiated". He continues:

> the renunciation of magical authority and political servitude is
> not easy, and . . . approaches finality only when the revolutionary

attack is raised to the level of symbolic action. The mere establishment of a new regime or the adoption of a new constitution
does not have the same effect. The former subjects of the king
must witness the destruction of kingship; they must somehow
share in the renunciation of their own servitude. (Walzer 1974:
88–9)

Although he never mentions Durkheim, his analysis might seem very
Durkheimian. Yet is it?

Killing people because they embody monarchy, Jewishness or whatever is a march straight to a new dark age. There was a double
iconocide. If enlightenment needs to demystify a king, how can it be
by the solemn, collective decapitation of a man?

One of the revolutionaries spoke of the "more impressive specta-
cle" of Louis "returning with his family to the class of citizens".[5]
There were many others who opposed the death penalty as a relic of
barbarism that would perpetuate the mentality of the old regime and
undermine hopes of a new, civilized and civilizing republic. Walzer
defends the execution as understandable, given existing norms and
their acceptance of capital punishment. But it is a curious view of a
revolution that it should go along with existing norms, and an even
curiouser view of a revolution committed to enlightenment that it
should go along with norms of this kind.

Durkheim's own opposition to capital punishment seems clear,
from the argument of his article on penal evolution ([1901a(i)]
1969c: 259; t.116) and from his explicit condemnation of all forms of
physical, corporal punishment in the lectures on moral education. All
such punishment is brutal, demeaning and degrading. It affronts "a
sentiment at the basis of our whole morality, the religious respect of
which the human person is the object". In virtue of this respect, any
violence exercised on a person is "like a sacrilege". It has nothing to
do with the development, in the citizens of a civilized, ethical republic, of a sense of "the dignity of man" (1925a: 208–9; t.182–3).[6]

Durkheim is very consistent about all this. It is why he condemns
suicide. It, too, is iconocide. But let us recall the note on the Revolution:

In these times of internal struggles and collective enthusiasm *the
individual personality had lost some of its value*. The interests of

country or of party came before everything. The many executions sprang, no doubt, from the same cause. One killed others as readily as oneself. (1897a: 247, n.1; t.228, n.34; italics added)

Is this only an explanation, or is it some sort of covert justification, of revolutionary violence? Either way it complicates the view of the Revolution as a creative ferment helping to usher in the human ideal, when part of the process is a devaluation of the person.

Again it may be that the enlightened republic cannot have a clear, clean beginning. Again, however, it may then seem all the more important to develop, through a cult of man, the basis of a civilized conduct of politics, and with it the confidence to look into the past and its murkiness without re-arousing its lethal partisan hates – a confidence that Durkheim, with all his emphasis on the Revolution's creativity, perhaps justifiably lacked at the time.[7]

In a study of republican symbolism, Rosemonde Sanson (1976) focuses on Bastille Day. In another, Maurice Agulhon (1979, 1989) concentrates on Marianne, the personification of liberty, the republic and France. He brings out how she was represented in two very different ways – as an insurrectionary figure, favoured by the left, and as a pacific, constitutionalist figure, favoured by moderates and the right – but also how she was part of a wider battle of symbols, rallying republicans of all factions against her ideological counterparts, including the other virgin, the other Mary. He writes:

The theoretical ideal of republicans was certainly rationalist ("philosophical" as it was said at the time). Emancipated minds do not need cults. But could an elitist ideal of philosophers have won the battle? It is only too true that enemies are never fought without resembling them a little ... To change the form of the State and its principle is to abolish its symbols and to have to invent others as a result. (Agulhon 1979: 232, 236)

This echoes Durkheim's remark: "the French Revolution felt the need to substitute a new cult for the old one that it wanted to destroy." Another need, however, is to develop some sort of consensus around an identity and symbolism within which the conflicts built into free, democratic politics can take place. A good example of an attempt to do so is the Third Republic's decision to create a national festival and the choice of 14 July. The day of the king's execution, 21 January, was never suggested. The day of the monarchy's overthrow by an armed, insurgent "people", 10 August, was preferred by the left. Moderates and conservatives preferred days such as 26 August, when the National Assembly adopted the Declaration of the Rights of Man and the Citizen. In the end, 14 July was endorsed with an overwhelming majority. The Bastille was a suitably unattractive symbol of the old regime, its fall was through the action of "the people", and yet the event belonged firmly to the more pacific, constitutionalist phase of the Revolution, with no overtones of the Terror (Sanson 1976: 25–38; Ory 1980).

Eugen Weber describes how long it took, after the Revolution, for most people in France to think of themselves as French – indeed even to speak French – and goes into the many processes involved in the eventual emergence during the Third Republic (and so in Durkheim's own lifetime) of an entrenched, widespread sense of such an identity. The battle of symbols played an essential part in the creation of the identity, and in discussing the battle of rites and festivals he judges 14 July "the clear winner" (Weber 1977: 390).

A fundamental point suggested by all this is that symbolism is not just necessary in an initial stage of struggle against old ideologies and towards an enlightened "rational" republic. It is necessary all along. It is part and parcel of the continuing conflict of ideas, movements and identities inherent in republican moral politics. It is at the same time essential for the norms of respect and due process governing the conduct of republican disputes. It lays the basis of these norms, and so of the very possibility of civilized politics, in the invention and reinvention of a common, overarching attachment and identity as citizens of the same human *patrie*. It is a form of myopia, which Durkheim encountered in his own day and which has continued since, to criticize his defence of the very idea of a *patrie*, as if we can be citizens without a city, or without, in our conflicts, a sense of a shared identity as members of it. The only question is: what city?

Global ethics

Durkheim asks us to endorse, as the local ethic of our place and time, a universalist ethic of man. Yet is there any contradiction? It is a commitment, not to an eternal moral law, valid from the beginning of history, but to an emerging global ideal and the central value of the human person throughout the modern world.

Is there a need, with global ethics, for a global *patrie*? Let us discuss this as cosmopolitanism. Durkheim comes close to imagining it in *The division of labour*, where he remarks, in doing so, that nothing dictates the continuation of "the intellectual and moral diversity of societies" ([1893b] 1902b: 402, n.2; t.406, n.6). Elsewhere, as in a lecture course of 1909, he rejects the idea (1975b, vol. 3: 224). What are the alternatives?[8]

In a debate of 1905, Durkheim distinguishes a *patrie* from a state, as well as from a nationality and a nation. A *patrie* is a political society involving sentiments of attachment to it and so, we could say, a sense of a common citizenship. A state is simply a legal–political organization that, like the Russian empire in Durkheim's own time, need not arouse these sentiments in its many and various subjects. A nationality is a community of civilization and historical memories that, like Poland in his own time, does not form a state, although it may have once done so. A nation is such a community, forming its own state (1905e: 27–9). So a nation is a *patrie*. But need a *patrie* be a nation in order to have the sense of citizenship and attachment that counts? It is possible to imagine the development, worldwide, of a system of human *patries* that is essentially segmentary since they are essentially alike and work with the same interpretation of the human ideal.

Durkheim, however, seems sufficiently impressed by continuing, relevant differences of civilization, outlook and collective memory to envisage something else. It might just be discussed as pluralism and finds expression, alongside cosmopolitanism, in *The division of labour*. Each "people" develops its own particular ideal and conception of man in line with its own temperament ([1893b] 1902b: 392; t.397). Durkheim often talks of "peoples" rather than "societies", but without an explicit distinction, and so interchangeably that it is difficult to infer what it might be. He talks of "societies" in arguing, in *The rules*, that they can still have the same identity despite far-reaching change. "Japan may borrow our arts, our industry, even our political organization; it will not cease to belong to a social type different from France and Germany" (1901c: 88, n.1; t.117, n.10). This again suggests a pluralism in which Japan, India, Iran, France and so on might all develop as human *patries*, but in their own ways and in working out different and distinctive versions of the human ideal.

They must all involve a recognizable regard for everyone as a person, in a society of persons, as a core value and belief. This mutual recognizability must develop as part of the evolution of global ethics itself, and perhaps it could do so without global updates of the Declaration of the Rights of Man, or any other form of cosmopolitanism. Is there nonetheless not a need for institutions, compatible with pluralism but amounting to a worldwide political society?

Some such global organization is in itself a symbol of our shared humanity, and there is every need for a powerful symbolism of this to do battle with all the sources, in the modern world, of inhumanity. These include the instrumentalism inherent in the market and in the social distance of interests working as an anomic, global force, just as they include the oppositions and hatreds inherent in anchorage in particular, communitarian identities. They block the development of republican society and remain a threat to it even to the extent that it is established. A basic Durkheimian concern is thus with a "virtuous circle" in which institutions, sentiments and symbolism feed on one another to entrench commitment in the modern world to its own ideal, and to motivate and sustain pressure for its realization. The symbolism of a cult of man is only part of this – but an essential part. And so is a cosmopolitan ethical citizenship, condemning inhumanity wherever it occurs and attaching us to one another worldwide.

In a debate on pacificism, Durkheim clearly talks of a "human *patrie*", in the sense that it is global, and that it is "only an ideal, but an ideal in process of realization" ([1908a(1)] 1970a: 294–5). He is unclear, however, in his attitude to it, since he is still against a cosmopolitanism rejecting roots in a particular society, and instead of exploring a cosmopolitanism retaining these he still looks forward only to each society as a human *patrie*. But a basic reason for a cosmopolitan expression of a shared identity is the same as for its expression in a local human *patrie*. It is the need in civilized moral politics to respect differences and to govern and conduct disagreements through an attachment to one another, a solidarity that transcends them.

"The hidden god"

The republic is the city of man, and Durkheim sometimes talks of man as its god. The obvious sense is that man is its central sacred value. Is not another sense that man is its central mythological truth? Either way the city is a place of symbols. So how can it be a place of transparency? An image that has become dominant is of a mysterious, tangled "forest of symbols". A Durkheimian urge is to clear the forest up and get to a republic, complete with bright festivals, in which there is at last a society with autonomous self-understanding. But is there not something about the numinous – the sacred, mythological and symbolic – that must always remain obscure?

Durkheim gives as examples of modern mythological truths "notions of *democracy, progress, class struggle*, etc." (1955a: 184; t.91). It is an interesting list – but not least because it leaves out man. Perhaps the reason is that it is fundamental to Durkheim's project to establish, as a scientific truth, a sociological understanding of the modern human ideal. Yet this ideal is why something must be done about the view that mythological truths are not to be questioned or discussed. Durkheim himself underlines the paradox when he talks of autonomy as the cult of man's first dogma, of freedom of enquiry and discussion as its first rite. The notion of man is in any case a central modern mythological truth in the way that matters most. It is not only a product of our society. It helps to constitute and create it.

Mythological truths connect with the periods of collective ferment going back to the review article on the Revolution, but also with the emergence, in the theses on Montesquieu and the division of labour, of the human ideal as an essential element of modernity's underlying, constitutive rationale. So if we sum up a Durkheimian account of the ideal, it is that it is rooted in the long-term, continuing processes of the division of labour, has sources of its own in times of great ferment such as the Revolution, as well as in the occasions that renew them, and becomes an active core element of our world's dynamic.

How, within the account, might man still remain elusive? Let us start with a very general epistemological point. Durkheimian sociology sets out, via empirical detective work, to get beyond the surface of things to an underlying reality and rationale. But it is not just because of this that its claims, however forcefully argued, must in a sense be bracketed, like any scientific claim. Durkheim is committed to the search for "scientific truth" – a belief in truth that is in its own way a mythological truth. It is basic to the meaning of science as an activity, making sense of and sustaining the attempt, the work, with all its disputes, risks, doubts and uncertainties, to develop an enlightened understanding of the world. But, he is explicit, it is not belief in a final, unchallengeable possession of the truth. It is a hope, a belief in *"progress"*. And it is in acceptance that there will always be "a free field open to our efforts". Hence man remains elusive if only because of the bracketing of any theoretical (including Kantian practical) claims about the world, even the well established.

Let us now turn to the need, which always exists, to go beyond the sphere of a more or less reasonably based knowledge itself. Then man remains elusive because Durkheim both seeks to bring the human ideal within this sphere and sees a continuing generation of aspirations, sentiments and movements and currents of opinion taking us beyond it.

But is there not something obscure at the core of the ideal itself, and so of its sociological understanding? The cult of "man" is of something so completely general and so completely abstract that it can seem a cult of a representation, which is precisely not a representation of any particular idea. It is a cult of "the person", the sacred word, the *logos*, that, magically, transforms us all into persons. But apart from the universalism that it enacts, and for which it is necessary, perhaps it has to be empty of any idea because it has to be a symbol of all the ideas it can be filled with. It brings into being a modern universal community of a formula, in a continuing development and diversity of ways of interpreting it. These beliefs around a common symbol in turn involve their own symbolisms, but which must at least have one shared symbol of the shared symbol, each individual human being as an icon of man.

The division of labour pushes to the extreme the necessary modern search for cohesion without consensus, and finds an alternative to a community of belief in a community of identity, attachment and interlocking connexions. This other argument pushes the same search to the extreme and finds an alternative to a community of belief in a community of symbols – the icon and the *logos*. The arguments can then come together, in a community of identity, attachment, interlocking connexions and symbolism, as the arena of the differences and conflicts around the modern human ideal and inherent in it, in whatever society at whatever time, as a community of belief. As in *The division of labour*, there is a "multitude" of such disagreements. As in the lectures on moral education, a society "without any conflict . . . would have only a quite mediocre morality" (1925a: 15; t.13). As in the debate with Parodi on equality, rival visions of this are built into our world and part of the same moral reality. As in "The introduction to Ethics", "the moral ideal is not fixed; it lives, evolves, forever transforms, despite the respect surrounding it" (1920a: 83; t.81).

It is idle to count on a consensus on issues at the core of the human ideal, with conflict just going on at the margins. Conflict takes place at the core itself, in disagreements over freedom, equality, justice, developing and flourishing, dignity, the individual as man and as woman . . . But this does not mean that there is not, in a particular society at a particular time, a community of belief with its own pattern of debate, centred in a consensus around some things and a range of conflicts over others, and so with its own sense of a moral agenda. Indeed, an essential part of the Durkheimian project is to try to understand such patterns in terms of an underlying rationale, so that an essential hope is that the agenda and centre of gravity of modern moral politics can move on, towards a republican realization of the rationale.

It is nonetheless a vision that, in seeing the moral ideal's development through constant stirrings of new, obscure aspirations, builds in limits to a society with autonomous self-understanding. This in any case depends on the constitution, through collective processes, of a collective body of knowledge and experience. It is something, in a society of persons, to which all of us might contribute and on which all of us might draw, but that goes beyond the limits of everyone's understanding as an individual. So the human ideal must remain, in various if not very mysterious ways, elusive. Man is the enlightened republic's hidden god.

Conclusion: from "is" to "ought"

Durkheim is not just one of the great founders of modern sociology. He has as good a claim as anyone to have developed a critical social science. This is partly because of the nature of his sociological theory itself. It is not least because of his development of an explicit ethical theory as a basis of critique and in a classic, enlightened commitment to the possibility of an informed, public, rational deliberation of ends.

This book shares that commitment. The task of the conclusion is not simply to recapitulate issues, themes and arguments outlined in the introduction and developed in subsequent chapters. It is to bring them together in an effort to show how Durkheim's project succeeds in its most fundamental, theoretical and practical ambition – a passage from "is" to "ought" that can establish and endorse the modern universalist ethic of the individual as man.

Situatedness and identity

Durkheim, as has been seen, is a persistent critic of our existing, actual society and a persistent advocate of reform. But where do the values and ideals of such criticism come from, and how might they be defended? It is possible just to refuse to discuss these questions and fall back on faith, or scepticism, or, indeed, a camouflage of value-judgements under a pretence of value-neutrality. Or it is possible, if we do try to address them, to appeal to intuition, metaphysics, human nature, universal reason . . . For Durkheim, however, the ideals in terms of which we criticize and seek to change our society must also arise from it. The ideal has its roots in the real although it is itself something real, and although it transfigures the real.

But a Durkheimian passage from "is" to "ought" – which he himself never fully sets out – involves at least three basic arguments. They concern situatedness, identity and the real and its rationale.

All three arguments emerge in his earliest writings and continue throughout his work. Let us start with situatedness and *The division of labour*'s original introduction:

> moralists of all schools . . . are obliged to take as the point of departure for their speculations a recognized, uncontested ethic, which can only be the one most generally followed in their time and milieu. It is from a summary observation of this ethic that they work up the law supposed to explain it. It supplies them with the material of their inferences; it is also where they return at the end of their deductions . . . Even when he [the moralist] seems to innovate, he only translates tendencies to reform that are at work around him. (1893b: 38; t.435).

Or, as in "The introduction to ethics":

> New ideas and aspirations stir up that lead to changes and even profound revolutions in existing morality. The role of the moralist is to make ready these necessary transformations . . . Through him, all the many currents cutting across society and over which minds are divided acquire consciousness of themselves and become expressed in reflection. It is indeed these currents that give rise to moral doctrines; it is to respond to them that they come into being. (1920a: 83; t.81)

Durkheim continues:

> The way man situates himself in the world, the way he conceives of his relations with other beings and with his fellow men varies according to conditions of time and place. Yet the moral ideal is always closely dependent on the conception men have of themselves and of their place in the universe. (*ibid.*: 89; t.86).

Thus the argument about situatedness can and does stress change. It is still to the effect that, even in the attempt to rise above their particular local social world, particular local ideas of human nature, universal reason, transcendental metaphysics and so on remain embedded in it.

On its own, and as a bridge between "is" and "ought", the argument fails. It is just mistaken to the extent that it suggests that it is impossible to escape our situation and reach out, in the imagination, to ways of life other than our own. On the contrary, history, anthropology, ethics itself and in general the human culture advocated by Durkheim demand, as a necessary postulate, that we can reach out, in the imagination, to other ways of life and transcend the confines of our own place and time.

But the argument is not mistaken to the extent that it is also an appeal to our identity, rooted in our situation, place and time. It is then an appeal to the limits not of what we can imagine but of what we can will. As in Durkheim's first publication: "The real man, the man truly man, is integrally part of a society which he wills as himself, since he cannot withdraw from it without degeneration and collapse" (1885a: 95). As in another early article: "The individual is integrally part of the society into which he is born; this penetrates him from all sides; to withdraw and isolate himself from it is to diminish himself" (1887a: 337). As in the paper on moral facts: "To will a morality other than that implied by the nature of society is to deny the latter and, in consequence, oneself" ([1906b] 1924a: 54; t.38).

This last passage is of especial interest, since, with its reference to what is implied by the nature of a society it brings together the arguments about situatedness, identity and the real and its rationale. All three arguments are necessary. The real and its rationale guide the will. Situatedness and identity are needed, in the first place, to supply it.

Thus behind the appeal to identity stands the whole theory of the self and the whole emphasis on attachment as "the very source of morality". An immediate implication, in the case of the modern world, is self-identification as liberal selves and attachment to its human ideal – autonomy, free thought, individualism and all. "Communitarians" such as Alasdair MacIntyre can dream as much as they like of other worlds and attack as much as they like the liberal individualism of our own. But they cannot escape its "penetration" from all sides, or the "deep, strong roots" it puts down within them. MacIntyre, it has been remarked, is a modernist despite himself (Larmore 1987: 36). The remark is not made from a Durkheimian perspective, but is apt enough in terms of it. A communitarian anti-individualistic attempt "to will a morality other than that implied by the nature of society is to deny the latter and, in consequence, oneself".

This, however, is to refer to modern liberal selves not as atoms or monads but as organic selves, interlockingly attached to one another, to society and to the universalizing collective representation of the person. Thus it is important to consider a passage in *The division of labour*'s original introduction, which discusses a conflict between social solidarity and individual independence and flourishing:

> But whatever this solidarity may be, whatever its nature and origins, it can be laid down only as a *fact* and this does not suffice to erect it into a *duty*. It is not enough to observe that in reality man is not completely master of himself to be entitled to conclude that he should not be completely master of himself. No doubt we are bound to our neighbours, our ancestors, our past; many of our beliefs, sentiments and actions are not our own but come to us from outside. But where is the proof that this dependence is something good? What gives it moral value? Why should it not be, on the contrary, a yoke we should seek to shake off, so that duty would then lie in a complete emancipation? This, it is known, was the doctrine of the Stoics. A reply is that the undertaking is unrealizable; but why should it not be attempted and carried through as far as possible? . . . [I]f my first duty is to be a person, I must reduce to a minimum all that is impersonal in me. (1893b: 8–9; t.414)

Durkheim goes on to insist that "solidarity is not only a duty not less obligatory than others, but is perhaps the very source of morality" (*ibid.*: 10; t.415). But it is only the development of *The division of labour*'s argument as a whole that answers his questions. It is society itself that is the source of "individual morality" and its ideals of personal developing and flourishing. In modern society, with its ideal of the individual as man, flourishing as a person is as a distinct, autonomous centre of thought and action. This can generate the pathological individualism of the "cult of the self" as an atom or monad. But the path to individuality and flourishing as a person lies in the social and ethical attachments of the organic self. This is certainly to shake off the "yoke" of a traditional, communitarian attachment. But it is to achieve emancipation through society itself, through a different solidarity and another identity.

Another important passage is in the preface, and comes just after talk of the new moral objectives that "science offers to the will":

> But, it is said, if science foresees, it does not command. This is true. Science tells us simply what is necessary for life. But how can it not be seen that, *on the assumption that man wills to live*, a very simple operation at once transforms the laws it establishes into imperative rules of conduct? No doubt it then becomes art; but the passage from one to the other is made without a break in continuity. It remains to be seen if we should will to live; even on this ultimate question, science, we believe, is not silent[1]. (1. We touch on it later.) ([1893b] 1902b: xl; t.34–5).

When we look up the reference, we find a discussion of hope as a source of the will to live, with the roots of both in social life itself (*ibid.*: 225–6; t.245–6). This then leads on to a long discussion of suicide, above all of "true suicide, the sad suicide", endemic in the modern world (*ibid.*: 226; t.247). The argument goes its own way, as part of Durkheim's attack on the idea of happiness as the driving force of social evolution, so that it is not made altogether clear how it touches on "the ultimate question", on which science is not silent, of whether we should will to live. Nor is the answer clear until the development of the argument of *Suicide* itself. It is not simply that to withdraw from society is to risk killing ourselves since, as in the earliest statement of the identity argument, we "cannot withdraw from it without degeneration and collapse". On the contrary, we risk losing the will to live and killing ourselves because we remain part of our society, with its individualist ideal – complete with individualism's pathologies – penetrating us from all sides. So the answer is again that the source of our ideals and identity – in this case, the human ideal and self-identification as individual and person – lies in our society itself.

We need a life-history to make life-plans, and we need anchorage in a core identity to be in a position to deliberate on particular ends, projects, views of the good and, indeed, interests. Identity precedes interests, as much as the other things, and the modern core identity is the individual as man. It inspires, for example, contractarian theories that postulate individuals in some sort of pre-social situation of choice of the just or the good society. But it is a social, not a pre-social, identity, and it already contains within it its own basic answer to the question of the just or the good society – a liberal society of persons. Durkheim especially attacks such theories – more or less all of them – when they "start" from the individual just as such rather than the person, or from atoms and monads rather than the organic self, or from the moral cripple, economic man. In any case he cuts through any ahistorical "rational reconstruction", whether or not a story of contract, to emphasize an identity that is sociohistorically formed and that is the unchosen context of choice and enlightened moral reflection. We cannot find criteria for such reflection in an empty, unsituated self, while although we can imagine very different identities from our own we cannot will them, given our own. Given this identity, along with the general argument for morality's source in solidariness and attachment, the ground is prepared for Durkheimian endorsement of the great, hegemonic moral ideals of our time.

The real and its rationale

The ground is only prepared by situatedness and identity, since although it is necessary to supply the will it is also necessary to guide it, which takes us, via Durkheim's internalist programme and view of autonomy, to the ethical principle: *the real and its rationale are the good.*

This, in the first place, is because for Durkheim a search to understand things must be a search for a rationale at work in them. But it is a search, in the internalist programme, to understand modern ideals and modern pathologies in terms of the same underlying, unfolding rationale, and to find a basis of critique of the actual, again in terms of this real rationale. From the standpoint of reform, it involves an ambivalence between optimism and despair: optimism, because the human ideal and its realization are written into modernity's dynamic; despair, because the forces that threaten this realization are written into it too. From the standpoint of ethics, it is to reject a perfectionist utopia. It is instead a vision of the coming, despite everything, of a republic of persons, which continues to secrete its characteristic pathologies, but which limits and contains them.

Yet what is the way in which it endorses the republic as a social and moral ideal?

Let us talk of moral cultures and ask what such a culture must contain, which is to ask, in effect, about morality's essential, universal elements. A Durkheimian answer looks for moral motivations, virtues and characters; ideas, in an objective discourse, of the right and the good; and an idea of the identity of the moral judge. Together these constitute a moral reality, with its own particular, culturally variable content. There is then a Durkheimian search for its rationale, but also for interrelationships with processes such as the division of labour, in a rationale of a wider, overall social and moral reality. This is an appeal, of the kind Hume dislikes about Montesquieu, to "certain *rapports* or relations" (Hume [1751] 1902: 197, n.1). But it is not an appeal, of the kind he condemns, to "eternal fitnesses and unfitnesses of things" (Hume [1739–40] 1978: 456). It is to look for a fitness of things in an ideal-typical dynamic of a local social and moral world. It is then a way of understanding and endorsing, as right, correct, appropriate in its place and time, the moral ideal that helps to form the dynamic and to power it.

It is thus not an attempt to judge between moral cultures, as if outside any, to pick one out as *the* ideal and condemn others – the error, we might say, of the vulgar universalist philosopher. The very identity of the moral judge is embedded in each different culture, so that such a *simpliste* universalism will be embedded in it too. Durkheim's form of universalism is a form of relativism that overcomes embeddedness, since it can and does claim objectivity in judgements of the fitness of things in terms of a real rationale, and so in judgements of an ethic as the right, appropriate ethic in its place and time. As such, it can and does endorse the modern universalist ethic of the individual as man, in that it is to endorse its universalism not as something timeless and retrospective but as a development globally and forwards.

It is also a form of rationalism that, in its very emphasis on an empirically based but also deductive search for an underlying real logic of things, must continue to involve its own brand of speculative or, as Durkheim often says in appealing to it, "dialectical" theorizing. Thus it is important to work out, if only "dialectically", the implications of autonomy as a proceduralism, since it is important to ask what substantive social and moral order it might endorse, and, it has been argued, it can endorse only the substantive social and moral ideal of a republic. This is no doubt like all the other arguments containing some or other liberal conclusion in their starting point. The arguments still matter, they are not easy or straightforward, and Durkheim's criticism of "moralists" is part of his campaign to develop a more sociological approach to ethics, not an attempt, in the name of science, to dispense with "art".

We can now commence the Durkheimian passage from "is" to "ought", which requires a first-level move, within the sphere of moral science, and its completion in a second-level move, within the sphere of ethics. An analogue, perhaps, is Kant's double route to the moral law in *The groundwork*, first through an anthropological search for the good will, then through pure practical reason's search for the ethical will. Another analogue is freedom's double status as a foundation and as a postulate.

The first-level move involves the arguments about situatedness, identity and a fitness of things. They are all within the sphere of moral science in that they are all at bottom judgements of reality, somewhat "metasociological" no doubt, but judgements of reality all the same. Yet their combined effect is to issue in a judgement of value, endorsing the human ideal as the modern ideal, in an autonomy of enlightened understanding and acceptance.

It is this that then takes us to the second-level move, via autonomy's two aspects, as enlightened understanding and acceptance and as freedom of the will itself. Autonomy, for Durkheim, depends on science, since it depends on an understanding of things: "thought is liberator of the will" (1925a: 136; t.119). But science "does not command" the will ([1893b] 1902b: xl; t.34). Autonomy is not just an understanding of things, or even just their enlightened acceptance. It is also, and as Durkheim himself discusses it, autonomy of the will.

Collective supersensible freedom

There has been talk of Durkheim's "sociological Kantianism", for example by Hans-Peter Müller (1986: 74). Puzzlement has been expressed at the idea, for example by Hans Joas (1993: 232) and elsewhere (Watts Miller 1993c: 148). Of course, there is often appeal to a sociology of "action" and "agency", and it often involves criticism of Durkheim. But is the criticism effective if it is just an affair of sociopolitical freedom? Durkheim looks for a modern sociopolitical freedom that is real and extensive. So is the criticism an affair of freedom of the will? Does the sociology of action in fact invoke a supersensible, transcendental, metaphysical liberty? Is it an expression, obscure, vague and intuitive, of a faith in freewill?

Certainly, few if any of those who criticize Durkheim and go on about "action" ever come out and come clean on this issue. How, after all, can social science combine with transcendental metaphysics?

Yet Kant himself seems committed to the combination, in that the causality of necessary connexion operates throughout the world, including the human social world. As he states the problem in *The groundwork*:

> Reason must therefore suppose that no genuine contradiction is to be found between the freedom and the natural necessity ascribed to the very same human actions; for it can abandon the concept of nature as little as it can abandon that of freedom. (Kant [1785] 1911: 456; t.116)

His solution involves two standpoints. From the standpoint of scientific theoretical reason and the sensible world we are subject to its causality. From the standpoint of practical reason and the intelligible or supersensible world we are free – unconditioned by the empirical world's causality, yet with a causal power to act on and through it.

Durkheim appears to reject all this, in insisting on an autonomy that develops in and through the world, and in understanding and acceptance of it. But autonomy is not a matter of sheer choice, of an arbitrary freewill, whether as an individual put-the-slave-on-the-cross *sic volo* or as a collective put-the-slave-on-the-cross *sic volumus*. It is a free acceptance in light of understanding of the moral ideal as the human ideal. Durkheim is here, in a way, very Kantian. The legislative will (*Wille*) discovers and declares the moral law – the universalizing morality of the person – as an objective necessary rationale. The executive will (*Willkür*) is autonomous to the extent that it chooses in light of this legislative understanding, respects its authority, and feels its necessitation and constraint.

A difference is that for Durkheim the legislative will discovers and declares the human ideal as a modern ideal, rooted in a modern logic of things. The difference is not so great if we take the route not of pure practical reason and the second *Critique* but of philosophical history and the third *Critique*. It is concerned, as Delbos points out, with freedom as a development rather than just a thing, *res aeterna*. It has also been argued that Durkheimian autonomy accommodates a development of the kernel, in everyone, of a free supersensible ability. Indeed it need not just accommodate this. It can lift it, through its involvement of a sociohistorical development in man as a species, from any purely individual level to transpose it into and emphasize a collective supersensible freedom.

Although, in talking of autonomy, Durkheim never talks of a supersensible freedom, the idea is there – above all as an idea of a collective supersensible freedom, and in the distinction between a social and moral world's rationale and an "alien" (even if internal) causality that threatens it. We achieve the autonomy of a collective supersensible freedom to the extent that our society achieves an understanding of its own rationale, realizes the ideals inherent in this, overcomes causalities opposing them, and becomes, in fact, a republic of persons.

The achievement of such autonomy is, and must always be, a struggle, a collective willed effort. The legislative effort, of discovering, working out and interpreting, in our conflicts and disputes, the universalism of the human ideal, faces the challenge, amongst others, of developing globally and as an unmonolithic universalism of different cultures and traditions. The executive effort of adherence to the ideal is not just an individual's battle against "sensible" desires, but returns us to the Durkheimian internalist programme and modernity's built-in risks, pathologies and "alien" causalities. The division of labour is not merely the other side of the market, yet is still tied up with it and its secretion of instrumentalism and an anomic, oppressive, class-divided society. Anchorage in particular connexions is essential, yet can lock us into narrow, hate-filled, communitarian identities instead of into the world. The cult of the individual courts atomization, can slide into all the forms of modern, not so postmodern, scepticism, and sets up libertarian demands for a freedom, without dignity, that undermines the whole central sacred value of the person. It is part of modernity's own logic of things that, as Durkheim fought hard not to admit, the republic might never come.

This intransigently optimistic streak has a place in the development of many of the concerns of his work: the spontaneous division of labour, the organic self, intermediate groups, a cult and culture of man, virtue ethics, secular science, autonomy . . . Yet it clearly has a place, too, in his constant appeals to effort, commitment, will. He is as much a sociologist of "action" as anyone. But it is of collective action, in the cause of individualism and an enlightened republic, and in an understanding that to have hope we must believe, and to believe we must have hope.

Notes

Introduction

1. "Ethics" generally refers here to a normative theory of morals; Durkheim's talk of *la morale* follows established usage in that it can sometimes refer to ethics, sometimes to morals.
2. References to works by Durkheim do not cite him by name. Translations from Durkheim are my own or, where it is gratuitous to depart from the published translation, my responsibility. This is also generally the case for other French authors. I am especially indebted to the translators of Kant, and appreciative of N. Rudd's translations of Juvenal. References to an English translation are indicated by "t", and references to A. Cuvillier's French translation of Durkheim's Latin thesis are indicated by "tf".
3. A common modern view of Hume is that, positivistically, he limits causation to regularities between observable phenomena, and refuses to go beyond these to a hidden, unobservable world of necessary connexions between things. This view has been challenged by recent commentators, including Galen Strawson (1989). But Hume is also taken (and defended) as subscribing to necessary connexion in Victor Cousin's *Philosophie écossaise* (1857: 385), based on lectures first given in 1819.
4. "The real is the rational is the good" was a slogan of the Scottish and English neo-Hegelians. J. MacTaggart, for example, wrote an article on Hegel for the first issue of the *Revue de métaphysique et de morale* (1893).

Chapter 2

1. The eventual French translation (1953a), by Durkheim's ex-student, Armand Cuvillier, is excellent. The English translation (1960b) appears to be based on this rather than the original and is less satisfactory.
2. Cuvillier appears correct to translate Durkheim as concerned with social facts, social science, etc. Bernard Lacroix is mistaken to suggest that the thesis really is about *scientia politica* rather than sociology (Lacroix 1981: 30). This ignores the opening list of *res politicae* (laws, *mores*, religions, etc.), the

whole argument of the thesis, and Durkheim's own use of the term *societas*, as in his criticism of Montesquieu for using governments to designate types of societies – *species societatum* (1892a: 40; tf.68; t.32). Indeed in talking of *scientia politica*, Durkheim seems out to redefine and reconceptualize it as social science.

3. The English translation botches Durkheim's contrast between a decree and an effort of the will in rendering "decree of the will" as an "act of the will". The idea of willed effort – *l'effort voulu* – is associated with Maine de Biran, a philosopher enjoying a revival at the time. For a discussion of his idea of this see the 1910–11 lecture course given by Victor Delbos (1931: 189–207).

4. The English translation omits the reference to the will.

5. Durkheim writes *videatur*, not *mihi videatur*! The French translation makes an uncharacteristic mistake in rendering "it seems" as "it seems to me", a mistake reproduced in the English translation as "to my mind". This attributes to Durkheim the very view he is criticizing.

6. "Leges sunt necessariae connexiones quae ex rerum natura sequuntur". Cf. Montesquieu (1748: I.1).

7. It goes back to Durkheim's own testimony that he owes to Boutroux the idea that each science explains according to its own principles (1907b: 613).

8. As in Durkheim's own testimony that he owes to Renouvier the axiom that the whole does not equal the sum of its parts (1913a(15): 326).

9. In a note (1892a: 55, n.2; tf.89, n.30) omitted from the English translation, but that should be at t.45.

10. Quoted in a note (1892a: 68, n.6; tf.107, n.16) omitted from the English translation, but that should be at t.59.

11. "Non sentit societatum naturam . . ." – another example of Durkheim's use of the term *societas*.

12. The English translation omits the phrase here italicized.

13. A letter of 1752 reads: "so that the sacred faculty can come up with something from such a multitude and variety of opinions concerning censure of the book entitled *Mens Legum*" (quoted in the original Latin by Robert Shackleton 1961: 369, n.6).

14. The note, omitted from the English translation, should be at t.45.

15. It is relevant, given Durkheim's rationalist view of science, that the meanings of "explanation" and "interpretation" are combined in *interpretatio*, a term standardly used in the thesis.

16. "Hoc est quo Monarchia differt a ceteris civitatibus: scilicet, laboris partitio". Durkheim does not say that the division of labour is how monarchy differs in its principle! – a confusion introduced in the French and repeated in the English translation.

17. "[N]on patriae, sed classis imago animos tenet."

18. Concern for "character" is to render the term *indoles*. The French translation also has trouble with this term, and the English translation just omits it. The trouble is rooted in honour ethics themselves, and debate over honour by natural make-up or by social breeding.

Chapter 3

1. Aristotle, *Politics* B, 1261a, 24–5. The passage was misleadingly removed in *The division of labour*'s 1973 9th edition to the top of the new preface. A misprint was introduced in the 1922 4th edition and has remained ever since. The passage is omitted from the English translation.
2. A regime has torn up the country's unwritten constitution, destroyed checks and balances, installed a Bonapartist state and spread social and moral malaise.
3. The original edition refers to emigration (1893b: 317), not as in some later editions to integration!
4. The reference to phalansteries is to the communities envisaged by the utopian socialist Charles Fourier.
5. The English translation has "narrow commercialism", which does not capture the meanness and grubbiness of *commercialisme mesquin*.

Chapter 4

1. Bosanquet read out a paper on sociology and philosophy that Durkheim was due to give to a meeting in London of the Sociological Society but was unable to attend (1905c).
2. Seth is ignored by his fellow countryman, Alasdair MacIntyre, in his Aristotelian *After virtue* (1981), which helped to get the current debate going.
3. Bik's Oxford D.Phil., supervised by Steven Lukes, was praised by Charles Taylor, who warms to the possibility of the holist route to individualism and says that theorists who explored it "occupy an extremely important place in the development of modern liberalism", but then gives as an example someone mentioned in a couple of footnotes in the thesis (Taylor 1989: 163). He says nothing about the man starring in it as the approach's greatest contributor. Perhaps this elimination of the Oxford thesis's Durkheim is a case for Inspector Morse to investigate.
4. Cf. Georges Deleuze (1953, vol. 2: 23–7); Philippe Saltel (1993: 33–4).
5. The quotations are from Rousseau's *Essay on the origin of languages* ([1781] 1870, vol. 1: 385), although Durkheim simply refers to chapter 9, and does not give any edition.
6. The English translation, perhaps understandably, renders the "sensible" individual as the "sensual" individual. But this obscures Durkheim's deliberate use of a Kantian term, conventionally rendered in both French and English translations of Kant as *sensible*.
7. There is of course a huge literature on *Suicide*, which it is neither possible nor necessary to cover here.
8. "Inordinate individuation", and not, as in the English translation, "inordinate individualism".
9. The liberal problematic of moderation versus strong sentiments of morals is discussed elsewhere (Watts Miller 1992).

Chapter 5

1. The English translation omits "sufficient".
2. The English translation makes nonsense of the passage, in rendering "if it is not noted . . ." as "if it is noted . . .".
3. This section of the original introduction is omitted from the part of it reprinted in 1975b, vol. 2, and is also omitted from the English translation.
4. Filloux talks of *hérédité sociale*, Cardi of *héritage sociale*, which seems preferable.
5. This is so, even though in England's current state his study would have to be about how working-class kids do not get working-class jobs.
6. For an earlier account see Watts Miller (1988).
7. But see the remark in the lectures on moral education: "There has often been scorn of the worker, who goes through the same motions day after day; but this is only a caricature, an exaggerated form of the kind of existence that we all lead to some extent" (1925a: 151; t.132).
8. For a more detailed critique of a corporatist reform in which the occupational group is the sole basis of politics, see Watts Miller (1993c).

Chapter 6

1. Cf. the note inserted in the 2nd edition of *The rules* (1901c: 88, n.1; t.117, n.10).
2. The English translation destroys Durkheim's point by omitting "it is not enough to say".
3. "Et propter vitam vivendi perdere causas" – quoted without reference ([1898b] 1970a: 275; t.197).
4. Juvenal, 8th Satire, lines 80–84, *Satires* (t. N. Rudd 1991).
5. Lecture notes taken by Armand Cuvillier, 1908–9.
6. Part of notes on a lecture course, "De l'enseignement de la morale à l'école primaire", reproduced by Steven Lukes in his D.Phil. thesis, and obtained from Raymond Lenoir, a student of Durkheim's and a friend of his son, André. Steven Lukes, in a personal communication, has expressed doubts about Lenoir's claim that all the notes were by Durkheim himself. A manuscript page in Durkheim's handwriting is reproduced as part of the publication of one of the lectures, "L'état", in the *Revue philosophique* **148** (1955), 432.

Chapter 7

1. The published translation eliminates Durkheim's Kantian talk of antinomies.
2. The discussion is about *volonté*, the will, and *vouloir* is here translated as "to will", whereas the published translation opts for it as to desire and wish.
3. The published translation again eliminates Durkheim's Kantian talk, rendering it as: "Our ascendancy has gained its goal."

Chapter 8

1. With the essay on perpetual peace, published in 1795. See A. Philonenko (1993, vol. 2: 264-9).
2. To a large extent through the influence of Victor Cousin, whose lectures on Kant, from 1818 on, were part of a series of lectures on Kant, Hegel and the Scots. See Paul Janet (1893).
3. Juvenal, 6th Satire, lines 219-24, *Satires* (t. N. Rudd 1991). The original is in fact "hoc volo, sic jubeo" (line 223).
4. Cf. the comment: "A strange obligation, which imposes obedience, and which is at the same time internal and not external, as an absolute law which a being gives to itself" (Boutroux 1926: 290).
5. The English translation omits the reference to the standard French translation of the time, by Barni, and corresponding with Kant ([1788] 1913: 32-3; t. 32-3).
6. A few pages on he seems to identify the *volonté bonne* with the *unbedingt guter Wille* (Boutroux 1926: 304) – the absolutely good or holy and humanly unrealizable will. But it is worth sticking to the *volonté bonne* as an ethical, humanly realizable, virtuous will.
7. Delbos translates *Willkür* as *libre arbitre*.
8. "Von dem Willen gehen die Gesetze aus; von der Willkür die Maximen."
9. The English translation's "we simply find it", instead of "we make it only in that we discover it", botches Durkheim's interpretative point.
10. "[E]in Ganzes aller Zwecke... in systematischer Verknüpfung."
11. The phrase *das glänzende Elend* recurs elsewhere in a similar context, for example in the third *Critique*, but translated as "shining misery" (Kant [1790] 1913: 432; t.320).
12. Despite the English translation's "association".
13. This is why, far from being "unDurkheimian", it is essential to appeal to everyone's natural potential to qualify and develop as a person in a republic of persons. *The division of labour* is very much involved in the argument against a reactionary and for a republican anthropology. Bouglé became even more involved in it, in his article "Anthropology and democracy" (1897) and in his later books *Egalitarian ideas* (1899) and *Democracy in view of science* (1909). A Kantian appeal to the free kernel in everyone is not just an alternative to a republican anthropology but may be an essential complement to it.
14. Kant, in such statements, was still well to the left of common elite opinion, but well to the right of the French Republic's Constitution of 1793, the first ever to proclaim universal male suffrage and full, active citizenship.
15. Kant gave up on the idea of a cosmopolitan state, as Philonenko explains (1993, vol. 2: 264). He moved over to something like the Durkheimian idea of an evolution of each society as a human *patrie* and of an international system of human *patries*. But this does not affect his basic resolution of the Rousseauan problem.

Chapter 9

1. But in *The elementary forms* Durkheim goes on to offer an explanation of belief in the immortal soul in terms of the perpetuity of the life of the group: "Individuals die; but the clan survives." Hence "this belief, despite its symbolic character, is not without an objective truth" (1912a: 384–5; t.304). He also links the soul itself with the idea of the personality, which is when he discusses the dualism of the person versus the individual (*ibid.*: 386–90; t.305–8). He returns to these points in the article on the dualism of human nature ([1914a] 1970a: 316–18; t.326–8).
2. For a further discussion, see Watts Miller (1992).
3. Thus by the 1930s, when *The elementary forms* had reached only its 2nd edition, the *Sketch* was into its 20th edition, and *The non–religion of the future* was into its 24th edition.
4. This translates the 1st edition of *Ethics*. The English translation is of the 2nd, revised edition (although the particular passage concerned remains the same). The 3rd edition is further revised.
5. His discussion makes clear that *l'irreligion de l'avenir* is better translated as the "non–religion" rather than the "irreligion" of the future.
6. The English translation is of the 2nd edition of the *Sketch*, revised and rearranged after Guyau's death by Fouillée, so that parts 1, 2, 3 and 4 become parts 2, 1, 4 and 3.
7. Guyau's attack on Scottish philosophy is mainly directed at Cousin, who popularized it in France. Guyau is fairer to the Scots, including Reid, in the not altogether aptly entitled *Contemporary English ethics* (1879). For a discussion of the influence of Scottish philosophy on French philosophy, see Boutroux (1897).
8. The point about monotheism is not just a throwback to Durkheim's "earlier" morphological days; its link with the arguments of the *Elementary forms* is noted by Cuvillier, the editor of the lectures on pragmatism (1955a: 177, n.2; t.87, n.3).
9. Durkheim picks up the Guyauan theme of risk in the lectures on moral education: "there are many careers in which the professional risk is quite considerable and which nonetheless recruit their members without difficulty . . . They prefer to expose themselves to certain and serious danger rather than give up their work, a form of activity which they enjoy" (1925a: 186: t.162)

Chapter 10

1. For a discussion suggesting how they might be overcome and defending Kant against standard criticisms, see Philonenko (1993, vol. 2: 166–70).
2. Mathiez was promptly accused of confusing religious phenemona with religion itself, in a review by Marcel Mauss (1905). But the accusation is not repeated by Durkheim in the *Elementary forms*.
3. For discussions, see, for example, Cornu (1956), Hermant (1978), Idzerda

(1954), Watts Miller (1994: 120–25), as well as Mathiez himself.

4. For other discussions of the king's trial and execution, see, for example, Fehér (1987), the Girault de Coursacs (1982), Soboul (1966), Walzer (1974).

5. J.-M. Rouzet, speech of 15 November 1792, in *Archives parlementaires*, 1st series, vol. 53 (Paris, 1898–9), 423.

6. As stated in the lectures on moral education, Durkheim's views on punishment in modern society have much in common with Guyau's views on the same subject, as stated in *Sketch of a morality without obligation or sanction*. That is, he is very much opposed to oppressive appeals to it, as distractions from the need for more fundamental social and moral reform. The best recent account of Durkheim on punishment is by David Garland (1990), although the very focus on the issue gives it far more importance than it has in Durkheim's overall, more positive ethical concerns.

7. Mathiez, in even raising the issue of revolutionary iconoclasm, was criticized for playing into the hands of the anti-republican right, and this might be part of the sub-text of the criticism of him by Mauss.

8. For another account, and the best recent discussion of Durkheim on nationalism, see Joseph Llobera (1994).

References

1. The dating-enumeration for works by Durkheim follows the system developed by Steven Lukes (1973) and W. S. F. Pickering (1984).
2. In the bibliography, as in the text, "t" refers to an English translation, "tf" to a French translation.

Agulhon, M. 1979. *Marianne au combat: l'imagerie et la symbolique républicaines de 1789 à 1880*. Paris: Flammarion.

—1989. *Marianne au pouvoir: l'imagerie et la symbolique républicaines de 1880 à 1914*. Paris: Flammarion.

Alexander, J. C. 1982. *Theoretical logic in sociology* [4 volumes]. London: Routledge & Kegan Paul.

Anon. 1895. Review of E. Durkheim, *Les règles de la méthode sociologique*. *Revue de métaphysique et de morale* 3, January supplement, 1.

Beck, U. 1986. *Risikogesellschaft: auf dem Weg in eine andere Moderne*. Frankfurt am Main: Suhrkamp (t.1992. *Risk society: towards a new modernity*. London: Sage).

Belot, G. 1905–6. En quête d'une morale positive. *Revue de métaphysique et de morale* 13 and 14.

—1907. *Etudes de morale positive*. Paris: Alcan.

Besnard, P. 1973. Durkheim et les femmes ou *Le suicide* inachevé. *Revue française de sociologie* 14.

—1987. *L'anomie: ses usages et ses fonctions dans la discipline sociologique depuis Durkheim*. Paris: Presses Universitaires de France.

—1993a. Les pathologies des sociétés modernes. See Besnard, Borlandi & Vogt (1993), 197–211.

—1993b. De la datation des cours pédagogiques de Durkheim à la recherche du thème dominant de son oeuvre. See Cardi & Plantier (1993), 120–30.

—1993c. Anomie and fatalism in Durkheim's theory of regulation. See Turner (1993), 169–90.

Besnard, P., M. Borlandi & P. Vogt (eds) 1993. *Division du travail et lien social: la thèse de Durkheim un siècle après*. Paris: Presses Universitaires de France.

Bik, M. 1987. *The liberal–communitarian debate: a defence of holistic individual-*

ism. D.Phil. thesis, University of Oxford.

Borlandi, M. 1993. Durkheim lecteur de Spencer. See Besnard, Borlandi & Vogt (1993), 67–109.

Bosanquet, B. 1899. *The philosophical theory of the state.* London: Macmillan.

Bouglé, C. 1897. Anthropologie et démocratie. *Revue de métaphysique et de morale* 5.

—1899. *Les idées égalitaires: étude sociologique.* Paris: Alcan.

—1903. Revue générale des théories récentes sur la division du travail social. *Année sociologique* 6.

—1909. *La démocratie devant la science: études critiques sur l'hérédité, la concurrence et la différenciation,* 2nd edn. Paris: Alcan.

—1914. Remarques sur le polytélisme. *Revue de métaphysique et de morale* 22.

Boutroux, E. [1874] 1895a. *De la contingence des lois de la nature,* 2nd edn. Paris: Alcan (t.1916. *The contingency of the laws of nature.* London: Open Court).

—1895b. *De l'idée de loi naturelle dans la science et la philosophie: cours professé à la Sorbonne en 1892–93.* Paris: Lecène, Oudin (t.1914. *Natural law in science and philosophy.* London: Nutt).

—1895c. Kant. *Grande Encyclopédie.* Paris: Lamirault; reprinted in Boutroux (1925).

—1897. *De l'influence de la philosophie écossaise sur la philosophie française.* Edinburgh: Willis & Norgate; reprinted in Boutroux (1925).

—1904. La morale de Kant et le temps présent. *Revue de métaphysique et de morale* 12.

—1908. *Science et religion dans la philosophie contemporaine.* Paris: Flammarion.

—1909. Contribution to discussion, Science et religion. *Bulletin de la société française de philosophie* 9; reprinted in Boutroux (1928).

—1925. *Etudes de l'histoire de la philosophie,* 4th edn. Paris: Alcan.

—1926. *La philosophie de Kant: cours professé à la Sorbonne en 1896–1897.* Paris: Vrin.

—1928. *Emile Boutroux: choix de textes avec une étude sur l'oeuvre,* introduction by P. Archambault. Paris: Rasmussen.

Brunschvicg, L. & E. Halévy 1894. Philosophie pratique. *Revue de métaphysique et de morale* 2.

Burns, R. [1795] 1986. *A man's a man for a' that.* In *The complete works of Robert Burns.* Alloway, Ayrshire: Alloway.

Cardi, F. 1993. Education, classes sociales et lien social chez Durkheim. See Cardi & Plantier (1993), 35–43.

Cardi, F. & J. Plantier (eds) 1993. *Durkheim, sociologue de l'éducation.* Paris: L'Harmattan.

Cladis, M. S. 1992. *A communitarian defense of liberalism: Emile Durkheim and contemporary social theory.* Stanford, Calif.: Stanford University Press.

Constant, B. [1819] 1980. De la liberté des anciens comparée à celle des modernes. In *De la liberté chez les modernes.* Paris: Le Livre de Poche (t.1988 in

Benjamin Constant: political writings. Cambridge: Cambridge University Press).

Cornu, M. 1956. Le père du vandalisme révolutionnaire. *Europe.*

Cousin, V. 1857. *La philosophie écossaise,* 3rd edn. Paris: Librairie nouvelle.

Cuin, C-H. 1987. Durkheim et la mobilité sociale. *Revue française de sociologie* 27.

—1991. Durkheim et l'inégalité sociale: les avatars et les leçons d'une entreprise. *Recherches sociologiques* 22.

Cuvillier, A. 1948. Durkheim et Marx. *Cahiers internationaux de sociologie* 4.

Darlu, A. 1898. De M. Brunetière et de l'individualisme. *Revue de métaphysique et de morale* 6.

Delbos, V. [1905] 1969. *La philosophie pratique de Kant,* 3rd edn. Paris: Presses Universitaires de France.

—1931. *Maine de Biran et son oeuvre philosophique.* Paris: Vrin.

Deleuze, G. 1953. *Empirisme et subjectivité: essai sur la nature humaine selon Hume.* Paris: Presses Universitaires de France.

Durkheim, E. 1885a. Review of A. Schaeffle, *Bau und Leben des sozialen Körpers,* vol. 1. *Revue philosophique* 19; reprinted in Durkheim (1975b), vol. 1.

—1885b. Review of A. Fouillée, *La propriété sociale et la démocratie. Revue philosophique* 19; reprinted in Durkheim (1970a).

—1885c. Review of L. Gumplowicz, *Grundriss der Soziologie. Revue philosophique* 20; reprinted in Durkheim (1975b), vol. 1.

—1886a. Les études de science sociale. *Revue philosophique* 22; reprinted in Durkheim (1970a) (first section, review of H. Spencer, *Ecclesiastical institutions,* t. in Durkheim 1975a).

—1886b. Review of G. De Greef, *Introduction à la sociologie. Revue philosophique* 22; reprinted in Durkheim (1975b), vol.1.

—1887a. La philosophie dans les universités allemandes. *Revue internationale de l'enseignement* 13; reprinted in Durkheim (1975b), vol. 3.

—1887b. Review of J-M. Guyau, *L'irréligion de l'avenir. Revue philosophique* 23; reprinted in Durkheim (1975b), vol. 2 (t. in Durkheim 1975a).

—1887c. La science positive de la morale en Allemagne. *Revue philosophique* 24; reprinted in Durkheim (1975b), vol. 1 (t. in 1993a. *Ethics and the sociology of morals.* Buffalo, NY: Prometheus Books).

—1888a. Cours de science sociale: leçon d'ouverture. *Revue internationale de l'enseignement* 15; reprinted in Durkheim (1970a).

—1888b. Le programme économique de M. Schaeffle. *Revue d'économie politique* 11; reprinted in Durkheim (1975b), vol. 1.

—1888c. Introduction à la sociologie de la famille. *Annales de la faculté des lettres de Bordeaux;* reprinted in Durkheim (1975b), vol. 3 (t. in 1978a. *Emile Durkheim on institutional analysis.* Chicago: University of Chicago Press).

—1889b. Review of F. Tönnies, *Gemeinschaft und Gesellschaft. Revue philosophique* 27; reprinted in Durkheim (1975b), vol. 1.

—1890a. Les principes de 1789 et la sociologie. *Revue internationale de l'enseignement* 19; reprinted in Durkheim (1970a) (t. in 1973a. *Emile*

Durkheim on morality and society. Chicago: University of Chicago Press).

—1892a. *Quid Secundatus politiciae scientiae instituendae contulerit: hanc thesim Parisiensi litterarum facultati proponebat.* Bordeaux: Gounouilhou (tf. in Durkheim 1953a [t.1960b]).

—1893b(1). *De la division du travail social: thèse présentée à la faculté des lettres de Paris.* Paris: Alcan.

—1893b(2). *De la division du travail social: étude sur l'organisation des sociétés supérieures.* Paris: Alcan – same as thesis, except for new sub-title; part of introduction reprinted in Durkheim (1975b), vol. 2.

—1893c. Note sur la définition du socialisme. *Revue philosophique* **36**; reprinted in Durkheim (1970a).

—1894a. Les règles de la méthode sociologique. *Revue philosophique* **37** and **38**.

—1895a. *Les règles de la méthode sociologique.* Paris: Alcan.

—1895b. L'enseignement philosophique et l'agrégation de philosophie. *Revue philosophique* **39**; reprinted in Durkheim (1975b), vol. 3.

—1897a. *Le suicide: étude de sociologie.* Paris: Alcan (t.1951a. *Suicide.* Glencoe, Ill.: Free Press).

—1897e. Review of A. Labriola, *Essais sur la conception matérialiste de l'histoire. Revue philosophique* **44**; reprinted in Durkheim (1970a) (t. in Durkheim 1982a).

—1897f. *Contribution to Enquête sur l'oeuvre de H. Taine. Revue blanche* **13**; reprinted in Durkheim (1975b), vol. 1.

—1898a(ii). La prohibition de l'inceste et ses origines. *Année sociologique* **1**; reprinted in 1969c (t.1963a. *Incest: the nature and origin of the taboo.* New York: Lyle Stuart).

—1898c. L'individualisme et les intellectuels. *Revue bleue* **10**(4); reprinted in Durkheim (1970a) (t. in Durkheim 1975a).

—1899a(ii). De la définition des phénomènes religieux. *Année sociologique* **2**; reprinted in Durkheim (1969c) (t. in Durkheim 1975a).

—1900a(30). Review of A. Lampérière, *Le rôle social de la femme. Année sociologique* **3**.

—1901a(i). Deux lois de l'évolution pénale. *Année sociologique* **4**; reprinted in Durkheim (1969c) (t. in 1983. *Durkheim and the law.* Oxford: Martin Robertson).

—1901a(iii)(28). Review of J. Lourbet, *Le problème des sexes. Année sociologique* **4**; reprinted in Durkheim (1975b), vol. 3.

—1901c. *Les règles de la méthode sociologique,* 2nd edn. Paris: Alcan (t.1982a. *The rules of sociological method.* London: Macmillan).

—1902b. *De la division du travail social,* 2nd edn. Paris: Alcan (t.1933b. *The division of labour in society.* New York: Macmillan – includes the part of the original introduction omitted in 2nd edn).

—1903a(i). De quelques formes primitives de classification: contribution à l'étude des représentations collectives. *Année sociologique* **6**; reprinted in Durkheim (1969c) (t.1963b. *Primitive classification.* London: Cohen & West).

—1903b. Pédagogie et sociologie. *Revue de métaphysique et de morale* **11**;

reprinted in Durkheim (1922a [t.1956a]).

—1904a(5). Review of L. Lévy-Bruhl, *La morale et la science des meours*. *Année sociologique* 7; reprinted in Durkheim (1969c) (t. in Durkheim 1979a).

—1904a(18). Review of C. Letourneau, *La condition de la femme dans les diverses races et civilisations*. *Année sociologique* 7; reprinted in Durkheim (1975b), vol. 3.

—1904a(40). Review of E. Durkheim, Pédagogie et sociologie. *Année sociologique* 7; reprinted in Durkheim (1975b), vol. 1.

—1905c. On the relation of sociology to the social sciences and to philosophy. *Sociological Papers* 1.

—1905e. Contibution to discussion, Sur l'internationalisme. *Libres entretiens* 2; parts reprinted in Durkheim (1970a) and (1975b), vol. 3.

—1906b. La détermination du fait moral. *Bulletin de la société française de philosophie* 6; reprinted in Durkheim (1924a [t.1953b]).

—1906d. Le divorce par consentement mutuel. *Revue bleue* 44(5); reprinted in Durkheim (1975b), vol. 2.

—1907a(4). Review of G. Belot, *En quête d'une morale positive*. *Année sociologique* 10; reprinted in Durkheim (1969c).

—1907b. Lettres au directeur de la Revue néo-scolastique. *Revue néo-scolastique* 14; reprinted in Durkheim (1975b), vol. 1.

—1907f. Cours d'Emile Durkheim à la Sorbonne. *Revue de philosophie* 7; reprinted in Durkheim (1975b), vol. 2.

—1908a(1). Contribution to discussion, Pacifisme et patriotisme. *Bulletin de la société française de philosophie* 8; reprinted in Durkheim (1970a).

—1908a(2). Contribution to discussion, La morale positive: examen de quelques difficultés. *Bulletin de la société française de philosophie* 8; reprinted in Durkheim (1975b), vol. 2 (t. in Durkheim 1979a).

—1908g. Contribution to discussion, L'inconnu et l'inconscient en historie. *Bulletin de la société française de philosophie* 8; reprinted in Durkheim (1975b), vol. 1 (t. in Durkheim 1982a).

—1910a(iii)(19). Review of Marianne Weber, *Ehefrau und Mutter in der Rechtsentwicklung*. *Année sociologique* 11; reprinted in Durkheim (1969c).

—1910a(iii)(20). Review of Gaston Richard, *La femme dans l'histoire*. *Année sociologique* 11; reprinted in Durkheim (1975b), vol. 3.

—1910b. Contribution to discussion, La notion d'égalité sociale. *Bulletin de la société française de philosophie* 10; reprinted in Durkheim (1975b), vol. 2 (t. in Durkheim 1979a).

—1911a. Contribution to discussion, L'éducation sexuelle. *Bulletin de la société française de philosophie* 11; reprinted in Durkheim (1975b), vol. 2 (t. in Durkheim 1979a).

—1911b. Jugements de valeur et jugements de réalité. *Revue de métaphysique et de morale* 19; reprinted in Durkheim (1924a [t.1953b]).

—1911c. Education. *Nouveau dictionnaire de pédagogie et d'instruction primaire*, published under the direction of F. Buisson. Paris: Hachette; reprinted in Durkheim (1922a).

—1912a. *Les formes élémentaires de la vie religieuse*. Paris: Alcan (t.1961b. *The elementary forms of the religious life*. New York: Collier).

—1913a(15). Review of S. Deploige, *Le conflit de la morale et de la sociologie*. *Année sociologique* 12; reprinted in Durkheim (1975b), vol. 1.

—1914a. Le dualisme de la nature humaine et ses conditions sociales. *Scientia* 15; reprinted in Durkheim (1970a) (t. in 1960c. *Emile Durkheim, 1858–1917*. Columbus, Ohio: Ohio State University Press).

—1918b. *Le Contrat social* de Rousseau. *Revue de métaphysique et de morale*, 25; reprinted in Durkheim (1953a [t.1960b]).

—1920a. Introduction à la morale. *Revue philosophique* 89; reprinted in Durkheim (1975b), vol. 2 (t. in Durkheim 1979a).

—1921a. La famille conjugale: conclusion du cours sur la famille. *Revue philosophique* 90; reprinted in Durkheim (1975b), vol. 3.

—1922a. *Education et sociologie*, introduction by P. Fauconnet. Paris: Alcan (t.1956a. *Education and sociology*. Glencoe, Ill.: Free Press).

—1924a. *Sociologie et philosophie*, preface by C. Bouglé. Paris: Alcan (t.1953b. *Sociology and philosophy*. London: Cohen & West).

—1925a. *L'éducation morale*, foreword by P. Fauconnet. Paris: Alcan (t.1961a. *Moral education*. New York: Free Press).

—[1928a] 1971d. *Le socialisme*, 2nd edn, edited with introduction by M. Mauss, new preface by P. Birnbaum. Paris: Presses Universitaires de France (t.1958b. *Socialism and Saint-Simon*. Yellow Springs, Ohio: Antioch Press).

—1938a. *L'évolution pédagogique en France* [2 volumes], introduction by M. Halbwachs. Paris: Alcan (t.1977a. *The evolution of educational thought*. London: Routledge & Kegan Paul).

—[1950a] 1969g. *Leçons de sociologie: physique des meours et du droit*, 2nd edn, foreword by H. N. Kubali, introduction by G. Davy. Paris: Presses Universitaires de France (t.1957a. *Professional ethics and civic morals*. London: Routledge & Kegan Paul).

—1953a. *Montesquieu et Rousseau*, edited by A. Cuvillier, introduction by G. Davy. Paris: Marcel Rivière (t.1960b. *Montesquieu and Rousseau*. Ann Arbor, Mich.: University of Michigan Press).

—1955a. *Pragmatisme et sociologie*, edited with preface by A. Cuvillier. Paris: Vrin (t.1983a. *Pragmatism and sociology*. Cambridge: Cambridge University Press).

—1969c. *Journal sociologique*, edited with introduction by J. Duvignaud. Paris: Presses Universitaires de France.

—1970a. *La science sociale et l'action*, edited with introduction by J-C. Filloux. Paris: Presses Universitaires de France.

—1975a. *Durkheim on religion*, edited with introduction by W. S. F. Pickering. London: Routledge & Kegan Paul.

—1975b. *Textes* [3 volumes], edited with foreword by V. Karady. Paris: Minuit.

—1979a. *Durkheim: Essays on morals and religion*, edited with introduction by W. S. F. Pickering. London: Routledge & Kegan Paul.

—1982a. *The rules of sociological method and selected texts on sociology and its method*, introduction by S. Lukes. London: Macmillan.

Fauconnet, P. 1920. *La responsabilité*. Paris: Alcan.

Fehér, F. 1987. *The frozen revolution*. Cambridge: Cambridge University Press.

Filloux, J-C. 1971. Démocratie et société socialiste chez Durkheim. *Revue européenne des sciences sociales: Cahiers Vilfredo Pareto* 25.

—1977. *Durkheim et le socialisme*. Geneva: Droz.

—1990. Personne et sacré chez Durkheim. *Archives de sciences sociales des religions* 69.

—1993. Inequalities and social stratification in Durkheim's sociology. See Turner (1993), 211–28.

Fishkin, J. 1987. Liberty versus equal opportunity. In *Equal opportunity*, E. F. Paul et al. (eds), 32–48. Oxford: Blackwell.

Fouillée, A. [1883] 1921. *Critique des systèmes de morale contemporains*, 7th edn. Paris: Alcan.

—1889. *La morale, l'art et la religion d'après M. Guyau*. Paris: Alcan.

—1911a. Sociologie théorique et sociologie pratique. *Revue de métaphysique et de morale* 19.

—1911b. *La pensée et les nouvelles écoles anti-intellectuelistes*. Paris: Alcan.

Fraisse, L. 1989. De l'imitation à l'organicisme: Montesquieu à la lumière des sociologues en 1880. *Revue d'histoire littéraire de la France* 89.

Friedmann, G. 1964. *Le travail en miettes*. Paris: Gallimard.

Gane, M. 1983. Durkheim: women as outsider. *Economy and Society* 12.

—1988. *On Durkheim's Rules of sociological method*. London: Routledge.

Garland, D. 1990. *Punishment and modern society: a study in social theory*. Oxford: Clarendon Press.

Girault de Coursac, P. & P. 1982. *Enquête sur le procès du roi Louis XVI*. Paris: Table Ronde.

Gurvitch, G. [1937] 1961. *Morale théorique et science des moeurs*, 3rd edn. Paris: Presses Universitaires de France.

—1938. *Essais de sociologie*. Paris: Sirey.

—1963. *La vocation actuelle de la sociologie* [2 volumes]. Paris: Presses Universitaires de France.

Guyau, A. 1913. *La philosophie et la sociologie d'Alfred Fouillée*. Paris: Alcan.

Guyau, J-M. 1879. *La morale anglaise contemporaine*. Paris: Ballière.

—1885. *Esquisse d'une morale sans obligation ni sanction*. Paris: Alcan (t.1898. *A sketch of morality independent of obligation or sanction*. London: Watts – based on 2nd edn, 1890, completely rearranged, with revisions and additions, by A. Fouillée).

—1887. *L'irreligion de l'avenir*. Paris: Alcan (t.1897. *The non-religion of the future*. London: Heinemann).

—1890. *La genèse de l'idée de temps*. Paris: Alcan.

Hall, R. T. 1987. *Emile Durkheim: ethics and the sociology of morals*. New York: Greenwood Press.

— 1991. Communitarian ethics and the sociology of morals: Alasdair MacIntyre and Emile Durkheim. *Sociological Focus* 24.

—1993. Introduction to *Ethics and the sociology of morals: Emile Durkheim*. Buffalo, NY: Prometheus Books.

Hermant, D. 1978. Destructions et vandalisme pendant la révolution française. *Annales: économies sociétés civilisations* 33.

Hume, D. [1739–40] 1978. *A treatise of human nature*, edited by L. A. Selby–Bigge and revised by P. H. Nidditch. Oxford: Clarendon Press.

—[1751] 1902. *Enquiry concerning the principles of morals*. In *Enquiries*, edited by L. A. Selby-Bigge. Oxford: Clarendon Press.

Idzerda, S. J. 1954. Iconoclasm during the French revolution. *American Historical Review* 60.

Isambert, F-A. 1990. Durkheim: une science de la morale pour une morale laïque. *Archives de sciences sociales des religions* 69.

—1992. Une religion de l'Homme? Sur trois interprétations de la religion dans la pensée de Durkheim. *Revue française de sociologie* 33.

—1993a. La naissance de l'individu. See Besnard, Borlandi & Vogt (1993), 113–33.

—1993b. Durkheim et l'individualité. See Pickering & Watts Miller (1993), 7–31.

—1993c. Durkheim's sociology of moral facts. See Turner (1993), 193–210.

Janet, P. 1893. *Victor Cousin et son oeuvre*, 3rd edn. Paris: Alcan.

Joas, H. 1993. Durkheim's intellectual development: the problem of the emergence of new morality and new institutions as a leitmotiv in Durkheim's oeuvre. See Turner (1993), 229–45.

Juvenal. 1991. *Satires*, translated by N. Rudd. Oxford: Clarendon Press.

Kant, I. [1784a] 1923. Idee zu einer allgemeinen Geschichte. In *Kant's gesammelte Schriften*, vol. 8. Berlin: Gruyter (t.1983).

—[1784b] 1923. Was ist Aufklärung? In *Kant's gesammelte Schriften*, vol. 8. Berlin: Gruyter (t.1983).

—[1785] 1911. *Grundlegung zur Metaphysik der Sitten*. In *Kant's gesammelte Schriften*, vol. 4. Berlin: Reimer (t.1948. *The moral law*. London: Hutchinson).

—[1786] 1923. Muthmassicher Anfang der Menschengeschichte. In *Kant's gesammelte Schriften*, vol. 8. Berlin: Gruyter (t.1983).

—[1788] 1913. *Kritik der praktischen Vernunft*. In *Kant's gesammelte Schriften*, vol. 5. Berlin: Reimer (t.1993. *Critique of practical reason*. New York: Macmillan).

—[1790] 1913. *Kritik der Urtheilskraft*. In *Kant's gesammelte Schriften*, vol. 5. Berlin: Reimer (t.1987. *Critique of judgment*. Indianopolis: Hackett).

—[1793] 1923. Über den Gemeinspruch: Das mag in der Theorie richtig sein, taugt aber nicht für die Praxis. In *Kant's gesammelte Schriften*, vol. 8. Berlin: Gruyter (t.1983).

—[1795] 1923. Zum ewigen Frieden. In *Kant's gesammelte Schriften*, vol. 8. Berlin: Gruyter (t.1983).

—[1797] 1914. *Die Metaphysik der Sitten*. In *Kant's gesammelte Schriften*, vol. 6. Berlin: Reimer (t.1991. *The metaphysics of morals*. Cambridge: Cambridge University Press).

—1983. *Perpetual peace and other essays*. Indianopolis: Hackett.

LaCapra, D. 1972. *Emile Durkheim: sociologist and philosopher*. Ithaca, NY: Cornell University Press.

Lacroix, B. 1981. *Durkheim et le politique*. Paris: Presses de la Fondation Nationale des Sciences Politiques.

Ladrière, P. 1990. Durkheim et le retour de l'individualisme. *Archives de sciences sociales des religions* 69.

Larmore, C. 1987. *Patterns of moral complexity*. Cambridge: Cambridge University Press.

Lehmann, J. 1994. *Durkheim and women*. Lincoln: University of Nebraska Press.

Lévy-Bruhl, L. [1903] 1910. *La morale et la science des meours*, 4th edn. Paris: Alcan (t.1905. *Ethics and moral science*. London: Constable – based on 1st edn, without new preface replying to critics).

Llobera, J. 1994. Durkheim and the national question. See Pickering & Martins (1994), 134–58.

Lukes, S. 1968. *Emile Durkheim: an intellectual biography* [2 volumes]. D.Phil. thesis, University of Oxford.

—1973. *Emile Durkheim: his life and work*. London: Allen Lane.

—1982. Introduction to *The rules of sociological method and selected texts on sociology and its method*. London: Macmillan.

MacIntyre, A. 1981. *After virtue*. London: Duckworth.

MacTaggart, J. E. 1893. Du vrai sens de la dialectique de Hégel. *Revue de métaphysique et de morale* 1.

Mathiez, A. 1904. *Les origines des cultes révolutionnaires 1789–1792*. Paris: Bellais.

Mauss, M. 1905. Review of A. Mathiez, *Les origines des cultes révolutionnaires*. *Année sociologique* 8.

Mill, J. S. [1861] 1975. *Considerations on representative government*. In *John Stuart Mill: Three Essays*. Oxford: Oxford University Press.

Milligan, D. & W. Watts Miller (eds) 1992. *Liberalism, citizenship and autonomy*. London: Avebury.

Montesquieu, C. S. [1748] 1951. *De l'esprit des lois*. In *Oeuvres complètes*, vol. 2. Paris: Gallimard (t.1989. *The spirit of the laws*. Cambridge: Cambridge University Press).

Müller, H-P. 1986. Gesellschaft, Moral und Individualismus: Emile Durkheims Moraltheorie. In *Gesellschaftlicher Zwang und moralische Autonomie*, H. Bertram (ed.), 71–105. Frankfurt am Main: Suhrkamp.

Ollé-Laprune, L. 1880. *De la certitude morale*. Paris: Eugène Belin.

O'Neill, O. 1992. Autonomy, coherence and independence. See Milligan & Watts Miller (1992), 203–25.

Ory, P. 1980. La république en fête: les 14 juillet. *Annales historiques de la révolution française* 52.

Parodi, D. 1920. *La philosophie contemporaine en France*, 2nd edn. Paris: Alcan.

Philonenko, A. 1993. *L'oeuvre de Kant* [2 volumes]. Paris: Vrin.

Pickering, W. S. F. 1984. *Durkheim's sociology of religion: themes and theories*.

London: Routledge & Kegan Paul.

—1990. The eternality of the sacred: Durkheim's error? *Archives de sciences sociales des religions* 69.

—1993a. Human rights and the individual: an unholy alliance created by Durkheim? See Pickering & Watts Miller (1993), 51–76.

—1993b. La morale laïque de Durkheim était-elle réellement laïque? See Cardi & Plantier (1993), 101–10.

Pickering, W. S. F. & H. Martins (eds) 1994. *Debating Durkheim*. London: Routledge.

Pickering, W. S. F. & W. Watts Miller (eds) 1993. *Individualism and human rights in the Durkheimian tradition: Individualisme et droits humaines selon la tradition durkheimienne*. Oxford: Centre for Durkheimian Studies.

Rauh, F. 1903. *L'expérience morale*. Paris: Alcan.

Renouvier, C. 1869. *Science de la morale* [2 volumes]. Paris: Ladrange.

Rousseau, J-J. [1781] 1870. *Essai sur l'origine des langues*. In *Oeuvres complètes*. Paris: Hachette.

Saltel, P. 1993. Introduction to *David Hume: La morale, Traité de la nature humaine, livre III*. Paris: Flammarion.

Sanson, R. 1976. *Les 14 Juillet (1789–1975): fête et conscience nationale*. Paris: Flammarion.

Seth, A. [1887] 1893. *Hegelianism and personality*, 2nd edn. Edinburgh: Blackwood.

Seth, J. 1894. *A study of ethical principles*. Edinburgh: Blackwood.

Shackleton, R. 1961. *Montesquieu: a critical biography*. Oxford: Oxford University Press.

Small, A. 1902. Review of E. Durkheim, *De la division du travail social*, 2nd edn. *American Journal of Sociology* 7.

Soboul, A. 1966. *Le procès de Louis XVI*. Paris: René Julliard.

Strawson. G. 1989. *The secret connexion: causation, realism and David Hume*. Oxford: Clarendon.

Susemihl, F. & R. D. Hicks 1894. *The Politics of Aristotle: a revised text with introduction, analysis and commentary*. London: Macmillan.

Tarde, G. 1893. Review of E. Durkheim *De la division du travail social* in Questions sociales. *Revue philosophique* 35.

Taylor, C. 1989. Cross-purposes: the liberal–communitarian debate. In *Liberalism and the moral life*, N. Rosenblum (ed.), 160–82. Cambridge, Mass.: Harvard University Press.

Tocqueville, A. [1835–40] 1961. *De la démocratie en Amérique*. Paris: Gallimard.

Turner, S. P. (ed.) 1993. *Emile Durkheim: sociologist and moralist*. London: Routledge.

Wallwork, E. 1972. *Durkheim: morality and milieu*. Cambridge, Mass.: Harvard University Press.

Walzer, M. 1974. *Regicide and revolution*. Cambridge: Cambridge University Press.

Watts Miller, W. 1988. Durkheim and individualism. *Sociological Review* 36.

—1992. Liberal vegetarianism: moderation versus strong sentiments of morals. See Milligan & Watts Miller (1992), 63–76.

—1993a. Iconocide: the case of the trial and execution of Louis XVI. *Cogito* 7.

—1993b. Durkheim: liberal–communitarian. See Pickering & Watts Miller (1993), 82–104.

—1993c. Les deux préfaces: science morale et réforme morale. See Besnard, Borlandi & Vogt (1993), 147–64.

—1994. Durkheim: the modern era and evolutionary ethics. See Pickering & Martins (1994), 110–33.

Weber, E. 1977. *Peasants into Frenchmen: the modernization of rural France 1870–1914*. London: Chatto & Windus.

Willis, P. 1977. *Learning to labour: how working class kids get working class jobs*. London: Saxon House.

Winch, P. 1958. *The idea of a social science*. London: Routledge & Kegan Paul.

Wundt, W. 1886. *Ethik: eine Untersuchung der Thatsachen und Gesetze des sittlichen Lebens*. Stuttgart: Ferdinand Enke; 2nd edn, revised, 1892 (t.1897–1901. *Ethics: An investigation of the facts and laws of moral life* [3 volumes]. London: Swan Sonnenschein); 3rd edn, further revised, 1903.

281

Index

abnormal forms of the division of labour
117, 121–31
abstract *v* real man 25–32
abstract society 45, 132–3
action, sociology of 258–61
aesthetic of the moral 82
age-based division of labour 75
Agulhon, Maurice 243
Alexander, Jeffrey C. 34
altruism 4, 97, 112–16
anomie 4, 12, 14, 112–16, 130–33, 214,
218, 224–6
anthropology 2, 191, 197, 202, 204–5,
267
anthroponomy 197, 202, 204
Aristotle 73, 99
art 74, 81–2, 125, 174, 180–81; *see also*
human culture
art (ethics) 17–18; *see also* moral science
attachment 7–8, 11, 17, 25, 30–2, 35–7,
86–90, 98–116, 149–54, 244, 248–9
authoritarianism 4, 12, 14, 80, 180–81
authority 11, 145, 149, 180, 186–8, 192–
5
autonomy, Durkheimian 1, 10–13, 31–2,
131–2, 149, 163–84; Kantian 186–206,
232–3; and *anomie* 12, 224–7; and the
real and its rationale 168, 170–71, 256–
61; and solidarity 31–2, 253–6

Bastille Day 243–4
Beck, Ulrich 14
Belot, Gustave 20
Besnard, Philippe 8, 10, 35, 74, 76, 111,
114, 130–31,
Bik, Mimi 99, 265
birth-rates 34
body and bodily parts 101, 107, 146, 160–
61, 239

Borlandi, Massimo 91
Bosanquet, Bernard 99, 265
Bouglé, Célestin 8, 13, 225, 226, 267
Boutroux, Emile 9, 33, 61–2, 84, 108,
185–6, 190–96, 223, 229–30, 233–4
Brunschvicg, Léon 56

Cardi, François 126, 266
causality, accidental/external causes 3, 60,
62–3, 183; contingency 3, 13, 60–61,
183–4; essentialist/internal causes 54–
7, 59, 63–4, 66–70; necessary
connexions 3, 13, 59–62, 182–4
certainty 13–14, 217–27, 234
character 10–11; *see also* virtues
chauvinism 33, 152, 246, 260
citizenship 1, 5–6, 41–2, 80–82, 133–4,
179–80, 204–5, 244–6, 267
Cladis, Mark S. 99
class 1, 4, 8–9, 70–71, 124–37, 202–3,
205–6, 247, 260
classification, in social science 28–9, 54–
9; in thought 211–12
cohesion without consensus 86–90, 215,
248–9; *see also* attachment
collective consciousness, and the individual 35–6, 50–51, 173–5; and the
modern human ideal 2, 36, 71, 78–9,
163–4, 225, 248–9; and "the person" as
a collective representation 105–9; and
religion and core beliefs 13, 207–9
collective ferment 19, 41, 89–90, 115,
239–40, 242, 247
collective supersensible freedom 258–61
communitarian 5, 88, 99, 104, 151–2,
248–9, 253–4, 260
Comte, Auguste 28, 56, 220
conscience collective (commune), *see*
collective consciousness

conflict 1, 4, 65–7, 77–8, 84–7, 92–3, 123–4, 129, 133–7, 198–9, 202–3, 239–44, 249, 260
consent 92–3, 119
conservatism 2, 38, 40, 43–4, 123–4, 175–6
Constant, Benjamin 6, 80
constitutive/creative 16; see also collective ferment; mythological truths; symbolism
contract 7, 27–8, 90–93, 119, 123, 129, 133, 255–6
cooperatives 42; worker-owned 126, 128–9
Cornu, Marcel 268
corporatist reform 5, 33, 41–3, 80–81, 126, 133–4, 180, 266
cosmopolitanism 16–17, 33, 153, 205, 245–6, 267
Coste, Adolphe 42
countervailing power 77, 135–6
Cousin, Victor 263, 267–8
Cuin, Charles-Henry 125–6, 129, 136
cult of man 4, 10, 12–13, 15, 143, 216, 234–49
Cuvillier, Armand 124, 263, 266, 268

Darlu, Alphonse 174–6
Davy, Georges 65
"Definition of religious phenomena" 154, 208, 220, 240
Delbos, Victor 185–6, 188–93, 195–7, 204, 232–3, 259
Deleuze, Georges 265
democracy 5–6, 41, 59, 80, 241
density of population 34, 52, 83–6
"Determination of moral facts" 26, 142, 148, 158, 172–8, 229, 253
developing and flourishing 8, 118, 132–7, 205–6, 260–61
dignity 29, 37, 160–61, 239
division of labour, see below
Division of labour 2, 5, 7–8, 17, 29–38, 41–2, 73–137, 172–3, 207, 245; the division of labour as a pattern of relationships 73–82; as a modern v world-historical dynamic 82–93; the organic self 95–110; the spontaneous v abnormal division of labour 117–37; original introduction's moral analysis 29–38
divorce 76
dogma 211, 213–18, 220–22, 227; see also mythological truths

doubt 14, 40, 216–27, 232–4
Dreyfus Affair 107; article on, see "Individualism and the intellectuals"
dualism of reason and sentiment 11, 13–15, 149–53, 196–7
Durkheim, Emile, books, see Division of labour; Elementary forms of the religious life; Ethics (introduction); Evolution of educational thought in France; Montesquieu (Latin thesis); Moral education; Pragmatism and sociology; Professional ethics and civic morals; Rules of sociological method; Suicide; lectures and articles, see inaugural lectures; "Definition of religious phenomena"; "Determination of moral facts"; "Individualism and the intellectuals"; "Judgements of value and judgements of reality"; "Principles of 1789 and sociology"; "Studies in social science"
duties to oneself 107, 131, 155–62
dutifulness, see virtues

education, see human culture
egoism 4, 33, 71, 97, 106, 112–16, 132–3, 157, 199, 226–7
Elementary forms of the religious life 16, 108–9, 208, 220, 234–40, 268; collective ferment 16; immortal soul 268; individual v person 108–9; religion and core, obligatory beliefs 208; religion and faith 220; religion, the sacred and symbolism 234–41
emblem, see symbols
ends, deliberation of 1, 147–8, 251, 255–8; fusion v conflict and balance 157–9; hierarchy v network 155–7, 194–5, 201–2
enlightenment, mechanical v organic 172–8
equality 8–9, 41–3, 74–7, 95–6, 119–20, 127–9, 132–3, 135–7, 202, 249
equilibrium, break in 83–5
estrangement 71, 80, 106, 133, 135–6, 156–7, 246, 260
Ethics (introduction) 17, 128, 249, 252
Evolution of educational thought in France 81, 181, 183.
exchange 7, 90–91, 93, 102–3, 119, 128–9, 134–6
explanation, forms of 64–7
exploitation 9, 93, 114, 129, 133–6, 202–3, 246, 260

factionalism, *see* patterns of relationships
faith 14, 39–41, 213–14, 217–27
family, *see* particular connexions
fatalism 4, 76, 112, 114, 116, 130, 134
Fauconnet, Paul 37
Fehér, Ferenc 269
Filloux, Jean-Claude 8, 108, 124–6, 266
Fishkin, James 127
Fouillée, Alfred 30, 34, 43, 51–2, 80, 185, 210, 212, 218, 268
Fourier, Charles 265
Fraisse, Luc 65
fraternity 9, 16–17, 31, 41–5, 95–6, 137, 205–6
freedom 1, 4, 30–2, 37, 71, 41, 80, 88–9, 95–6, 115–6, 119, 134–6, 163, 222, 249, 258–9; *see also* autonomy; freewill
freewill and necessity 13, 163–4, 182–4, 192–3, 197–8, 258–61
French Revolution 1–2, 114–15, 213, 239–44; article on, *see* "Principles of 1789 and sociology"
Friedmann, Georges 130
friendship, *see* particular connexions

Gane, Mike 47, 74
Garland, David 269
Girault de Coursac, Paul and Pierrette 269
global ethics 16–17, 244–6, 257
God 8, 10, 13, 15, 141–3, 203, 207, 214, 216–17, 229–34
Gumplowicz, Ludwig 26
Gurvitch, Georges 1, 10, 21, 36, 96, 124, 170
Guyau, Augustin 34
Guyau, Jean-Marie 12, 14, 39–41, 210–27, 233–4; *anomie* 12, 218, 224–6; faith *v* doubt 217–22; hope 233–4; religion and non-religion 39–41, 210–17; risk society 222–7

Halbwachs, Maurice 124
Halévy, Elie 56
Hall, Robert T. 21, 99
happiness 83, 202; *see also* virtue and happiness
Hegel, G. W. F. 53, 99
Hermant, Daniel 268
history 28; *see also* philosophical history; world history
holy beings/wills 12, 187, 192–3, 197
homme de clan 104, 151–2, 199
homo economicus 27, 30
homosexuality 102

honour 50, 67, 70–1
hope 2, 9, 15, 180, 226–7, 229–34, 255–6, 260–61
human culture 1, 4, 12, 81–2, 136, 180–81, 194, 215, 224–5
human *patrie* 1, 16–17, 33, 137, 151–4, 244–6
humanity, *see* virtues
Hume, David 1, 3, 5, 11, 61, 104, 113, 149, 151, 196, 199, 257, 263; necessary connexions 3, 61, 263; particular connexions 5, 104, 151, 199; post-Pyrrhonian scepticism 113; sentiment 11, 149, 196

icon, *see* symbols
iconocide 241–2
iconoclasm 240–41
identity 7, 26, 30–32, 79, 84, 89–90, 93, 95, 98, 103–5, 151–54, 221, 239–46, 253–6, 258
Idzerda, Stanley J. 268
Ihering, Rudolf von 31
image, *see* symbols
immortal soul 10, 141, 207, 230, 268
inaugural lectures, at Bordeaux 25- 28, 31, 35, 44; at the Sorbonne 81, 180
individual, and person 105–10; and society, *see* identity; organic self; situatedness
"individual morality" 11, 159–161, 174
individualism and individuality 95–99
"Individualism and the intellectuals" 30, 90, 107–8, 115, 154, 156, 158, 208, 222, 236–7
individualism, methodoligical *v* moral 30
individualism's pathologies 110–16
inequality, *see* equality
inherited wealth 43–4, 126–9, 136
injustice, *see* justice
instrumentalism 7, 9, 16, 129, 131, 133–6, 246, 260
integrity, *see* virtues; whole man
interest 1, 4, 7–8, 27, 71, 87, 90–93, 114, 131, 134–5, 246
intermediate groups, *see* particular connexions
internalist programme 3–4, 33, 71, 79–80, 111, 116, 118–21 *et seq.*, 222–27, 256
Isambert, François-André 13, 21, 35, 95
isomorphism 118–9, 127–8

Janet, Paul 267

Joas, Hans 258
"Judgements of value and judgements of reality" 16, 236–7
justice 7–8, 41–3, 88, 92–3, 96, 119, 122, 129, 134–5, 158, 249; *see also* virtues
Juvenal 186, 223, 266

Kant, Immanuel 1, 3, 9–13, 15, 61, 100, 107–9, 182–206, 229–34, 259; autonomy 186–206; freedom as a postulate 232–3; God 10, 229–34; immortal soul 10, 230; kingdom of ends 9, 194–5; necessary connexion 3, 61; necessity and freewill 13, 182–4, 192–3, 259; philosophical history 197–9; teleology 200–6; virtue, happiness and hope 229–34; the will 189–94; Durkheim's critique 186–8; Guyau's critique 218–19, 225; *see also* Boutroux; Delbos

labour, degaded 129–31, 137
Labriola, Antonio 53
LaCapra, Dominick 114
Lacroix, Bernard 263
Ladrière, Paul 109
Larmore, Charles 253
Lehmann, Jennifer 74
Letourneau, Charles 75–6
Lévy-Bruhl, Lucien 18, 21, 51, 143, 185
liberal 6, 12–13, 30–31, 44–5, 88, 99, 132–3, 135–6, 147 175–81
liberal-communitarian debate 99, 265
libertarian 4, 96, 99, 160–1
life-history and life-plans 132–3, 136, 255
Llobera, Joseph 269
logos, see symbols
loyalty, *see* virtues
luck 129
Lukes, Steven 8, 47, 265–6

MacIntyre, Alasdair 253, 265
MacTaggart, J. E. 53, 263
Maine de Biran, Françoise-Pierre 264
Marianne 154–23
market 6–8, 16, 128–30, 134, 136, 161, 246, 260
marriage, *see* particular connexions
Marxists 8, 53
materialism 33–5, 134
Mathiez, Albert 239–40
Mauss, Marcel 30, 268–9
mechanical social processes 33–4, 83–5,

117, 199
mechanical solidarity 32, 73; *see also* patterns of relationships, segmentariness
merit 127–9, 134
Mill, John Stuart 6, 60, 126
Montesquieu, Charles Secondat de, *see below*
Montesquieu (Latin thesis) 2–3, 18, 47–71, 77, 120–21; necessary connexion and the internalist programme 59–67; social facts as will-independent "things" 48–54; social types and two routes to the normal 54–9; the "structure" and "principle" of a social rationale 67–71
Moral education 9–12, 82, 111–12, 141–72, 186–8, 229, 242, 249, 258, 266, 268–9; autonomy 10, 162–72; critique of Kant 186–8; duty and the good 11, 144–62; might ethics destroy morals? 10–12, 141–4; God 142, 229; the real and its rationale 121, 165–71; the sacred and modern society's cult of man 142–3; virtue, happiness and the whole man 81–2, 146–7, 155–9; the will 145–7, 168–9, 258
moral judge, the 10–11, 148–9, 171–2, 177–8, 193–5
moral law, the 145, 186–8, 192–7, 202–5
moral motivation 10–11, 13–15; *see also* attachment; cult of man; hope; obligatoriness
moral science, as key to ethics 1, 17–21, 251–61
morality, early analysis 25–38; universal elements of "duty" and "the good" 141–62; autonomy as enlightened acceptance 163–84; a secular cult and religion 207–49
morphology 34, 52–3, 55–6, 83–6
Müller, Hans-Peter 258
mythological truths 16, 220–2, 247–8

nation/nationalism 33, 79, 151–2, 245; *see also* social change and enlargement
natural abilities/potential 119, 204, 267; and free supersensible ability 204
necessary connexions, *see* causality
normal, the 18–21, 28–9, 47, 54–70, 120–37 *passim* 165–71

obligatoriness 11–12, 35–7, 39, 145, 187–8, 192–3, 196
occupational groups and milieux, *see*

particular connexions
Ollé-Laprune, Léon 185, 217
O'Neill, Onora 100
optimism *v* pessimism 8–9, 33, 226, 233, 256, 260
organic self 4–5, 7, 11, 26, 95–116, 135–6, 155–7
organic solidarity 32, 73; *see also* division of labour
Ory, Pascal 244

Parodi, Dominique 20, 54, 61, 127, 134
Parsons, Talcott 34
particular connexions 5, 31–33, 41–3, 76–8, 80–81, 101–5, 125–7, 133–6, 151–3, 244, 248–9, 260; of friendship 5, 101–4, 155–6; of marriage and family 5, 76–7, 101–5, 126–7, 151, 153, 156; of occupational/intermediate groups 5, 41–3, 70, 78, 80–81, 125–7, 133–6, 152–3, 215
patterns of relationships, factionalism 77–80, 87, 98, 123–4, 133–4, 175–8, 208–9, 239, 242–4, 249; pluralism 77–9, 87, 98, 208–9, 214, 224–5, 245; segmentariness 77–9, 87, 104, 151–2, 199, 245; *see also* division of labour
personalism 108–10
phenomena 3
Philonenko, A. 232–3, 267–8
philosophical history 197–206
Pickering, W. S. F. 13, 81–2
pluralism, *see* patterns of relationships
polytelism 224–5
"Positive moral science in Germany" 26–7, 31, 34, 37–9, 43–4, 48, 209–10
positivism 3, 52–3, 263
post-modernism 4, 181, 260
post-Pyrrhonianism 113
Pragmatism and sociology 16, 36, 176–8, 208, 220–2, 247–8; individual *v* collective thought 36; individualism, science and organic enlightenment 176–8; "mythological" truths 16, 208, 220–2, 247–8
pride, *see* virtues
"Principles of 1789 and sociology" 16, 18–21, 41, 44–5, 240
Professional ethics and civic morals 41–2, 59, 80, 93, 157, 159, 161; citizenship 59, 80; consent and contract 93; corporatist reform 41–2; duties to oneself 159, 161; mysticism of cult of society 157

punishment 242, 269

raison raisonnante 43–4, 221
Rauh, Frédéric 21, 173
(the) real and its rationale 3–4, 18–21, 47, 56–70, 120–37 *passim* 165–71, 256–8
register of the sacred 15, 235
relativism, *see* universalism
religion 13–16, 35, 39–41, 43–5; as core beliefs 207–9; as faith 217–27; and hope 229–34; as the sacred 234–9; and Guyau's account 210–16
Renouvier, Charles 61, 108, 185, 195
responsibility 37
rhetoric 15, 235–6
Richard, Gaston 76
rights 7, 11, 87–8, 97
risk 14, 110–11, 181, 222–7, 260–61, 268
ritual, *see* symbols
Rousseau, Jean-Jacques 13, 44, 104–5, 105, 109, 153, 156, 199, 205
Rules of sociological method 2–3, 28, 47–8, 50–56, 60–64, 70, 121, 148, 245; Durkheim a "rationalist" 3; necessary connexion and causality 60–64; routes to the normal 70, 121; social facts 50–54; social types and comparative sociology 28, 55–6

sacred 13, 15–16, 142–3, 207, 216, 234–9
sacrifice 158, 237
Saltel, Philippe 265
sanctions 35–7; *see also* punishment
Sanson, Rosemonde 243–4
scepticism 4, 14, 113, 181, 227, 260
Schaeffle, Albert 4, 26, 32–3, 38, 41–3, 59, 79, 133
segmentariness, *see* patterns of relationships
Seignobos, Charles 50
self-discipline, *see* virtues
self-ownership 160
self-respect, *see* virtues
Seth, Andrew 53
Seth, James 99, 265
sexuality 100–1, 161
situatedness 2, 25–6, 30–33, 103–5, 251–6, 258
Small, Albion 87
Soboul, Albert 269
social change and enlargement 32, 79, 83–6, 88, 152, 244–5

social facts 3, 19, 26, 38, 48–55, 57–8, 70, 163–4
social inheritance 126–7, 129
socialism 4, 33, 42–4, 265
Socialism 41–2, 44
sociomorphism 211–12
Socrates 148–9
solidarity, *see* attachment
specialization, *see* division of labour; human culture; whole man
Spencer, Herbert 28, 31, 39, 44, 91
spirit of association and of discipline, *see* virtues
state 4–6, 42, 56–9, 65, 68, 79–80, 91, 96, 205, 245
Strawson, Galen 263
structures and ideas/"principles" 19–20; 33–5; 38–40; 67–70; 83–6; 89–90; 117–20; 260–1
struggle for existence, *see* conflict
"Studies in social science" 25, 29, 35, 39–44
Suicide 2, 4, 41–2, 55, 75, 79, 106–16, 125, 134, 142, 152, 183, 242–3; conceptual structure and *Moral education* 111–12; individual person and organic self 106–9; individualism's pathologies 4, 110–16; man's first appearance as "god for men" 142; note on freewill 183; note on French Revolution 115, 242–3; sociology of risk 110–11; women 75, 102;
symbolism, of God 15, 229, 232; of the immortal soul 207, 230, 268; and the sacred 15–16, 234–9; and the socially creative/constitutive 16, 239–46; and the transparent *v* the hidden 247–9
symbols, the emblem 16, 53, 236–7; the icon 16, 237–9, 248; the image 236, 243; the *logos* 16, 238, 248; the ritual 16, 236, 238–9, 241–4; the temple 236–9

Tarde, Gabriel 8, 86–7
Taylor, Charles 265
telos, man's *v* modern man's 27, 67, 132, 141, 190, 200–6

teleology 66–7, 83–5, 197–203
temple, *see* symbols
Tocqueville, Alexis de 6
tolerance 78, 98, 176–8, 208–9
Tönnies, Ferdinand 45
trilemma 127

universalism, and global ethics 16–17, 244–6, 257; and relativism 2, 10, 29, 143, 163–5, 190–91, 193, 197–206, 244–5, 252–3, 257

vie sérieuse and *vie légère* 81–2, 180–81
virtue ethics 10–11, 141–62
virtue and happiness 146–7, 155, 158–9, 229–34
virtues, of dutifulness, justice and self-discipline 134, 144–9; of loyalty, humanity and attachment/spirit of association 151–4; of self-respect, integrity and pride 131, 134, 155–62
virtuous and vicious circles 33, 153
volume of population 34, 52, 83–6; *see also* birth-rates

Wallwork, Ernest 21, 29
Walzer, Michael 241–2
Watts Miller, William 99, 241, 266, 268–9
Weber, Eugen 244
Weber, Marianne 76
whole man, the 81–2, 136, 147, 157
will, the 2, 9, 11, 26, 47–54, 146–50, 163–4, 168–9, 253–61; and collective supersensible freedom 258–61; and identity and situatedness 26, 169, 253–5; and the imagination 2, 9, 26, 169, 253; and the real and its rationale 168, 256–8; and self-discipline 11, 146–50; and social facts as "things" 26, 38, 48–54; *see also* autonomy; freewill; Kant
Willis, Paul 126
Winch, Peter 53
women 74–77, 79, 100–2, 161, 186, 249
world history 34–5, 52–3, 67, 82–6, 141, 197–206, 244–5
world spirit 27, 34, 52, 82
Wundt, Wilhelm 27, 37, 209–10

.